Move More, Learn More!

Harnessing the Brain–Body Connection in Early Childhood

EDITED AND CO-AUTHORED BY
Mike Kuczala and Lynne Kenney

Foreword by Cindy Hovington
Afterword by Ronald S. Fischler

Published by Teachers College Press,® 1234 Amsterdam Avenue, New York, NY 10027

Copyright © 2026 by Mike Kuczala and Lynne Kenney, except as noted below.

Copyright © for "Physical Activity, Neuroplasticity, and Brain Growth: The Key Connections" by Ty Melillo

Copyright © for "Enhancing Sensory-Motor, Cognitive, and Social Skills in Young Children Through Physical Activity" by Joann McFee, Kelly Barnhart, and Lynne Kenney

Copyright © for "Using Music Interventions to Strengthen Cognition, Co-Regulation, and Self-Regulation: The PreK SEND Program" by Angelo Molino

Copyright © for "Using Movement and Rhythm to Enhance Language and Reading Skills in Young Children" by Stacy Fretheim

Copyright © for "Handwriting and Movement: Addressing Delays and Difficulties" by Mary Mountstephen

Copyright © for "Activity Gym and Cross-Body Activities for Children" by Eleonora Palmieri and Piero Crispiani

Copyright © for "Rhythm and Movement for Early Childhood Self-Regulation Development" by Kate Williams

Copyright © for "'MovementWorks' for Neurotypical and Neurodivergent Learners" by Ali Golding of MovementWorks® with Joanne Lara

Copyright © for "Promoting Social Connections Through Group Activities" by Andy Milne

Copyright © for "Creating Meaningful Movement Experiences Before, During, and After School" by Andrew Vasily

Front cover: Shadows by Jerin Chowdhury / Shutterstock. Children (left to right) by onlyyouqj, evgenyatamanenko, Rawpixel, and Deagreez, all via iStock / Getty Images.

All rights reserved. No part of this publication may be reproduced or transmitted in any form or by any means, electronic or mechanical, including photocopy, or any information storage and retrieval system, without permission from the publisher. For reprint permission and other subsidiary rights requests, please contact Teachers College Press, Rights Dept.: tcpressrights@tc.columbia.edu

Library of Congress Cataloging-in-Publication Data is available at loc.gov

ISBN 978-0-8077-8405-1 (paper)
ISBN 978-0-8077-8367-2 (hardcover)
ISBN 978-0-8077-8406-8 (ebook)

Printed on acid-free paper
Manufactured in the United States of America

Contents

Foreword: Why Movement Matters: What Every Teacher, Clinician, and Parent Should Know About Children's Brains   *Cindy Hovington* v

Acknowledgments vii

Introduction 1
Mike Kuczala

PART I: WHAT TO KNOW

1. **Light a Fire! The Scientific Basis for Integrating Movement Into School and Clinical Settings** 7
   Lynne Kenney, United States

2. **Physical Activity, Neuroplasticity, and Brain Growth: The Key Connections** 20
   Ty Melillo, United States

3. **Enhancing Sensory-Motor, Cognitive, and Social Skills in Young Children Through Physical Activity** 32
   Joann McFee, Kelly Barnhart, and Lynne Kenney, United States

4. **Using Music Interventions to Strengthen Cognition, Co-regulation, and Self-Regulation: The Pre-K SEND Program** 51
   Angelo Molino with Lynne Kenney, United States

PART II: WHAT TO DO (ACADEMIC DEVELOPMENT)

5. **Implementing Cognitive-Physical Activities to Strengthen Executive Function Skills for Better Learning and Behavior** 67
   Lynne Kenney with Mike Kuczala, United States

6. **Using Movement and Music to Enhance Language and Reading Skills in Young Children** — 92
   Stacy Fretheim, United States

7. **Handwriting and Movement: Addressing Delays and Difficulties** — 109
   Mary Mountstephen, UK

8. **Activity Gym and Cross-Body Activities for Children** — 126
   Piero Crispiani and Eleonora Palmieri, Italy

9. **The Kinesthetic Classroom: Teaching and Learning Through Movement** — 141
   Mike Kuczala, United States

PART III: WHAT TO DO (SELF-REGULATION AND SOCIAL-RELATIONAL DEVELOPMENT)

10. **Rhythm and Movement for Early Childhood Self-Regulation Development** — 153
    Kate Williams, Australia

11. **"MovementWorks" for Neurotypical and Neurodivergent Learners** — 167
    Ali Golding, UK

12. **Promoting Social Connections Through Group Activities** — 186
    Andy Milne, United States

13. **Creating Meaningful Movement Experiences Before, During, and After School** — 198
    Andy Vasily, Belgium

Conclusion: Putting It All Together So Kids Will *Move More to Learn More* — 211
   Mike Kuczala, United States

Afterword: The Pediatric Perspective of the Family Experience and Why Returning to Our Roots in Pediatrics Matters for Children *Ronald S. Fischler* — 215

Index — 217

About the Editors and Contributors — 226

Foreword
Why Movement Matters
What Every Teacher, Clinician, and Parent Should Know About Children's Brains

One of the most striking insights I've come to understand as a neuroscientist and mom of three is this: *Movement is not just a physical activity—it is foundational to brain growth and the connections it builds*. When a baby crawls, we don't realize how many parts of the brain act in synchrony to make this happen. It is a whole-brain activity that involves the integration of motor, sensory, visual, and cognitive functions. Repetition of these moments builds neural pathways foundational to the brain's growth and development. Yet, despite this understanding, our modern approach to education and parenting increasingly limits the very elements that spark this growth: movement through play and exploration.

I recently visited Italy with my three kids, and when we were at a park in the northern part of Italy near the Austrian border, I was struck by something. The park pushed my children's physical boundaries ("Am I strong enough to push this structure?"). It created various risks they had never encountered ("Can I walk across this without falling?"). More important, it was fun for them. Each visit to this park in Italy opened a new imaginary world for my kids. In contrast, most of the parks here in Montreal look the same. They all have the same structure that has one ladder, one slide, and a small bridge connecting the two parts. Kids not only need to move, but they also need to be placed in situations that help them understand how their body moves and what their physical limits are—all of which helps them build confidence and resilience. This is the power of gross motor movement.

Music is another powerful way to incorporate movement in our children's lives. Learning to play an instrument is a powerful activity for brain development because it engages multiple areas of the brain at once, promoting both cognitive and motor growth. It requires the coordination of fine motor skills—precise movements of the fingers and hands—which strengthens the motor cortex and improves hand–eye coordination. At the same time, reading music and keeping rhythm activates areas responsible for auditory processing, timing, memory, and emotional regulation. These complex tasks require the brain's hemispheres to communicate efficiently, strengthening the corpus callosum, which supports higher-order thinking skills like problem-solving and focus. Over time, playing an instrument can enhance neuroplasticity (the brain's ability to form new connections), boosting learning, attention, and even emotional resilience. When combining music and movement, they naturally enhance the inherent beauty and best qualities of each.

Today, many of our educational settings and parenting norms ask children to sit still, follow rigid schedules, and focus on structured learning far too early—well before their bodies and brains are ready. We are raising children in environments that prioritize stillness over exploration, repetition over creativity, and outcomes over experiences. We ask young children to sit still before their bodies are developmentally ready. We confine learning to desks and worksheets, while the brain is begging to learn through the body. Yet what we know from research is that a child who can coordinate their body is also learning to coordinate their thoughts, emotions, and behavior.

It's time we reconsider what we define as learning. As you will read in this book, if we want to raise thoughtful, emotionally intelligent, creative, and resilient children, we must build learning environments that reflect how the brain works. That means reintroducing movement, music, art, and play—not as extras or rewards, but as essential elements of development. These are not luxuries; they are necessary for a child's healthy development.

What Mike Kuczala and Lynne Kenney have done is to gather some of the best and brightest minds in the world for a practical, scientific discussion on movement and the impact that it can have on early-childhood learners. From cognition and social-relational health to co-regulation, executive function, reading, handwriting, and much more, this book delivers a one-stop shop for why and how movement has a much greater impact on early childhood learning than we ever imagined. Educators, clinicians, parents, caregivers, and, most important, our children will all benefit from this relevant and timely project.

—Cindy Hovington
Founder & CEO of Curious Neuron
Host of the *Reflective Parenting* Podcast

Acknowledgments

MIKE KUCZALA

I would like to thank the following people: Sarah Jubar, our editor, for her guidance and partnership on this project; and Dr. Lynne Kenney, whose brilliance I admire every day. To our contributors, I cannot thank you enough! What you've given to this book has made an immeasurable difference. To Diana Ramsey, for creating and maintaining the dynamic organization, Regional Training Center, which allows me to continue to grow professionally. To Traci Lengel for her friendship, professional partnership, and collaboration on the Kinesthetic Classroom books. To Jean Moize for her mentorship and for showing me a path forward. To my dear friend Don Stratman, my very first superintendent, who started me down the road of leading and training. And to Cyndy, Scott, and Demi, the absolute wind beneath my wings.

LYNNE KENNEY

One could not hope to work with a more talented and down-to-earth editor than Sarah Jubar. I am grateful that Sarah understood the importance of movement in the lives of children. To my mentors, Ann Alexander, MD; Annette Brodsky, PhD; John Callaghan, PhD; Kathy Gilbride, PhD; Carl Hoppe, PhD; Raun Melmed, MD; Karen Saywitz, PhD; Ron Schouten, MD; and Edward Shafranske, PhD: thank you for sharing your wisdom and talents with me. Your knowledge continues to impact the children with whom I work. I wish to warmly thank our contributors. They are accomplished, busy professionals who generously gave of their time and knowledge to bring this book to fruition. To Mary Mounstephen, who conferenced with me at odd hours in the UK, Singapore, and Malaysia, providing essential support and guidance. To Olivia Markan for her valuable editorial ideas, activity conceptualization, and research contributions. To my colleagues at Wellington-Alexander Center who transform lives every day, including mine. To the families, teachers, and children with whom I have worked for over 30 years, you are the inspiration for this book. To my husband for his unwavering support, even when I'd wake him up at 4:00 a.m. on video calls to the UK, Australia, and beyond. To my daughter Alexis, my brothers Doug and Greg, and my dad (Grampa) for encouraging, rooting for, and supporting me. I love you, Family, this book is for you and all the children whose lives we will positively impact with applied neuroscience.

Introduction

Mike Kuczala

If we want our children to move mountains, we first have to let them out of their chairs.

—Nicolette Sowder

It's time to move mountains. It is a safe assumption, based on decades of extensive and ongoing research, that the brain and body are intricately linked in the teaching and learning process. To truly enhance education, we must recognize the contributions the body makes to learning and cognition. Learning, in fact, does not happen from the neck up, but from the feet up. From the time a child enters this world, a significant portion of learning, adapting, and cognitive growth happens because of physical experiences or observations of others' physical experiences. Rather than fight this, we believe educators, clinicians, parents, and caregivers should consider embracing the idea of learning based in movement.

While modern daycares and early childhood classrooms have evolved, children still spend a good part of their day in chairs. The research is clear that movement and learning go hand-in-hand. We now know that not only can movement stimulate focus and attention, but it can also help to support and generate neural connections, regulate emotion, develop social skills, enhance executive function, and prepare the brain for learning.

Move More, Learn More creates a path for readers to embrace the idea of learning in and through movement to create a better world for all our children to positively grow cognitively, socially, emotionally, and physically. Early childhood educators, clinicians, and parents deserve a resource where they can find answers to critical questions they have been asking for decades, and one that will serve them for many years. It is our hope that *Move More, Learn More* does both. While early childhood is often defined as preschool to 3rd grade, the reader will see that much of the research and activities in *Move More, Learn More* apply to older students as well. Activities are adaptable; we anticipate that you will apply your knowledge and experience to apply them as appropriate to your students and setting. You will find QR codes for activities so that you can make your own personalized binder.

We are extremely grateful to have assembled a team of some of the best and brightest minds in the field of movement from all over the world. Their shared insights and knowledge have been a treasure trove of information. The great minds that have contributed to this book cover cognition, co-regulation, play, executive function, reading, writing, music, neurodivergent learners, classroom-based physical activity, and physical education. As we wrote, revised, and edited content, we could barely contain our excitement. In the spirit of joy, optimism, and utility, the book is divided into three sections:

- Part I: What to Know
- Part II: What to Do (Academic Development)
- Part III: What to Do (Self-Regulation and Social-Relational Development)

Chapter 1 lays the foundation for the rest of the book. For 50 years, science has established the importance of movement in learning. What continues to generate excitement is the fact that our brain and body are connected; the brain continues to develop because we move. This relationship is essential for observation, learning, decision-making, and life. For far too long, the brain and body have been treated, especially in schools, as two separate entities. We now understand that the brain and body share a reciprocal relationship that truly cannot be separated in any aspect of life. This first chapter makes the scientific case for both the brain/body connection and the rest of the book.

Chapter 2 picks up right where Chapter 1 leaves off by showing that active play isn't just fun, but neurologically essential. The early years are a core period when movement and sensory experiences literally shape brain architecture. The author places this developmental sequence in a real-life context before exploring the neurobiology of the process.

Chapter 3 follows by exploring the downside of what happens when motor skills aren't as developed as they have been in previous generations. More screen time, reduced opportunities for outdoor play, and briefer periods of unstructured play are just a few of the reasons why children are experiencing sensory-motor deficits. After a discussion of how sensory and motor systems work in unison, the authors provide a narrative about the motor-skill learning connection and finish with examples of rhythmic movement activities.

Chapter 4 concludes Part I by describing music's impact on cognition, learning, and behavior, from the synergistic power of music to how it impacts neurodiverse children and enhances cognitive development and self-regulation through musical play and improvisation.

Part II focuses on academic development. Chapter 5 provides not only the science of cognitive-motor movement and how it supports executive function, but also describes how rhythmic movement with cognitive demands strengthens cognition. It also provides rhythmic activities, songs, and dance that "Dr. Lynne" has created in her clinical work with children for over 30 years.

Chapter 6 continues the discussion on rhythm and timing by describing the relationship between language and vocabulary development, and movement and music, including building phonological skills through music and movement. Sample activities are provided for building phonemic representations and awareness, and the chapter presents an overview of the Alexander Integrated Method, a literacy approach that aligns with how the brain naturally develops language and reading skills.

Chapter 7 shows how secure motor skills are crucial to the development of cognitive skills and how that applies to handwriting. Discussion centers on Specific Learning Differences (SpLDs), dyslexia, school readiness, and research from physical education. Activities are also shared from the Early Movements, Young Minds™ program.

Chapter 8 follows with the Crispiani Method, based on the Praxis-Motor Theory, to improve reading and processing fluency in children with dyslexia, dyspraxia, dysgraphia, and dyscalculia through a dynamic combination of word reading and rapid coordinated movement. A detailed discussion follows on the cognitive and motor skills the method aims to improve and the activities that make this possible.

Finally, Chapter 9 explores the concept of the Kinesthetic Classroom as it applies to early childhood teaching and learning. Both the history of how the Kinesthetic Classroom came to be and how it might be implemented are explored. Though the Kinesthetic Classroom framework consists of six parts, the primary focus is on four components: (1) providing brain breaks, (2) creating class cohesion, (3) reviewing content, and (4) teaching content.

Part III focuses on self-regulation and social-relational health. Two current or former physical educators, among others, add their experience and expertise in this section. Self-regulation skills control attention, emotions, and behavior. These skills are critical to academic and social success.

Chapter 10 discusses the science behind the use of rhythmic movement for self-regulation and social development. Highlighted topics include spontaneous motor tempo, beat synchronization, and entrainment. The evidence-based RAMSR (which stands for Rhythm and Movement for Self-Regulation) program for self-regulation is presented.

Chapter 11 highlights the challenges and opportunities of creating movement experiences for neurotypical and neurodivergent learners. After presenting the challenges of current school readiness and the learning loss that occurred during the COVID-19 pandemic, the author underscores recent research that cognitive and motor development are more closely related than previously assumed. This essence is captured by the fact that our brains evolved to move. The author presents two evidence-based dance and movement programs.

Chapter 12 focuses on creating and emphasizing social connections through group activity. After briefly highlighting what children are capable of at different ages regarding social activity and cooperative play, the author focuses on the critical attributes of connection and cooperation through a physical activity lens. He then offers a discussion of the practical nature of cooperation and play in group activity through creating teams, tag games, walking activities, relay games, parachute play, recess, and team-based and sport-inspired activities.

The other physical education–minded chapter is Chapter 13, which focuses on principles applicable to any teaching and learning experience in early childhood. It is based on the setting of before-, during-, and after-school movement activities, but the true core of this chapter centers on a specific framework that puts the child at the center of their own learning. Assessment has evolved from testing what a child learned to using ongoing assessment tools as a guide to how best to design teaching and learning to help ensure a child's success. This chapter dives into self-assessment to help students reflect on their learning, adjust, and continually improve their skills with the goal of helping students find more meaning and joy during movement experiences.

Move More, Learn More concludes with Chapter 14 by presenting a vision for a better world for early childhood learners through movement. We outline a comprehensive picture based on the previous chapters, with essential steps to make your roadmap clearer. Creating learning environments that encourage movement takes time and must be intentional and well planned.

We hope this final chapter integrates the most essential parts of this book to create a brighter future for all our children.

Part I

WHAT TO KNOW

CHAPTER 1

Light a Fire!
The Scientific Basis for Integrating Movement Into School and Clinical Settings

Lynne Kenney, United States

You have been right all along. Your intuition, years of experience in education, clinical practice, and/or as a parent speaks the truth. There is a plethora of research uniting play, sensory stimulation, singing, rhyming, being in nature, and movement to cognitive, academic, and social development (Fiveash et al., 2023; Ladányi et al., 2020; Macdonald et al., 2018; Willoughby et al., 2021; Zelazo et al., 2024). The question is, how did we get so far afield from what we know to build strong brains, healthy bodies, and happy, confident kids?

The answer is complex. The cultural constellation of our classrooms shifted, educational technology expanded to the tune of billions of dollars, classroom sizes increased, free play outdoors diminished, and we lost sight of what we know children need most: movement, art, music, free play, building, making, creating, nature, and more. For many children—possibly millions of children—recess and physical education classes are more fundamental to their academic achievement than the hours they are expected to sit in a classroom. Children need developmental movement experiences to build the subcortical structure of the brain upon which cognition and learning develop.

HISTORY IS IMPORTANT

Having valued being an intern and fellow in my thirties and training interns and fellows in my fifties, the most important lesson I bring to our new psychologists, internal medicine doctors, and psychiatrists is that research is translational. If one only studies in their respective fields or country, they have an incomplete picture of applied neuroscience. It is only through the integration of knowledge and experience across *multiple disciplines*—kinesiology, speech/language pathology, occupational therapy, neuropsychology, cognitive science, auditory neuroscience, educational leadership, learning and motivation, and developmental psychology—that we shift a generation. It is not one factor—many parts make a meaningful whole.

In 1974, Rainer Martens and his wife, Marilyn, founded Human Kinetics and began publishing about the importance of movement and cognition in sport psychology. Martens drew upon his German history of oppression and escape to create some of the most seminal works in the field of sport psychology. This fact is relevant because Martens and his colleagues at the University of Illinois were foundational in establishing the importance of physical activity in health and sport.

Other influential colleagues and researchers who were instrumental in raising the profile of movement in cognitive, health, and social outcomes are Darla Castelli, Jean Moize, Charles Hillman, Carla Hannaford, Robert Pangrazzi, Paul Rosengard, John Ratey, and Phillip Tomporowski. In the associated fields of auditory neuroscience and language, meaningful contributions related to the work in *Move More, Learn More* can be found in the work of Ann Alexander, Sheila Allen, Fleur Bouwer, Alex Doman, Anna Fiveash, Reyna Gordon, Usha Goswami, Assal Habibi, Tiffany Hogan, Nina Kraus, G. Reid Lyon, Louisa Moats, Aniruddh Patel, Michael Thaut, and Adam Tierney, to name a few.

Remember When You Were Young?

You would play outdoors, paint, sing rhyming songs, draw with chalk on the sidewalk, play hopscotch, read books with your parents, and play music as a family. If you were of our era, you would come home from school and change out of your school clothes into your play clothes, and your adult loved one would say, "I'll ring the cowbell when dinner is ready, and you will be promptly on time." You rode bikes in the street, climbed trees, and played kick the can in the alley. Free unstructured play was abundant. That was then; we need more of that now.

There are benefits to technological evolution. You get your news faster. You can learn about cool things like astronomy, geography, travel, and cooking. You no longer must open the *Thomas Guide* in Los Angeles or stop at the gas station to ask for directions. Yet there are costs for our children. Humans are agricultural beings. We were designed to roam the earth and hunt for berries. Historically, we moved from place to place following our food sources. Now we go to the grocery store, unaware of how the food got to our plates.

Developmental Growth Is Sequential

While the size of the human brain and body has changed over millions of years, especially in the early stages of human evolution, there has been a remarkable lack of change in the last 100,000 to 150,000 years (Mitteroecker & Fischer, 2024). Brain size has not significantly shrunk recently, and brain shape has remained relatively stable. The human brain continues to develop from the bottom up and inside out. The brainstem and cerebellum are among the first brain regions to develop and function, playing crucial roles in regulating essential bodily functions like breathing, heart rate, and movement coordination.

For these two critical regions to develop, they require movement. *Without movement, the brainstem and cerebellum do not establish the necessary neural pathways to support higher-order cognitive function.* Without proper movement experiences, which are largely sequential in nature, especially during the first years of life, the brain may not fully develop the necessary connections to support functions like attention, executive control, and language (Cundari et al., 2023; Jylänki, 2022; Kuhl, 2010; Mastrangelo et al., 2024; McClelland et al. 2021; Tao et al., 2025).

I was reminded this week of a parent who gleefully exclaimed, "My son walked at 7 months." This is not always a good thing. Children are not designed to walk at 7 months. An array of sensory-motor skills needs to be developed before a child walks. They need to roll over, crawl, and pull to a stand. When infants and toddlers develop these skills sequentially, we know that the brainstem and cerebellum are maturing in a direction that will support cognition and learning. As UK child development expert Mary Mountstephen points out, "Faster is not better." *As a society, we need to go slower.* We need to get on the ground and play with our children. We need to let them bang pots and pans, hum and sing rhyming songs, skip, and jump rope. Children need to climb up the slide, not just slide down it. They need to swing from trees and jump off swings. This is what teaches them about their body positioning in space. These vestibular, proprioceptive, fine, and gross motor activities lay the foundation for the whole child.

When we go slower, children can integrate the lower brain and subcortical structures, stimulated by movement in the natural environment to grow into well-regulated, thinking humans who care about relationships and have empathy and respect.

We need to allow children the time to develop the motor skills to support the cognitive skills needed for learning. You cannot rush development. Building a brain is done through experience; it takes time.

In *Move More, Learn More* we provide teachers, clinicians, and parents with the evidence to say, "Children need to play and move to learn and grow; we will no longer allow our young children to sit at desks all day."

THE SCIENCE

Physical activity plays a transformative role in early childhood development. Far from being merely recreational, movement and physical engagement with the environment represent foundational processes through which children develop physically, cognitively, and socially. This section examines the scientific evidence underpinning the profound impact of physical activity across multiple developmental domains, drawing on research from neuroscience, developmental psychology, exercise physiology, and educational theory.

Neuroplasticity and Brain Development

Physical activity profoundly influences brain development through multiple mechanisms. Neuroscientific research has established that movement experiences trigger neurochemical cascades that support neuroplasticity—the brain's ability to form new neural connections and modify existing ones.

Animal and human studies demonstrate that exercise increases brain-derived neurotrophic factor (BDNF), a protein essential for neuronal growth, differentiation, and survival (Cotman & Berchtold, 2002). In young children, higher physical activity levels correlate with increased hippocampal and basal ganglia volume, regions critical for memory formation and procedural learning (Chaddock et al., 2010; Dadkhah et al., 2023; Pontifex et al., 2014).

The cerebellum, traditionally viewed as primarily involved in motor coordination, has extensive connections with prefrontal regions involved in executive function. Physical activities that challenge coordination and balance appear to strengthen these cerebellar-cortical networks, potentially explaining the observed relationship between motor proficiency and cognitive function (Diamond, 2000; Latino & Tafuri, 2024).

Executive Function

Executive function skills, including self-regulation, attention, working memory, inhibitory control, and cognitive flexibility, represent some of the core cognitive capacities for school readiness and academic success (González-Del-Castillo & Barbero-Alcocer, 2025; Greenfader et al., 2019; Kenney & Comizio, 2016). In a study of 2,470 Danish children, researchers identified a consistent positive association between exercise capacity and cognitive performance across all measured cognitive domains, including psychomotor function, attention, working memory, and visual learning (Lind et al., 2025). A growing body of evidence shows that physical activity or energetic play is associated with these capacities in children. Improved self-regulation in young children is also essential (Becker et al., 2014; Ludwig & Rauch, 2018; McGowan et al., 2024; Montroy et al., 2016). Developing self-regulation skills during early childhood is important because it supports a child's capacity to regulate their cognition, emotion, and behavioral systems. As we have stated, self-regulation and other executive function skills are highly correlated with academic success (see McGowan et al., 2023: Spiegel et al., 2021; Tomporowski et al., 2015; Zelazo et al., 2016).

Physically active play requiring complex movements and decision-making particularly benefits executive function development (Best, 2010; Mao et al., 2024). For example, games involving rules, team coordination, and strategic thinking (like simplified versions of tag or follow-the-leader) appear especially beneficial for developing inhibitory control and cognitive flexibility (Leong et al., 2022).

Research has also demonstrated that martial arts training (such as tai chi and dance), which combine physical activity with attention-focusing and self-regulation, produced significant improvements in executive function compared to standard physical education programs (Martín-Rodríguez et al., 2025; Pujari, 2024). The structured increase in cognitive complexity of such activities, combined with their physical demands, appears to create an optimal context for executive function development (Diamond & Ling, 2016; Kenney & Comizio, 2016; Kuczala & Kenney, 2020).

ACADEMIC READINESS AND ACHIEVEMENT

For many students, the cognitive benefits of physical activity translate into measurable impacts on academic readiness and achievement.

Children with ADHD demonstrate some of the most robust academic improvements from physical activity interventions. The dopaminergic and noradrenergic systems that are dysregulated in ADHD are directly targeted by exercise. Studies show that even single bouts of moderate aerobic exercise can improve attention, reduce hyperactivity, and enhance working memory for several hours afterward. A 2023 study of the effects of exercise in ADHD showed that cognitively engaging exercise is effective in improving attention problems in school-aged children with ADHD (Li et al., 2023).

Structured physical activity programs for children with ADHD have shown significant improvements in on-task behavior, reduced need for medication adjustments, and better performance on measures of inhibitory control (Zhao et al, 2025). The effects are often more pronounced than in neurotypical populations, suggesting that these children may be particularly responsive to the cognitive benefits of movement.

Given the heterogeneity of interventions, more research is needed on the quantitative and qualitative characteristics of physical activity to determine what type of interventions work best for students with various neurobiological presentations.

Particularly noteworthy is the relationship between physical activity and language development. Studies by Carson et al. (2016) reveal that physically active play correlates with enhanced vocabulary acquisition and verbal fluency in preschoolers. One proposed mechanism involves the embodied cognition framework, which suggests that sensorimotor experiences provide concrete references for abstract language concepts, facilitating deeper linguistic understanding (Dove, 2023; Lebert & Vilarroya, 2024; Leisman et al., 2016; Mavilidi et al., 2018). In 2020, Ladányi and her colleagues proposed the Atypical Rhythm Risk Hypothesis (ARRH), showing that difficulties with rhythm processing, including perception and production, are a risk factor associated with developmental speech/language disorders (DSLDs). ARRH suggests that atypical rhythmic abilities in children may lead to difficulties in language acquisition, particularly in areas like phonological awareness and speech production. Many of the contributors in *Move More, Learn More* observe deficits in rhythm, tempo, and timing in children with and without neurodevelopmental diagnoses.

Mathematics performance also shows positive associations with physical activity levels. Resaland et al. (2016) found that integrating physical activity into mathematics instruction improved numerical cognition and problem-solving abilities in the lowest third of learners when compared with peers. These findings align with theories that spatial-temporal reasoning, developed through movement experiences, underlies many mathematical concepts (McCluskey et al., 2023).

SENSORY-MOTOR INTEGRATION AND PERCEPTUAL DEVELOPMENT

Physical activity provides essential multisensory experiences that help children develop efficient sensory processing systems. According to sensory integration theory, developed by occupational therapist A. Jean Ayres, active engagement with the environment through movement is crucial for integrating information from different sensory modalities (Ayres, 1972).

Research shows that vestibular stimulation during activities like swinging, spinning, and balancing activates multiple brain regions and helps establish proper sensory integration patterns (Wiener-Vacher et al., 2013). These experiences are particularly important for developing appropriate sensory thresholds and responses, explaining why physically active children often demonstrate better attentional capacity and fewer sensory processing difficulties.

MOTOR SKILL DEVELOPMENT

Fundamental motor skills developed through physical activity form the building blocks for more complex movement patterns throughout life. These skills typically develop in a sequential pattern, with mastery of basic movements (running, jumping, throwing) preceding more complex skills.

Capio et al. (2024) reported that participation in a motor skill intervention led to higher rates in the development of object control skills and executive function in 185 children aged 36 to 60 months. A dose-response relationship was found in which those children who displayed greater development of object control skills over time also displayed greater development of executive function. Longitudinal research by Barnett et al. (2009) demonstrates that motor skill proficiency in early childhood predicts physical activity levels and fitness in adolescence. Children who develop strong fundamental movement skills are more likely to participate in sports and physical activities later in life, creating a positive developmental cascade.

The quality of early movement experiences significantly impacts this developmental trajectory. Structured physical activities that provide appropriate challenges and feedback appear most effective for motor skill development (Dapp et al., 2021). However, unstructured play also offers unique benefits, allowing children to experiment with movement solutions and develop movement creativity.

Physical activity enhances the integration of perceptual information with motor output, a critical capacity for skilled movement. Activities requiring eye-hand coordination (catching, throwing), spatial awareness (navigating obstacle courses), and rhythm perception (dancing) strengthen neural pathways connecting sensory processing and motor execution systems.

Perceptual-motor training programs significantly improved visual-motor integration, spatial awareness, and fine motor control in preschool children (Sutapa et al., 2021). These improvements transferred to improvements in graphomotor skills essential for writing and drawing, demonstrating the connection between gross motor experiences and fine motor development.

SOCIAL AND EMOTIONAL DEVELOPMENT

Physical activity provides natural opportunities for children to experience, express, and regulate emotions. Vigorous play often produces states of physiological arousal similar to emotional excitement or stress, offering children practice in recognizing and modulating these states.

Research indicates that regular physical activity is associated with reduced anxiety and depressive symptoms even in young children. One mechanism appears to involve the regulation of stress response systems; physically active children typically show more moderate cortisol responses to stressors and quicker returns to baseline (Spring & Staiano, 2024).

Physical activities requiring persistence through challenging tasks also build emotional resilience. Children who regularly engage in physically challenging play develop greater frustration tolerance and persistence in the face of difficulties across multiple domains.

Social Skill Development

Movement-based play provides rich contexts for social interaction and skill development. Group games and team activities require children to negotiate rules, take turns, communicate effectively, and consider others' perspectives.

A systematic review by Lubans et al. (2016) found consistent evidence that participation in structured physical activities improved social competence measures in children, including cooperation, assertion, responsibility, and self-control. These benefits were especially pronounced in programs emphasizing team play and cooperative goals rather than individual competition.

Rough-and-tumble play—a physically active form of play involving running, chasing, and playful wrestling—makes a unique contribution to social development (Smith & St. George 2022). This play form helps children learn to recognize social cues, modulate physical force, and distinguish between playful and aggressive interactions, skills fundamental to social competence.

Self-Concept and Identity

Physical activity influences how children perceive themselves and their capabilities. According to self-determination theory, experiences of competence in physical domains contribute to intrinsic motivation and positive self-concept (Ryan & Deci, 2000).

Children who view themselves as physically capable are more likely to engage in and enjoy physical activities, creating a positive feedback loop supporting continued development. Perceived physical competence in early childhood predicts physical activity participation throughout development (Palmer et al., 2021). Physical activities also provide opportunities for children to explore different social roles and contexts. Team sports, dance, martial arts, and other movement forms each offer distinct cultural contexts and value systems that contribute to children's developing sense of self within their social world.

CONCLUSION

Our children need to play! They need movement, art, music, social problem-solving, digging, tunnelling, swinging, climbing, and jumping rope to develop the integrated brain structures to support learning and prosocial behavior, self-confidence, and happiness. The scientific evidence strongly supports the fundamental role of physical activity in multiple domains of child development. From strengthening bones and muscles to enhancing executive function, from refining sensory integration to building social skills, physical movement serves as a primary developmental mechanism during early childhood. These findings carry significant implications for educational, clinical, and parenting practices.

Ensuring that children have ample opportunities for varied physical activities, both structured and unstructured, represents not merely a recreational luxury but a developmental necessity.

Physical education programs, active learning approaches, and environmental designs that facilitate movement deserve recognition as essential components of developmental support systems rather than supplementary enrichment.

As research continues to illuminate the mechanisms connecting physical activity to developmental outcomes, a more integrated, movement-positive approach to childhood development becomes increasingly imperative. We have the evidence. It's time for children to move more so that they can learn more!

REFERENCES

Álvarez-Bueno, C., Pesce, C., Cavero-Redondo, I., Sánchez-López, M., Martínez-Hortelano, J., & Martínez-Vizcaíno, V. (2017). The effect of physical activity interventions on children's cognition and metacognition: A systematic review and meta-analysis. *Journal of the American Academy of Child & Adolescent Psychiatry, 56*(9), 729–738.

Ayres, A. (1972). *Sensory integration and learning disorders*. Western Psychological Services.

Barnett, L., van Beurden, E., Morgan, P., Brooks, L., & Beard, J. (2009). Childhood motor skill proficiency as a predictor of adolescent physical activity. *Journal of Adolescent Health, 44*(3), 252–259.

Becker, D., Miao, A., Duncan, R., McClelland, M. (2014). Behavioral self-regulation and executive function both predict visuomotor skills and early academic achievement. *Early Childhood Research Quarterly, 29*(4), 411–424.

Best, J. (2010). Effects of physical activity on children's executive function: Contributions of experimental research on aerobic exercise. *Developmental Review, 30*(4), 331–351.

Capio, C., Mendoza, N., Jones, R., Masters, R., & Lee, K. (2024). The contributions of motor skill proficiency to cognitive and social development in early childhood. *Scientific Reports, 14*, 27956.

Carson, V., Hunter, S., Kuzik, N., Wiebe, S. A., Spence, J. C., Friedman, A., Tremblay, M., Slater, L., & Hinkley, T. (2016). Systematic review of physical activity and cognitive development in early childhood. *Journal of Science and Medicine in Sport, 19*(7), 573–578.

Chaddock, L., Erickson, K., Prakash, R., Kim, J., Voss, M., Vanpatter, M., Pontifex, M., Raine, L., Konkel, A., Hillman, C., Cohen, N., & Kramer, A. (2010). A neuroimaging investigation of the association between aerobic fitness, hippocampal volume, and memory performance in preadolescent children. *Brain Research, 1358,* 172–183.

Cotman, C., & Berchtold, N. (2002). Exercise: A behavioral intervention to enhance brain health and plasticity. *Trends in Neurosciences, 25*(6), 295–301.

Cundari, M., Vestberg, S., Gustafsson, P., Gorcenco, S., & Rasmussen, A. (2023). Neurocognitive and cerebellar function in ADHD, autism and spinocerebellar ataxia. *Frontiers in Systems Neuroscience, 17,* 1168666.

Dadkhah, M., Saadat, M., Ghorbanpour, A., & Moradikor, N. (2023). Experimental and clinical evidence of physical exercise on BDNF and cognitive function: A comprehensive review from molecular basis to therapy, *Brain Behavior and Immunity Integrative, 3,* 100017.

Dapp, L., Gashaj, V., & Roebers, C. (2021). Physical activity and motor skills in children: A differentiated approach. *Psychology of Sport and Exercise, 54*(2020), 101916.

Diamond, A. (2000). Close interrelation of motor development and cognitive development and of the cerebellum and prefrontal cortex. *Child Development, 71*(1), 44–56.

Diamond A., & Ling, D. S. (2016). Conclusions about interventions, programs, and approaches for improving executive functions that appear justified and those that, despite much hype, do not. *Developmental Cognitive Neuroscience, 18,* 34–48.

Dove, G. O. (2023). Rethinking the role of language in embodied cognition. *Philosophical Transactions of the Royal Society of London. Series B, Biological Sciences, 378*(1870), 20210375.

Fiveash, A., Ferreri, L., Bouwer, F., Kösem, A., Moghimi, S., Ravignani, A., Keller, P., & Tillmann, B. (2023). Can rhythm-mediated reward boost learning, memory, and social connection? Perspectives for future research. *Neuroscience and Biobehavioral Reviews, 149,* 105153.

González-Del-Castillo, J., & Barbero-Alcocer, I. (2025). Effects of school-based physical activity programs on executive function development in children: A systematic review. *Frontiers in Psychology, 16,* 1658101.

Greenfader, C. (2019). What is the role of executive function in the school readiness of Latino students? *Early Childhood Research Quarterly, 49,* 93–108.

Jylänki, P., Mbay, T., Hakkarainen, A., Sääkslahti, A., & Aunio, P. (2022). The effects of motor skill and physical activity interventions on preschoolers' cognitive and academic skills: A systematic review. *Preventive Medicine, 155,* 106948.

Kenney, L., & Comizio, R. (2016). *70 play activities for better thinking, self-regulation, learning & behavior.* PESI Publishing.

Kuczala, M., & Kenney, L., (2020). *Brain primers.* Moving Minds.

Kuhl, P. (2010). Brain mechanisms in early language acquisition. *Neuron, 67*(5), 713–727.

Ladányi, E., Persici, V., Fiveash, A., Tillmann, B., & Gordon, R. (2020). Is atypical rhythm a risk factor for developmental speech and language disorders? *Cognitive Science, 11*(5), e1528.

Latino, F., & Tafuri, F. (2024). Physical activity and cognitive functioning. *Medicina (Kaunas, Lithuania), 60*(2), 216.

Lebert, A., & Vilarroya, Ó. (2024). The links between experiential learning and 4E cognition. *Annals of the New York Academy of Sciences, 1541*(1), 37–52.

Leisman, G., Moustafa, A. A., & Shafir, T. (2016). Thinking, walking, talking: Integratory motor and cognitive brain function. *Frontiers in Public Health, 4*, 94.

Leong, A., Yong, M., & Lin, M. (2022). The effect of strategy game types on inhibition. *Psychological Research, 86*(7), 2115–2127.

Li, D., Li, L., Zang, W., Wang, D., Miao, C., Li, C., Zhou, L., & Yan, J. (2023). Effect of physical activity on attention in school-age children with ADHD: A systematic review and meta-analysis of randomized controlled trials. *Frontiers in Physiology, 14*, 1189443.

Lind, R. R., Andersen, T. R., Beck, M. M., Madsen, M., Madsen, E. E., Lundbye-Jensen, J., Geertsen, S. S., Krustrup, P., & Larsen, M. N. (2025). The influence of physical, psychological and sociocultural factors on cognitive performance: A nationwide cross-sectional analysis in 10-12-year-old Danish children. *Early Human Development, 209*, 106339.

Lubans, D., Richards, J., Hillman, C., Faulkner, G., Beauchamp, M., Nilsson, M., Kelly, P., Smith, J., Raine, L., & Biddle, S. (2016). Physical activity for cognitive and mental health in youth: A systematic review of mechanisms. *Pediatrics, 138*(3), e20161642.

Ludwig, K., & Rauch, W. A. (2018). Associations between physical activity, positive affect, and self-regulation during preschoolers' everyday lives. *Mental Health and Physical Activity, 15*, 63–70.

Macdonald, K., Milne, N., Orr, R., & Pope, R. (2018). Relationships between motor proficiency and academic performance in mathematics and reading in school-aged children and adolescents: A systematic review. *International Journal of Environmental Research and Public Health, 15*(8), 1603.

Mao, F., Huang, F., Zhao, S., & Fang, Q. (2024). Effects of cognitively engaging physical activity interventions on executive function in children and adolescents: A systematic review and meta-analysis. *Frontiers in Psychology, 15*, 1454447.

Martín-Rodríguez, A., Herrero-Roldán, S., & Clemente-Suárez, V. J. (2025). The role of physical activity in ADHD management: Diagnostic, digital and non-digital interventions, and lifespan considerations. *Children (Basel, Switzerland), 12*(3), 338.

Mastrangelo, S., Peruzzi, L., Guido, A., Iuvone, L., Attinà, G., Romano, A., Maurizi, P., Chieffo, D. P. R., & Ruggiero, A. (2024). The role of the cerebellum in advanced cognitive processes in children. *Biomedicines, 12*(8), 1707.

Mavilidi, M., Okely, A., Chandler, P., Cliff, D., & Paas, F. (2018). Effects of integrated physical exercises and gestures on preschool children's foreign language vocabulary learning. *Educational Psychology Review, 30*(2), 413–426.

McClelland, M., Gonzales, C., Cameron, C., Geldhof, G., Bowles, R., Nancarrow, A., Merculief, A., & Tracy, A. (2021). The head-toes-knees-shoulders revised: Links to academic outcomes and measures of EF in young children. *Frontiers in Psychology, 12*, 721846.

McCluskey, C., Kilderry, A., Mulligan, J. & Kinnear, V. (2023). The role of movement in young children's spatial experiences: A review of early childhood mathematics education research. *Mathematics Education Research Journal, 35*, 287–315.

McGowan, A. L., Chandler, M. C., & Gerde, H. K. Infusing physical activity into early childhood classrooms: Guidance for best practices. (2024). *Early Childhood Education Journal, 52*, 2021–2038.

McGowan, A. L., Gerde, H. K., Pfeiffer, K. A., & Pontifex, M. B. (2022/2023). Meeting 24-hour movement behavior guidelines in young children: Improved quantity estimation and self-regulation. *Early Education and Development, 34*(3), 762–789.

Mitteroecker, P., & Fischer, B. (2024). Evolution of the human birth canal. *American Journal of Obstetrics and Gynecology, 230*(3), Supplement, S841–S855.

Montroy, J. J., Bowles, R. P., Skibbe, L. E., McClelland, M. M., & Morrison, F. J. (2016). The development of self-regulation across early childhood. *Developmental Psychology, 52*(11), 1744–1762.

Palmer, K., Nunu, M., Scott-Andrews, K., & Robinson, L. (2021). Perceived physical competence predicts gains in children's locomotor but not ball skills across an intervention. *International Journal of Environmental Research and Public Health, 18*(11), 5990.

Pontifex, M., Parks, A., O'Neil, P., Egner, A., Warning, J., Pfeiffer, K., & Fenn, K. (2014). Poorer aerobic fitness relates to reduced integrity of multiple memory systems. *Cognitive, Affective and Behavioral Neuroscience, 14*(3), 1132–1141.

Pujari, V. (2024). Martial arts as a tool for enhancing attention and executive function: Implications for cognitive behavioral therapy—A literature review. *Journal of Pharmacy & Bioallied Sciences, 16*(Suppl 1), S20–S25.

Resaland, G. K., Aadland, E., Moe, V. F., Aadland, K. N., Skrede, T., Stavnsbo, M., Suominen, L., Steene-Johannessen, J., Glosvik, Ø., Andersen, J. R., Kvalheim, O. M., Engelsrud, G., Andersen, L. B., Holme, I. M., Ommundsen, Y., Kriemler, S., van Mechelen, W., McKay, H. A., Ekelund, U., & Anderssen, S. A. (2016). Effects of physical activity on schoolchildren's academic performance: The Active Smarter Kids (ASK) cluster-randomized controlled trial. *Preventive Medicine, 91*, 322–328.

Ryan, R., & Deci, E. (2000). Self-determination theory and the facilitation of intrinsic motivation, social development, and well-being. *American Psychologist, 55*(1), 68–78.

Smith, P., & St. George, J. (2022). Play fighting (rough-and-tumble play) in children: Developmental and evolutionary perspectives. *International Journal of Play, 12*(1), 113–126.

Spiegel, J. A., Goodrich, J. M., Morris, B. M., Osborne, C. M., & Lonigan, C. J. (2021). Relations between executive functions and academic outcomes in elementary school children: A meta-analysis. *Psychological Bulletin, 147*(4), 329–351.

Spring, K., & Staiano, A. (2024). Physical activity and depressive symptoms in youth. *Translational Pediatrics, 13*(6), 1007–1011.

Sutapa, P., Pratama, K., Rosly, M., Ali, S., & Karakauki, M. (2021). Improving motor skills in early childhood through goal-oriented play activity. *Children (Basel, Switzerland), 8*(11), 994.

Tao, Y., Zhang, Y., Qian, H., & Cao, Z. (2025). Long term effects of physical activity types on executive functions in school aged children. *Scientific Reports, 15*(1), 30303.

Timmons, B. W., Leblanc, A. G., Carson, V., Connor Gorber, S., Dillman, C., Janssen, I., Kho, M. E., Spence, J. C., Stearns, J. A., & Tremblay, M. S. (2012). Systematic review of physical activity and health in the early years (aged 0-4 years). *Applied Physiology, Nutrition, and Metabolism = Physiologie Appliquee, Nutrition Et Metabolisme, 37*(4), 773–792.

Tomporowski, P. & Pesce, C. (2015). *Enhancing children's cognition with physical activity games.* Human Kinetics

Wiener-Vacher, S., Hamilton, D., & Wiener, S. (2013). Vestibular activity and cognitive development in children: Perspectives. *Frontiers in Integrative Neuroscience, 7,* 92.

Willoughby, M., Hudson, K., Hong, Y., & Wylie, A. (2021). Improvements in motor competence skills are associated with improvements in executive function and math problem-solving skills in early childhood. *Developmental Psychology, 57*(9), 1463–1470.

Zelazo, P., Blair, C., & Willoughby, M. (2016). *Executive function: Implications for education (NCER 2017–2000).* National Center for Education Research, Institute of Education Sciences, U.S. Department of Education.

Zelazo, P., Calma-Birling, D., & Galinsky, E. (2024). Fostering executive-function skills and promoting far transfer to real-world outcomes: The importance of life skills and civic science. *Current Directions in Psychological Science, 33*(2), 121–127.

Zhao, K., Li, Y., Wang, P., & Zhang, P. (2025). Exercise prescription to improve inhibitory control in children and adolescents with ADHD: a network meta-analysis. *Frontiers in Psychiatry, 16,* 1601765.

CHAPTER 2

Physical Activity, Neuroplasticity, and Brain Growth
The Key Connections

Ty Melillo, United States

Physical activity, neuroplasticity, and brain growth are interconnected elements in childhood development. Regular physical activity stimulates neural growth and strengthens connections between brain regions, enhancing cognitive function, learning capacity, and emotional regulation. Children's brains possess remarkable neuroplasticity, the ability to reorganize and form new neural pathways in response to experiences, making the early years a core period when movement and sensory experiences literally shape brain architecture. This biological window of opportunity means that active play isn't just fun, but also neurologically essential, as it provides the sensory input and physical challenges that optimize brain development, the foundation for cognitive, motor, and emotional skill development.

This chapter provides educators, clinicians, and parents with an understanding of how the brain develops, why neonatal reflex integration is important, and how brain development influences learning. I introduce the role of the nervous system in learning and reflect on how an imbalance in brain architecture contributes to neurodevelopmental disorders as well as developmental differences.

But before we dive into neurobiology, let's apply what you are about to learn in a real-life context. Biological development follows a distinct pattern in the first 3 years. For some children, even a 1-month delay in any milestone can be indicative of an array of other developmental issues (Khan & Leventhal, 2023). Let me explain.

The developmental sequence follows a predictable pattern where physical milestones directly influence cognitive and emotional development. In the first 12 months of life, the progression of skills is quite predictable and beautiful. Infants first use their sense of smell to navigate their ability to seek the milk provided by their mothers in the first few hours of life. In the first month of life, infant vision is blurry. They can see black and white images about 8–12 inches away. During months 1–2, an infant's sight is developed such that they begin to see faces. This is important, as it contributes to language skill development and attachment. Infants then develop the skills to reach, push, and pull between 3 and 4 months of age. This assists with their ability to roll back and forth on their tummies, supporting vestibular and motor strengthening. In months 5–6, infants learn to creep and crawl, which facilitates development across the two hemispheres of their brains. At 7–9 months, infants exhibit goal-directed actions such as reaching for a toy while seated or pulling to a standing position (Voight et al., 2018).

By 9–11 months, infants are moving their bodies in space, enjoying object play, laughing and smiling in social interactions, and preparing to walk by pulling to stand with the support of their caregivers or objects in their environments, such as the couch. You can picture this: an infant-toddler pulling up on the couch and walking while holding onto it. This is a special time; a lot of sensory-motor and brain development has led to this task. What is important to know is that these patterned, sequential motor, cognitive, and social development skills rest on the development of the brainstem. Now, we are ready to explore the science!

UNDERSTANDING NEONATAL REFLEXES AND BRAIN DEVELOPMENT

Brain development follows a clear pattern, like a skyscraper constructed from the foundation up. Neonatal reflexes are a foundational element of brain architecture. Neonatal reflexes are newborns' automatic responses, like grasping your finger or the startle reflex, primarily controlled by the brainstem, specifically in regions known as the medulla and pons. Think of the brainstem as the brain's "command center" for basic survival functions. It develops early in pregnancy and is one of the most primitive parts of the brain.

When we observe delayed or persistent neonatal reflexes in children, we're actually seeing information about the maturity of their brainstem structures, or lack of maturity away from these neonatal reflexes and into a further developed or maturing brain. This is significant because the brainstem houses other crucial control centers:

1. The vestibular nuclei, which regulate balance and spatial orientation.
2. Autonomic nuclei, which control automatic functions like breathing, heart rate, and digestion.

The Bottom-Up Pattern of Brain Development

The human brain develops in what's called a "caudal to rostral" direction. "Caudal" refers to the lower, more primitive regions (like the brainstem).

"Rostral" refers to the higher, more advanced regions (like the cerebral cortex). This "bottom-up" development pattern means that the most basic survival functions develop first, providing a foundation for more complex brain functions to build upon later.

Brainstem Maturation

Understanding this developmental pattern helps explain why certain skills and behaviors emerge in a predictable sequence. A child must develop strong brainstem functions before they can fully develop higher-level cognitive skills. When you observe persistent reflexes or developmental delays in children ages 3–9, you might be seeing evidence of immature brainstem development that could affect learning, attention, and behavior.

The brainstem, which houses neural circuits for basic survival functions and reflexes, should naturally inhibit primitive reflexes (like the Moro reflex or the ATNR [Asymmetrical Tonic Neck Reflex]) as higher brain regions mature. However, when these reflexes remain active beyond their expected time frame, it signals that the neural maturation process—which follows a bottom-up sequence from brainstem to cortex—has been interrupted or delayed. This neurological immaturity often manifests in difficulties with posture, balance, coordination, and sensory processing, which can subsequently impact higher cognitive functions like attention, language processing, and academic learning (Blythe et al., 2009).

UNDERSTANDING THE AUTONOMIC NERVOUS SYSTEM'S ROLE IN DEVELOPMENTAL DISORDERS

When we talk about children with developmental disorders, there's an important pattern happening inside their bodies that affects their overall health and development. Let me explain this in a way that connects to what you might observe in your classroom.

The Body's Control Systems

Our bodies have what's called an "autonomic nervous system" that works automatically without our conscious control. Think of it as having two main settings:

1. **Fight or Flight Mode (Sympathetic):** This is our body's emergency response system. When activated, it
   - Diverts blood from digestion to muscles
   - Increases heart rate

- Raises blood pressure
- Releases stress hormones
- Makes us feel alert or anxious

2. **Rest and Digest Mode (Parasympathetic):** This is our body's restoration system. When activated, it
   - Conserves energy
   - Helps us feel calm and relaxed
   - Promotes digestion
   - Slows heart rate
   - Supports immune function

The Imbalance in Children With Developmental Disorders

Research shows that children with developmental disorders (like autism, ADHD, and learning disabilities) often have an imbalance in these two systems. Their bodies tend to stay in "fight or flight" mode too much of the time. This is like having a car in neutral, but your foot is pressing the accelerator, so the car is idling but the motor is revved up.

How This Connects to Immune Function and Inflammation

When the body stays in "fight or flight" mode for extended periods, it affects physical health in several ways:

- **Immune System Changes:** The immune system doesn't function optimally when the body is constantly in alert mode. This can lead to frequent illnesses, longer recovery times, and possible autoimmune responses (Alotiby, 2024).
- **Increased Inflammation:** Chronic stress triggers inflammatory responses in the body. Think of inflammation as the body's internal "fire alarm" that should turn on briefly when needed, but in these children, it may stay on too long, causing digestive problems, sleep disturbances, brain fog, attention problems, mood lability, or physical pain. These might be silent problems that can take years to fully manifest. They can be subtle and challenging to diagnose.

Autonomic Nervous System Imbalance

When you have students with a developmental difference who are constantly on edge, get overwhelmed easily, have trouble transitioning, have digestive issues, have difficulty regulating their emotions, and/or are frequently ill, you're likely seeing the effects of an autonomic system imbalance. Their nervous system is stuck in a heightened state of alertness, which affects both their learning ability and their physical health.

How You Can Help

Understanding this connection helps explain why calming strategies can be so beneficial for these students. You can help a child move from "fight or flight" into a more balanced state by having predictable and consistent routines at home and in the classroom. Teaching deep breathing exercises and mindfulness activities can serve as accessible ways to calm down in the moment. Providing frequent movement breaks (i.e., taking a break from sitting still to move their bodies) can also facilitate better self-modulation and self-regulation. You're not just helping them behaviorally—you're supporting their physical health and immune function as well. This holistic understanding shows why addressing the nervous system's balance is vital for supporting children with developmental disorders in your classroom.

HUMANS ARE A UNIQUE SPECIES

Humans are unique as a species because we are bipedal (i.e., use two legs for walking). We move in a very specific way compared to any other animal. This movement requires a sophisticated nervous system and proprioceptive awareness to achieve bipedalism. Humans require a specific sequence of sensory-motor development to build the mental, sensory-motor map of our bodies correctly, so we can ambulate and speak efficiently. Humans are born in a relatively immature state compared to other mammals, such as horses, that can walk around within the first 100 minutes of birth. Homo sapiens have the biggest head-to-body size of any other primate; however, because of bipedalism, humans have the smallest birth canal, which presents a problem when it comes to the birthing process. As an evolutionary adaptation, we are born with relatively underdeveloped brains and nervous systems and have very soft and small skulls to help with successfully getting through the birth canal; however, this also means we are born with virtually no ability to move in a coordinated fashion for several months and won't walk for approximately 1 year.

The human brain and nervous system need to receive sufficient sensory-motor stimuli to mature and develop the sensory-motor cortex to move with intent. Although we do not have a well-developed cortex at birth, there are many essential primitive functions in the brainstem that have been programmed while in the womb. This is why there is no need to teach a baby how to breathe or grasp. If you put your finger in the palm of an infant's hand, they will grasp; if the mother chooses to nurse the child, they will often latch on with no physical or verbal instruction.

Evolutionary Role of Neonatal Reflexes

The actions described above (e.g., an infant grasping a finger and latching to nurse) are known as the neonatal reflexes that are covered in depth in Chapter 3. They are also an evolutionary precaution to help with the drawbacks of being so underdeveloped at birth. They help infants participate in the birthing process without having volitional control over their movements. If the child is in a breech position or if the cord is wrapped around the baby's neck, and if these neonatal reflexes persist, then we may assume that these neonatal reflexes did not come online properly, which may delay normal developmental milestones and may result in cognitive or developmental disorders later in life (Chinello et al., 2018).

Something that is well-known in embryology and early life development is that the right hemisphere takes the lead in development in the first 2–3 years. During this time, we do not form conscious memories until around the age of 3, since the left hemisphere takes the lead in development for the next 2–3 years, when the hippocampus is coming online and we start forming conscious memory. There are areas in the right hemisphere, such as the parietal-temporal-occipital (PTO) and insular cortex, that are mostly associated with attachment and nonverbal communication with the mother.

For example, an infant, from the moment of birth, needs to be able to nonverbally communicate with their caregivers when they are in pain, hungry, thirsty, cold, hot, need to be changed, tired, etc.; this is known as interoception. These internal and environmental sensory stimuli require the baby to properly feel these sensory signals to communicate their needs, even nonverbally, to their parents and form the foundation of attachment (Yoshida & Funato, 2021). The summary here is that *you can't teach higher cognitive processes in an underdeveloped brain/immature brain*. Brain development is critical from the brainstem to the cortical structure. Posterior to anterior. The brain can't receive or process higher-order cognitive concepts if it hasn't developed that center in the cortex. You must learn to move first, then you can learn to think. Moving your body develops your brainstem and sets the brain on a proper developmental course.

Asymmetric Hemispheric Development

The right hemisphere of the brain has a whole sensory-motor map of the body compared to the left, where there's more of a half body map in the sensory motor strip. This is one reason why the right hemisphere should be more active during the first 3 years of life, as it supports the development of interoception and proprioception as well as attachment formation—all essential survival functions that the left hemisphere cannot provide. Brief examples of left hemisphere functions are reading, speech, motor planning, and handedness (if right-handed—we don't see a dominance profile at an early age because the left hemisphere has not matured enough to the point where we see a dominance profile arising).

From an evolutionary and survival perspective, it makes sense that the right hemisphere should be the main hemisphere online, since it receives more sensory input from the environment, which is also highly related to how the infant is moving and interacting with their environment. The type of genes involved in regulating brain growth and development make up a majority of our total genes and are stimulated by environmental and sensory input. They are classified as *experience-dependent* genes. This concerns the topic of epigenetics. Epigenetic factors influence the expression of genes and are more malleable and changeable than true genetic disorders/mutations, since they are more related to lifestyle and environmental exposure (Negi & Guda, 2017).

Many developmental disorders are related to lifestyle, delayed early motor milestones, and retained neonatal reflexes. Therefore, if you can properly understand this relationship, then you can intervene and potentially avoid or even therapeutically treat developmental disorders such as ADHD, autism spectrum disorder (ASD), or dyslexia (Melillo et al., 2022).

The Connection to Immunity

Here's where it gets fascinating: These same autonomic nuclei in the brainstem don't just control heart rate and breathing—they directly influence how our immune system functions.

When the brainstem sends signals through these pathways, it can trigger or suppress inflammation. The brainstem also controls the production of stress hormones that affect immunity. Importantly, the brainstem also regulates our gut, where most of our serotonin is produced and where our immune system resides.

This level of autonomic regulation eventually falls under the control of the cortex and the corticoreticular pathway, top-down regulation. If the medulla is delayed in maturity and if there is not proper bottom-up completion, top-down regulation from the cortex over the brainstem, autonomic, and immune functions may be impacted. The parasympathetic nervous system is cortically regulated in the right hemisphere, particularly the insula and the left insula, which is more connected to the sympathetic nervous system and promotes inflammation. The field of neuroimmunology is an exploding field where we are further exploring how different neurological disorders are directly related to immune system dysfunction.

The concept of *leaky gut* has been proven and accepted, since lactose-mannitol tests show that larger-than-normal proteins are able to get through the gut lining and into the bloodstream/urine. Because the sympathetic nuclei in the brainstem, the rostral ventral lateral medullary nuclei, are fully active at birth, they inhibit the parasympathetic dorsal motor nuclei, and the gut functions are inhibited. The infant naturally starts life with a "leaky gut," partly because the infant does not produce their own antibodies, which they must get from the mother's breast milk. These antibodies would not pass through a fully mature, closed stomach lining. Infants are not producing digestive enzymes and acid at this time, since they would digest the antibodies, which would be counterproductive.

At the time solid foods are introduced to babies, their gut lining should've closed up, and they should've started producing digestive enzymes and acid. At that point of maturation, their adaptive immune system should begin operation. Leaky gut is an issue that many people deal with, and it is largely correlated to autoimmune disorders and systemic hyperinflammation. Therefore, a condition such as leaky gut is much more of a maturational delay in how the nervous system regulates the intercellular junctions of the intestinal cells, rather than an issue that arises later in life.

Neurological Foundations

This bottom-up and top-down development is known as vertical integration of neurological development, and it is essential. Early neonatal reflexes, motor milestones, and environmental stimuli are essential factors in the brainstem maturing and developing in early life. They set a foundation for the cortex and more complex structures of the brain to play their role in parasympathetic regulation and volitional movement that further directly correlates with cognitive function and neurotypical development. If disruptions occur in these early steps of life, then bottom-up/top-down regulation does not properly mature. Simultaneously, horizontal, right-left integration of the nervous system and brain should be progressing as well.

Neonatal reflexes play an important role in babies' positioning themselves in utereo as well as playing a role in the birthing process. Neonatal reflexes are important for movement and survival outside of the womb when babies do not have full control of their bodies after birth. As examples, the spinal galant helps infants wiggle out of the birth canal, and then the rooting reflex helps them to eat. The neonatal reflexes are designed to emerge in utero and then integrate within the first year of life. If the onset and integration of neonatal reflexes are delayed, they can lead to missed motor milestones. Horizontal integration of the hemispheres may also be negatively impacted, which is known as a *functional disconnection of networks*. Horizontal integration is essential for things like a dominance profile and asymmetrical functions of the brain.

The less immature a brain is, the less lateralized it is. Your brain develops at midline and from back to forward, as your brain grows, the hemispheres develop specific functions. Lateralization is the process of the brain developing specific functions unique to each side of the brain. Two examples are Broca's and Wernicke's areas, which reside in the left hemisphere. Again, this fact explains why we see ambidextrous handedness in the first few years of life in human infants—their brains have not reached a maturational state of lateralization. Once the neonatal reflex integrates and movement becomes more complex, a dominant hand, foot, eye, and ear should arise. If the baby still has their neonatal reflexes, they will be held back from achieving more volitional and complex movements. There is a saying in neuroscience: "Complex movement, complex brains; simple movement, simple brains." If a child never reaches a certain level of complexity of movement due to skipped, delayed motor milestones or retained neonatal reflexes, the impact on the right brain will be greater than on the left, since this is during the peak of right hemisphere development. The right hemisphere is where most of the early sensory information is processed, and it requires proper mechanoreception to create a sensory motor map of the body, as well as the interoception of visceral organs such as the stomach and bladder.

FUNCTIONAL DISCONNECTION SYNDROME

The best way to understand a developmental disorder such as autism spectrum disorder (ASD) is to first realize the asymmetrical nature of the two hemispheres of the brain. The right hemisphere plays a big role in the parasympathetic nervous system, attachment, self-awareness, socialization, proprioception, interoception, and anti-inflammatory events. All or most of these neurological functions are found to be very deficient in individuals diagnosed with ASD. This implies that the right hemisphere of these individuals is developmentally delayed. We can use a quantitative electroencephalogram (qEEG) to measure slow brain wave activity in both hemispheres, but even more so in the right hemisphere of individuals with ASD, which is indicative of a more immature cortex.

While the brain is complex, based on human traits, individuals with ASD can be overactive in left-hemisphere skills (Leisman et al., 2023). Symptoms of tics; self-stimulating behavior, or stimming; obsessive-compulsive disorder (OCD); and anger outbursts could result, which are all produced by left hemisphere areas. Documentation exists of such individuals displaying extremely high levels of IQ, hyperlexia, savant algorithmic math skills, and photographic memory (Treffert, 2009). Savant gifts, or splinter skills, may be exhibited in the following skill areas or domains: memory, hyperlexia (i.e., the exceptional ability to read, spell, and write), art, music, mechanical or spatial skills, calendar calculation, mathematical calculation, sensory sensitivity, athletic performance, and computer ability.

These skills are correlated with structures in the left hemisphere of the brain, such as Broca's and Wernicke's areas. The left hemisphere of the brain is more dopaminergic as well, where certain disorders such as tics, stims, hyperactivity, and Tourette's are correlated to dopamine and its effect on the direct pathway in the basal ganglia. The left hemisphere is also more associated with activating the sympathetic nervous system, which plays a role in the inflammatory cascade of the immune system. The imbalance that can develop between the right and left hemispheres occurs in a diagnosis such as ASD. These individuals tend to be in highly sympathetic states along with a clear representation of this imbalance in their cognitive and social functions.

Clinical Implications

It is well documented that early intervention in developmental disorders is critical; therefore, we believe that the earlier we can identify developmental delays, the earlier we can intervene.

Neonatal reflex integration and early motor milestones are essential keys to determining whether the brain is developing normally. If prebirth movements are disrupted, this may be the first sign of a delay in the onset of neonatal reflexes due to the epigenetic factors inhibiting gene expression in the developing brain. Once the child is born, if they continue to miss/skip or have abnormal development of motor milestones, this is again a clue that there is a delay in the maturational development in the brain, which may lead to neurobehavioral disorders later in life.

If the reflexes do not emerge on time at the proper strength, they will not become integrated at the proper time—or at all. Poor integration will keep movement in a more immature or less complex state and therefore lead to less complex interaction with the environment and sensory stimulation. The brain may remain in a more immature and less complex state as well, thus delaying the emergence of higher-level cognitive skills. If this vertical integration is delayed, then it will also have an impact on the horizontal integration of the right and left sides of the nervous system and the hemispheres.

This maturational delay leads to maturational imbalances, which are often seen with asymmetric development of the neonatal reflexes and muscle tone asymmetry. These developmental imbalances are what produce most of the symptoms that we see in neurobehavioral disorders later in life. We see that these disorders are a result of underdeveloped and underactive areas of the cortex on one side and overactivity on the other. Determining which hemisphere is overactive and which is underactive can explain most of the varieties of neurobehavioral disorders we see. To correct this imbalance, we must use multimodal sensory stimulation and motor activation to activate one side, which has the effect of downregulating the correlated activities on the other side. Current research argues that the earliest intervention is to stimulate delayed neonatal reflexes to promote proper development of these reflexes and normal motor milestones. By activating the reflexes, we encourage their use, which ultimately leads to integration of the reflexes and maturation of the brainstem and the brain.

Clinical Applications

The good news is that research shows that we can improve this. We have seen one to two standard deviation improvements in children and adolescents with evidence-based interventions. Treating conditions nonpharmacologically, using targeted neurostimulation instead of systemic drugs, is a hallmark of the growing field of bioelectronic medicine (Levine et al., 2020). We can use targeted brain stimulation devices such as transcranial direct current or photobiomodulation tools to activate one side and downregulate the other in the matrix of electromagnetic frequencies. As a result of this immaturity in the brainstem, particularly the medulla and the pons, an imbalance may exist between the sympathetic and parasympathetic functions.

Immaturity in the brainstem keeps the individual in a more dominant sympathetic state; the subsequent autonomic nervous sytem imbalance can explain almost every biomedical issue that is well documented as present in neurodevelopmental disorders. Leaky gut, reduced acid and enzymes, food sensitivities, poor digestion, malabsorption, constipation, dysbiosis, low heart rate variability, and chronic inflammation are all direct results of this sympathetic dominance and parasympathetic deficit. Vagal stimulation is another tool that can help, but ultimately, the answer is to promote the maturation of the brainstem and stimulate the development of the parasympathetic nuclei in the medulla. As you will read in other chapters, language intervention, music, and rhythmic cognitive-motor interventions also improve the brain and the functioning of the student.

Other biomedical tools can also help; elimination diets, digestive enzymes, and vitamin supplementation can all be useful, but gut dysfunction is not the root cause of these problems. The root cause is the immaturity in the brainstem and its impact on brain development and cortical regulation of the autonomic system.

The first step must begin with (1) neonatal reflex stimulation and integration, (2) movement therapy to promote more complex movement, and (3) sensory stimulation to help encourage the proper development of interoception in the right insula and the sensory map in the parietal lobe. If the sensory map does not develop, the motor map in the frontal cortex will not develop properly either, and the individual will not be able to sense their body or purposefully move their body. We have shown that this is the primary reason why some children with autism cannot speak. We must develop these maps so that children can control and gain agency over their bodies and their behavior. Movement interventions will evolve as the child's competencies develop. When children approach age 4, adding rhythmic coordinative movement is central to their continued cognitive, motor, and social development.

CONCLUSION

In America and globally, children need to move more throughout the day. We need to get back to the developmental skills associated with our phylogenetic roots. Our children need stimulation of their vestibular, proprioceptive, and motor systems to support their higher-order language and cognitive systems. If we continue to keep our children in carriers, limit tummy time, and eliminate climbing, foraging, and cross-patterned motor movement, we will continue to interfere with the natural development of our children.

REFERENCES

Alotiby, A. (2024). Immunology of stress: A review article. *Journal of Clinical Medicine*, *13*(21), 6394. https://doi.org/10.3390/jcm13216394

Blythe, S., Beuret, L., & Blythe, P. (2009). *Attention, balance and coordination: The A.B.C. of learning success*. John Wiley & Sons Ltd.

Chinello, A., Di Gangi, V., & Valenza, E. (2018). Persistent primary reflexes affect motor acts: Potential implications for autism spectrum disorder. *Research in Developmental Disabilities*, *83*, 287–295.

Kelly, M., Breathnach, C., Tracey, K., & Donnelly, S. (2022). Manipulation of the inflammatory reflex as a therapeutic strategy: Cell reports. *Medicine*, 3(7), 100696.

Leisman, G. (2024). Neurodiversity and autism spectrum disorder: An ostriches' head in the sand? *Journal of Integrative Neuroscience*, *23*(10), 186.

Leisman, G., Melillo, R., & Melillo, T. (2023). Prefrontal functional connectivities in autism spectrum disorders: A connectopathic disorder affecting movement, interoception, and cognition. *Brain Research Bulletin*, *198*, 65–76.

Leisman, G., Moustafa, A., & Shafir, T. (2016). Thinking, walking, talking: Integratory motor and cognitive brain function. *Frontiers in Public Health*, *4*, 94.

Leisman, G., & Sheldon, D. (2022). Tics and emotions. *Brain Sciences*, *12*(2), 242.

Levine, Y., Faltys, M., & Chernoff, D. (2020). Harnessing the inflammatory reflex for the treatment of inflammation-mediated diseases. *Cold Spring Harbor Perspectives in Medicine*, *10*(1), a034330.

Melillo, R., Leisman, G., Machado, C., Machado-Ferrer, Y., Chinchilla-Acosta, M., Kamgang, S., Melillo, T., & Carmeli, E. (2022). Retained primitive reflexes and potential for intervention in autistic spectrum disorders. *Frontiers in Neurology*, *13*, 922322.

Negi, S., & Guda, C. (2017). Global gene expression profiling of healthy human brain and its application in studying neurological disorders. *Scientific Reports*, *7*, 897.

Treffert, D. (2009). The savant syndrome: An extraordinary condition. A synopsis: past, present, future. *Biological Sciences*, *364*(1522), 1351–1357.

Voight, R., Macias, M., Meyers, S., & Tapia, C. (2018). *AAP developmental and behavioral pediatrics* (2nd Ed.). American Academy of Pediatrics.

Yoshida, S., & Funato, H. (2021). Physical contact in parent-infant relationship and its effect on fostering a feeling of safety. *iScience*, *24*(7), 102721.

CHAPTER 3

Enhancing Sensory-Motor, Cognitive, and Social Skills in Young Children Through Physical Activity

Joann McFee, Kelly Barnhart, and Lynne Kenney, United States

Over the past decade, we've observed a significant decline in children's fundamental motor skills, which directly impacts their learning readiness and academic success. Research shows today's children are entering school with notably weaker motor skills compared to previous generations (Koolwijk et al., 2024). This is evident in several ways. Children have decreased core strength and postural control needed for sitting and attending to lessons. In children, diminished balance and coordination can significantly affect their ability to participate in physical activities like skipping, hopping, jumping, playing sports, climbing, and even activities of daily living such as dressing themselves and making their beds.

Our children's worlds have shifted to more time spent on digital devices, briefer periods of unstructured play, reduced opportunities for outdoor play, and less time in "risky" motor activities like spinning, jumping off a swing, and climbing up a slide. Our current child-rearing practices substantially limit opportunities for gross motor, vestibular, and proprioceptive input starting at birth, with less tummy, or belly, time; movement restricted by car seat carriers and strollers; and more sleeping on one's back. We are creating sensory-motor deficits in our children. These sensory-motor limitations influence motor milestones, cognition, self-regulation, attention, and overall development.

Our occupational therapy clinics have many more referrals for children with greater sensory-motor deficits than a decade ago. Teachers tell us that up to 30% of their classrooms have language, motor, and social skill deficits. Where there used to be one or two children in a classroom of 20–25 with neurodevelopmental needs requiring accommodation or interventions, now there may be six or more. We are contributing this chapter to share strategies that will help address this issue. There are evidence-based ways to improve sensory-motor function in all children. Providing more opportunities for fine and gross motor activities alongside movement that stimulates various developmental systems can shift a generation. The QR code below will bring you to a glossary of terms for this chapter. This material may also be accessed under the "Downloads" tab at htttps://www.tcpress.com/move-more-learn-more-9780807784051.

THE FIRST 1,000 DAYS

The first 5 years of a child's life represent a window for sensory-motor development, during which the brain establishes fundamental neural pathways that will shape future learning and behavior (Shonkoff, 2000). During this period, the child's brain undergoes rapid synaptogenesis, forming more than one million neural connections per second.

The brain's capacity and structure develop at an extraordinary rate during the early years. In the first 1,000 days of life, 80% of the brain's growth occurs—which includes not only an increase in size but also the refinement of neural connections. During this critical period, the brain's architecture and potential are shaped, and a lack of opportunity for movement and exploration can increase developmental vulnerability, limiting the brain's ability to fully develop (de Rooij, 2022).

Did you know that the first 1,000 days are preceded by a period of 3–6 months before conception, which lays the biological foundation for how a fetus will develop in utero? Then, after the first 1,000 days, there are "the next 1,000 days" from ages 2 to 5. While this chapter will not delve into preparing the body for conception, it is an important field of science. If you wish to know that body of research, you may choose to visit Neurologicalhealth.org.

Technically, 1,000 days from birth are up to 2 years and 9 months of age. This period entails heightened neuroplasticity, allowing sensory input and motor experiences to directly shape the neural architecture through the pruning of little-used brain pathways and the strengthening of frequently used connections. Thus, the stimulation of the sensory and motor pathways, alongside language and cognition, is critical in the early years. When opportunities for movement are provided to children, the myelination of nerve fibers increases, improving neuronal signal transmission, speed, and efficiency. Studies utilizing advanced neuroimaging techniques have demonstrated that children who engage in structured sensory-motor activities show increased activation in areas associated with executive function and improved cross-hemispheric integration (Alsaedi, 2025; Schach et al., 2023).

In this chapter, we will discuss the sensory-motor underpinnings for language, cognition, and social understanding, offering recommendations for varied interactions with people and the environment to build the sensory and motor skills central to the brain and body architecture children need to learn, thrive, and behave.

HOW THE SENSORY AND MOTOR SYSTEMS WORK IN UNISON

The sensory and motor systems work in concert with each other to provide the brain with high-quality information about the world, allowing individuals to make adaptive responses to a variety of incoming stimuli. The sensory-motor systems function in a complex and fascinating interplay that supports development and learning (Bigelow & Agrawal, 2015).

The foundation begins with exposure to sensory experiences, often called sensory inputs, where the body receives information through multiple channels. These inputs are sometimes classified into two categories: far senses and near senses. Far senses refer to sensory inputs that arrive from outside the body, such as our basic senses of vision, hearing, touch, taste, and smell. The near senses, sometimes called the hidden senses, tend to be less understood and arise from inputs from our own bodies, including the vestibular and proprioceptive senses.

- **Visual System:** The visual system processes what children see in the environment. This includes much more than just visual acuity; visual processing also includes the task of interpreting visual stimuli to understand forms, patterns, movement, and more to allow individuals to navigate the world.

  The brain processes this information through multiple pathways:
  » Visual acuity (sharpness of vision)
  » Form recognition (identifying objects)
  » Pattern processing (recognizing relationships and sequences)
  » Movement detection (tracking motion)
  » Spatial awareness (understanding position and relationships)
- **Vestibular System:** The vestibular system in the inner ear detects head position and movement, essentially establishing one's relationship with gravity. It has a markedly important relationship with the visual system, as information from a well-functioning vestibular system allows individuals to stabilize their gaze during body movement. Vestibular function also relates to the cognitive domain of visuospatial ability, which includes spatial memory, navigation, mental rotation, and mental representation of three-dimensional space. Substantial evidence suggests that the vestibular system has an impact on attention and cognitive processing ability.

- **Proprioceptive System:** The proprioceptive system provides awareness of body position through muscle and joint feedback. This proprioceptive information from muscles, tendons, and joints allows the brain to create and modify a map of the body to understand how body parts are moving in relation to one another. The more detailed and accurate a body map is, the better able an individual is to unconsciously make adjustments to movement to enhance accuracy.
- **Tactile System:** The tactile system processes touch sensations through the skin, including sensations such as light touch, pressure, temperature, and vibration, allowing us to perceive the texture and qualities of objects we encounter.
- **Auditory System:** The auditory system processes information delivered as sound waves. The auditory system is responsible for hearing by converting vibrations in the air into electrical signals that are interpreted by the brain as sound; this process begins with the outer ear capturing sound waves and continues through the middle ear where vibrations are amplified, finally reaching the inner ear where the sound is transformed into neural signals sent to the brain for interpretation. The brain uses central auditory processing to recognize, interpret, and organize sounds. This includes skills like auditory discrimination, binaural processing, and temporal aspects of audition.

These sensory inputs converge in the central nervous system, particularly in areas like the cerebellum and motor cortex, which then coordinate with the muscular system to produce refined movements. This process is known as *sensorimotor integration*. While it is helpful to learn about these systems in isolation, it is important to understand that these various sensory inputs are generally arriving *simultaneously* and must be managed simultaneously in a process called multisensory processing.

A DEEPER DIVE INTO THE MOTOR SYSTEM

The motor system allows an individual to interact with and react to the world. This includes obvious examples, such as walking to get to a desired location or speaking to make needs known, as well as unseen examples, such as contraction of the smooth muscles of the intestines to aid in digestion and reflexive changes to blood pressure during position changes. Despite the diversity of movements that the human body performs, motor control is often regarded as simple; however, even simple movements require significant computations to coordinate the action of multiple muscles (Hall, 2023). It is through the support of a strong sensorimotor foundation that a child can optimize both conscious and unconscious motor functions and development.

It is well established that sensory input both initiates motor movements and shapes movement over time (Fiorentino, 1972). This cyclical relationship between sensory processing and motor development is integral. As varying sensory inputs are received, a child must adapt to the new experiences with motor responses. These new motor responses create novel sensory inputs, which, again, require adaptive motor responses.

Typical motor development progresses in a cephalocaudal (head to tail) and proximodistal (center outward) pattern. Head control is the first skill to develop, and motor control progresses downward the spine. The center of the body (the musculature of the head and trunk) develops prior to the periphery of the body (the upper and lower extremities). Delays in the development of head control and midline stability can have subsequent effects on the development/stability of the distal joints, impacting overall motor performance.

Tummy time is a primary means of developing head and trunk control in infancy.

The Back to Sleep campaign, instituted in 1994, was a public health initiative in response to research indicating that infants who slept on their stomachs were at a higher risk for sudden infant death syndrome (SIDS). While the program was hugely successful, reducing SIDS rates by 50%, an unintentional consequence was that babies lost opportunities to practice the head and trunk control development that occurs while in a prone position. This has directly contributed to an increase in positional diagnoses such as plagiocephaly (flattening of the head) and torticollis (tightness in the muscles on one side of the neck yielding a tilted head posture).

The development of head control in different postural positions is essential, as it enables infants to practice postural reactions and refine their vestibular system. For instance, a baby carried on their mother's hip must constantly adjust their head and body in response to its movements, experiencing rotational, linear, and inversion movements. This provides important input for developing postural control and balance. In contrast, a baby in a child carrier is passively supported, primarily experiencing linear movement and having fewer opportunities to actively engage in postural adjustments.

In addition, building strong flexor and extensor musculature is crucial for postural endurance. Children with weak extensor muscles often have difficulty sitting upright at their desks, resulting in poor posture, slouching, and fatigue. The development of the extensor system—essential for maintaining upright posture and counteracting gravity—begins early in life through experiences such as tummy play. Early weight-bearing activities, such as pushing up on extended arms during tummy time, play a vital role in strengthening the upper body, particularly the shoulders, arms, and hands, to support fine motor development. The stability and strength built through these movements boost neural development and influence later abilities such as coordination, concentration, and motor planning, highlighting the link between physical and cognitive development (Shonkoff & Phillips, 2000).

Diminished opportunities for developing head and trunk control appear to have had a general impact on the development of motor skills in many children, as this foundational stability sets the stage for higher-level motor skills such as crawling. These changes in typical motor development are so widespread that the Centers for Disease Control and Prevention (CDC, 2022) altered the checklist of traditional developmental milestone acquisition. Due to data about variability in crawling patterns among children, the CDC removed crawling as an essential marker of motor development. From the therapeutic perspective, this is a concerning change because of the variety of motor benefits that crawling provides. This change in the milestones normalizes pathology.

Crawling is a key developmental skill for building shoulder and hip strength, coordination, balance, and spatial awareness. It also engages the core muscles and enhances proprioception, laying the groundwork for more advanced motor skills. The absence of crawling in early development can lead to challenges with bilateral coordination and cross-pattern movements, affecting tasks like climbing stairs, swimming, and even riding a bicycle.

Crawling is a foundational skill that builds the strength, balance, and coordination necessary for babies to progress to pulling themselves up to stand and, eventually, independent walking. Crawling also supports reaching and moving in various planes of movement: verticals, horizontals, diagonals, and cross-body upper and lower body movements.

Additionally, children with language and learning disabilities often struggle with bilateral coordination and laterality, leading to difficulties such as letter and number reversals and word transposition. Since physical movement is closely tied to brain development, a decline in these foundational activities can have cognitive consequences as well.

A CLOSER LOOK AT SENSORY PROCESSING

Sensory processing is a term that refers to the way the nervous system (brain and spinal cord) receives messages from the senses (often referred to as *input*) and turns them into appropriate motor and behavioral responses (often referred to as *output*). Usually, sensory processing occurs automatically and unconsciously in typically developing students through the course of ordinary childhood activities. When the process is disorganized, several problems in overall development, learning, and behavior may result, all of which can affect a child's future skill development (See Ayres, 1971, 1972, 1975; Passarello et al., 2022).

When any part of this process is inefficient, a wide array of challenges can arise. If sensory information provided to the brain is unreliable or inaccurate, it is a stressor. As a result, the brain must allocate more neural resources to respond to the stressor, leaving fewer resources available for other processes. Ideally, sensory and motor systems develop efficiently to reach a state of automaticity, which reduces the cognitive load involved in motor planning, thereby allowing the development of higher-order skills.

As we shift into a discussion of fine and gross motor learning, it is helpful to understand their differences. The distinction between fine and gross motor movement are a matter of motor units. This refers to a single nerve fiber interfacing with a muscle fiber or fibers. It is the activation of a nerve fiber that yields muscle contraction. If a nerve fiber goes into a large number of muscle fibers, this large contraction produces a gross motor movement. Conversely, a nerve fiber that interfaces with a limited number of nerve fibers produces a smaller but more precise contraction, allowing for fine motor movement.

Gross motor development involves the large musculature of the body for tasks such as running, jumping, and climbing. Maintaining static and dynamic balance is also critical. Gross motor skill development is reliant on a strong foundation of effective sensory processing. These large movement skills develop as the sensory systems inform the motor systems via connections to the cerebellum, allowing these skills to be continuously monitored and optimized with repetition. The brain's ability to adapt and change, known as *neuroplasticity*, allows neural pathways to strengthen through repetition, leading to more efficient sensorimotor integration and improved sensory-motor skills.

THE MOTOR-SKILL LEARNING CONNECTION

During childhood development, sensory-motor skill integration manifests in several key ways, such as the following:

- **Physical Development:** When a child learns to catch a ball, they must coordinate multiple factors: visual input (tracking the ball), proprioceptive feedback (awareness of arm position), and motor output (moving arms to intercept the ball). The brain continuously adjusts and refines motor commands based on sensory feedback, creating smoother, more accurate movements over time.
- **Balance, Core Strength, and Coordination:** Balance, core strength, and coordination are essential elements of physical development required for foundational movements. Standing and walking require constant integration between the vestibular system, visual input, proprioception, and motor output. The brain processes information about head position, visual environment, and body position to maintain balance and adjust muscle activity accordingly.

- **Fine Motor (FM) Skills:** FM skills support many elements of learning. The hands are an incredibly important human feature that allow individuals to experience and skillfully manipulate the environment. The proficient use of the hands, often termed fine motor development or dexterity, is an essential skill that warrants attention. For individuals with fine motor challenges, components of hand function must be assessed and addressed.

Factors such as hand strength, arch development, and in-hand manipulation skills are often relatively familiar to parents and teachers; however, often overlooked factors, such as trunk stability or the optimal function of the joints of the shoulder, elbow, and wrist, provide important foundational stability from which fine motor abilities can more easily unfold.

When a child learns to write, they must integrate multiple skills: visual input (seeing the paper and letters), tactile feedback (feeling the pencil), proprioception (knowing where their hand is), and motor control (making precise finger movements). Visual-motor integration and visuospatial skills also play a key role in this complex task. In addition, core strength is necessary to maintain a sturdy upright posture, while upper extremity strength provides proximal stability, enabling fluid hand and finger movements for writing. This complex integration improves with practice, leading to better handwriting. However, it is essential that balance, posture, and core strength are secure before focusing on the fine motor skills required for handwriting activities.

During early childhood, the sensory and motor systems become increasingly refined through repeated exposure to experiences that support maturation. Neural pathways strengthen through repetition, leading to more efficient sensorimotor integration. This process is particularly active during early childhood, which is why movement experiences are so important for development. When children engage in activities such as climbing, crawling, rolling, spinning, swinging, and jumping, they are constructing and refining vital sensory-motor connections that constantly refine the child's abilities to interact efficiently in their environment. The development of these integrated systems also supports cognitive and social development.

"The Power 3"

While all the foundational senses are highly important, some are more well known than others. From a therapy standpoint, a primary focus is attending to and providing students, parents, and teachers with education and resources concerning the lesser-understood sensory systems. We call them "the Power 3" because interventions using these systems can have long-lasting impacts.

They are:

1. The vestibular system
2. The proprioceptive system
3. The tactile system

These three systems, combined with all the other senses, form a complex interconnected network that fundamentally underpins learning in children (Wiener-Vacher et al., 2013).

> Occupational therapists report the effects of addressing these areas can extend long after the intervention, with vestibular input impacting the brain for up to 8 hours and proprioceptive and tactile interventions affecting the brain for up to 90 minutes afterward (See Lane et al., 2019).

As previously mentioned, all the sensory systems are working simultaneously and must be organized and managed as such through multisensory processing. Certain foundational sensory systems do, however, have special relationships via structural proximity or neurological pathways and can be skillfully used to better understand and support development.

Vestibular-Proprioceptive-Visual Systems. The vestibular system, paired with the proprioceptive and visual systems, work together to constantly provide the brain with information regarding the body's position in space and how it is moving through space. The vestibular system is the primary source of descending neural control for paraspinal muscles, spinal erectors, and extensors, so optimizing vestibular function has huge implications in postural stability. A well-functioning vestibular system allows the development of a vertical central axis, or midline, which is the foundation for 3D orientation and movement. All organization of our neuromuscular system moves from the vertical axis. Together, these systems enable stable posture during learning tasks.

When a child sits at a desk to read or write, these systems work together to maintain head and body position without conscious effort. The vestibular system and proprioception support eye tracking while reading. The vestibular system stabilizes vision during head movement, coordinating with proprioception to skillfully guide eye movements. These systems also contribute to spatial awareness. Their combined input helps children understand their position in space, which is essential for developing fundamental skills like reading and writing. This spatial awareness aids in distinguishing letter orientation (like telling *b* from *d*), tracking text from left to right across a page, maintaining proper distance from reading materials, and organizing written work on paper.

When a child has difficulties in carrying out academic tasks such as reading and writing, it would be appropriate for the teacher/practitioner to observe the child's posture: Are they slumped over the desk or perched on the edge of the chair? Are their legs wrapped around the chair legs to stabilize their balance? How secure are static/dynamic balance skills? There may be underlying issues that need addressing.

Vestibular-Auditory-Integration. The vestibular and auditory systems share anatomical proximity in the inner ear and have significant functional connections. They aid in balance and movement; they facilitate rhythm, tempo, and timing; and they influence attention. Another key role of this duo is vibration detection. A well-functioning vestibular system is crucial for understanding our surroundings. Without it, sights and sounds become fragmented, lacking connection to each other and to a cohesive understanding of the world. Since movement is integral to virtually all our activities, the vestibular system underpins all behavior and skill acquisition. It also plays a vital role in organizing the constant influx of sensory information we receive.

Proprioceptive-Auditory Relationship. While less direct than the vestibular-auditory connection, proprioception and auditory processing interact in important ways. The proprioceptive and auditory systems respond to musical rhythm; they coordinate planning of movement (praxis) in response to auditory cues. Together, the proprioceptive and auditory systems support speech development by providing feedback regarding the placement of the mouth, tongue, and vocal muscles that allow for the accurate production of speech.

Visual-Proprioception-Tactile. This important relationship connects both near and far senses to integrate internal and external sensory inputs that allow for enhanced motor control, especially relating to eye-hand coordination. It is this relationship that first facilitates a functional reach in babies, the very foundation of visual motor integration. While also integral for developing large motor skills, this relationship is often observed in the classroom during fine and visual motor tasks, such as handwriting. The coordination of visual skills (shifting eyes from far- to near-point vision) for a task such as copying from the board must combine with well-developed body maps of the arm and hand, as well as tactile input from a writing implement. A weak link in any part of this chain can result in difficulty in carrying out academic tasks.

How Do These Systems Relate to Classroom Performance?

The integration of sensory input with motor responses allows children to construct mental representations of concepts, develop spatial awareness, and establish the sensorimotor schemas necessary for abstract thinking. When sensory-motor systems function optimally, children can better sustain attention, process information efficiently, and organize their thoughts—all prerequisites for academic learning.

Academic Skills. Efficient reading requires stable posture, core strength, and skillful control of eye movements, combined with auditory processing for phonological awareness. Proprioceptive feedback guides hand movements, while vestibular feedback is used to maintain head position during writing and drawing. Spatial awareness from vestibular-proprioceptive integration supports numerical concepts and geometric understanding (Lindner et al., 2022). Static and dynamic balance contribute to overall stability, coordination, and the ability to perform everyday activities safely and effectively, as they enable the body to maintain control both while stationary (static) and during movement (dynamic). As children progress developmentally in their ability to be stable within and beyond the sagittal, coronal, and transverse planes, they are better able to remain balanced as they walk, reach, kick, hop, jump, and run. This ability to efficiently change direction while remaining in balance contributes to functional movement across various activities of daily living (Kenney & Comizio, 2016; Wiener-Vacher et al., 2013).

Fine Motor Skills. Fine motor skills play a central role in early academic development. Diminished capabilities in this area can significantly impact a child's learning experience across multiple domains. When children struggle with fine motor control, the physical act of writing becomes laborious and frustrating, resulting in illegible handwriting, incorrect letter formation, and slower work completion. This mechanical challenge diverts cognitive resources away from content learning, as the child must concentrate intensely on the physical act of writing rather than the ideas they wish to express.

Grip Strength. Grip strength is considered a valuable indicator of overall muscle strength and can predict future health outcomes, including cardiometabolic health, bone health, and cognitive function. Studies have shown that millennials, compared to previous generations, tend to have significantly weaker grip strength, with data indicating a decline in hand strength, particularly among young men, likely due to increased reliance on technology and less manual labor in their daily lives. This means that millennials generally have a weaker grip than older generations when squeezing something with their hands, which impacts handwriting skills.

Research conducted by Fain (2016) found that young adults (millennials) between the ages of 20 and 34 had significantly weaker hand grips than those tested in 1985. Experts attribute this decline to increased technology use in daily activities, which leads to less hand muscle engagement compared to previous generations, who performed more manual labor.

When These Systems Are Challenged

Learning difficulties can emerge when these systems aren't working optimally together:

- Challenges with tracking while reading
- Decreased ability to follow verbal instructions while moving
- Difficulty maintaining attention during seated work
- Problems with handwriting or fine motor tasks
- Reduced participation in physical activities that support learning

Supporting Integration

To support healthy integration of these systems, children benefit from the following:

- Activities that combine listening with movement
- Fine motor activities with varying postural demands
- Games that challenge balance and spatial awareness
- Movement opportunities throughout the learning day
- Rhythmic activities that incorporate whole-body movement

Understanding these relationships helps educators and caregivers create learning environments that support the development and integration of these crucial sensory systems. When these systems work together effectively, they create a stable foundation for learning across all domains. The QR code below will bring you to a printable PDF version of the Rhythmic Movement Activities. This material may also be accessed under the "Downloads" tab at https://www.tcpress.com/move-more-learn-more-9780807784051.

RHYTHMIC MOVEMENT ACTIVITIES

Activity #1: Back-to-Back Ball Passing

Overview: Back-to-Back Ball Passing is a simple yet effective partner activity that builds coordination, communication, and core strength.

Benefits

- Promotes coordination and motor planning
- Strengthens core muscles
- Encourages communication between partners
- Provides vestibular *and* proprioceptive input, especially with a weighted ball
- Can be adapted for different ages and abilities

Materials Needed

- A 4–6-inch diameter or playground ball (regular or 2 lb. weighted)
- A partner

Instructions

1. Stand back-to-back with your partner, with your spines touching.
2. One person starts with the ball.
3. Pass the ball to your partner by twisting to either side.
4. Your partner receives the ball and twists to pass it back.
5. Continue passing in rhythm, alternating sides when possible.
6. Count out loud: "1-2-3-4; 2-2-3-4; 3-2-3-4; 4-2-3-4."

Tips

- Keep feet planted shoulder-width apart for stability.
- Engage your core muscles during the twisting motion.
- Communicate verbally to coordinate passes.
- Use a weighted ball to increase resistance and provide heavy work input.
- Challenge older kids by increasing the distance between partners or changing body positions (i.e., tall kneel, half kneel).

Activity #2: Belly Crawling

Overview: Belly crawling is a developmental activity where the person moves forward while keeping their belly on the ground, providing important sensory input and building coordination.

Benefits

- Can be calming and organizing for the sensory system
- Develops motor planning and body awareness

- Promotes bilateral coordination between both sides of the body
- Provides rich tactile input through continuous floor contact
- Strengthens core, shoulder, and neck muscles
- Supports neurological development through cross-lateral movement

Materials Needed

- Open floor space with a clean surface
- Optional: mat, carpet, or soft blanket for comfort

Instructions

1. Lie face down on the floor with belly touching the ground.
2. Keep arms extended forward or bent at the elbows near shoulders.
3. Use a combination of arm pulling and leg pushing to move forward.
4. Alternate left and right limb movements (opposite arm and leg working together).
5. Keep belly in contact with the floor throughout the movement.
6. Crawl toward a specific target or follow a designated path.

Tips

- Start with short distances and gradually increase.
- Ensure that the surface is comfortable but provides some resistance.
- Encourage proper cross-pattern movement (right arm/left leg, left arm/right leg).
- Make it fun by creating an obstacle course or story context.

Activity #3: Animal Walks

Overview: Animal walks are movement activities that mimic different animals, encouraging upper extremity weight-bearing while providing proprioceptive input and building strength.

Benefits

- Creates purposeful movement opportunities in the classroom setting
- Develops upper-body strength and endurance
- Enhances motor planning and coordination
- Improves proximal stability in shoulders and core
- Promotes bilateral integration
- Provides substantial proprioceptive feedback to joints and muscles

Materials Needed

- Open space for movement
- Optional: Markers for paths or stations; poly spots to mark the spot

Instructions

Crab Walk
- » Sit on the floor and place hands behind you.
- » Lift hips off the ground.
- » Walk backward, forward, or sideways using hands and feet.
- » Keep belly facing upward.

Bear Walk
- » Start on hands and knees.
- » Lift knees slightly off the ground.
- » Walk forward or backward with opposite hand and foot moving together.
- » Keep back flat and head in line with spine.

Wheelbarrow Walk (Partner Activity)
- » One person lies on stomach.
- » Partner lifts person's legs between ankles and thighs.
- » Person walks forward on hands while partner holds legs.
- » Switch roles after a designated distance.

Three-Legged Animal Walks (Challenge)
- » Perform any of the walks using only three limbs.
- » Example: Bear walk with one arm tucked or crab walk with one leg lifted.

Tips

- Maintain proper form with shoulders directly over wrists.
- Start with short distances and gradually increase.
- Use as transitions between classroom stations or activities.
- Add fun elements like moving like specific animals or racing.

Activity #4: Rocking Eggs

Overview: Rocking Eggs is a fun body awareness activity where children create an "egg" shape with their bodies and practice controlled rocking movements without "breaking" their form.

Benefits

- Builds coordination and balance
- Develops core strength and stability
- Enhances vestibular processing
- Improves body awareness and control
- Promotes self-regulation through rhythmic movement
- Strengthens neck and back muscles

Materials Needed

- Soft surface (mat, carpet, or padded floor)
- Optional: pillows for safety

Instructions

1. Have the child sit upright on the floor with knees bent.
2. Ask them to look down at their belly button.
3. Guide them to wrap their arms around their knees, hugging them close to their chest.
4. The body should now resemble an "egg" shape.
5. Encourage the child to slowly rock backward until their upper back touches the floor.
6. Then have them rock forward to return to the upright position.
7. Challenge them to maintain the tight "egg" shape throughout the rocking motion.
8. Practice rocking back and forth several times.

Tips

- Demonstrate the movement first.
- Emphasize keeping the body tight and compact like an egg.
- Use the cue "don't break your egg" to help maintain form.
- Start with small movements and gradually increase the range.
- Ensure adequate space and padding for safety.

Activity #5: Rolling on Diagonals

Overview: Log Rolling Diagonal combines vestibular input with visual tracking by having participants roll across the room diagonally while focusing on visual targets along the way.

Benefits

- Challenges multiple sensory systems simultaneously
- Combines physical activity with academic content
- Develops core strength and body awareness
- Enhances spatial awareness
- Improves bilateral coordination
- Integrates visual processing with movement
- Provides intensive vestibular stimulation

Materials Needed

- Open space with clear diagonal paths
- Visual targets (flash cards, large-print words, pictures)
- Optional: exercise mat or carpet for comfort

Instructions

1. Clear a diagonal path across the room.
2. Place visual targets at intervals along the path or have a partner hold them.
3. Have the participant lie flat on their back with arms extended overhead.
4. Keep the body straight and rigid like a "log."
5. Begin rolling sideways across the diagonal of the room.
6. While rolling, pause briefly at rhythmic intervals (1, 2, 3, Flash card) to
   - Focus on flash cards
   - Read large-print words
   - Identify images or symbols
7. Continue rolling until reaching the opposite corner.
8. Return by rolling along another diagonal path.

Tips

- Maintain a straight body position throughout the roll.
- Keep arms and legs extended.
- Roll in a slow, controlled manner.
- Be ready to respond to the visual targets (flash cards with stimuli).
- Position visual targets so they're visible during brief pauses.
- For beginners, start with shorter distances and fewer targets.
- Ensure the rolling area is free of obstacles.

CONCLUSION

To help children and older students thrive in various environments—such as the classroom, playground, cafeteria, or at home—it's essential to integrate regular, challenging activities into their daily routines that enhance the development of the Power 3. There is a growing shift toward more intentional active learning, with early educators, teachers, occupational therapists, speech pathologists, school psychologists, and other professionals recognizing that today's fast-paced society demands learners to quickly adapt, engage, and respond in diverse ways.

Emphasizing the movement dimension of learning allows us to be confident that we are working to meet children's needs more effectively. This chapter included a small selection of our clinical activities. The reader is encouraged to consider how these can be integrated into the school year calendar and lesson planning, working toward a whole-school ethos of active learning.

REFERENCES

Alsaedi, R. (2025). Relation between executive functioning, sensory processing, and motor performance in children with autism. *BMC Pediatrics, 25*, 457.

Ayres, A. (1971). Characteristics of types of sensory integrative dysfunction. *American Journal of Occupational Therapy, 25*, 329–334.

Ayres, A. (1972). *Sensory integration and learning disorders*. Western Psychological Services.

Ayres, A. (1975). Sensorimotor foundations of academic ability. In W. Cruikshank & D. P. Hallahan (Eds). *Perceptual and learning disabilities in children. vol. 2: research and theory*. Syracuse University Press.

Bigelow, A., & Agrawal, K. (2015). Sensorimotor integration in infancy. *Child Development Perspectives, 9*(3), 187–192.

Centers for Disease Control and Prevention. (2022). *CDC's developmental milestones.* https://www.cdc.gov/act-early/milestones/

de Rooij, S. (2022). Are brain and cognitive reserve shaped by early life circumstances? *Frontiers in Neuroscience, 16*, 825811.

Fain, E. (2016). Grip strength in millennials. *American Journal of Occupational Therapy, 70*(4), 1–7.

Fears, N., Sherrod, G., Templin, T., Bugnariu, N., Patterson, R., & Miller, H. (2023). Community-based postural control assessment in autistic individuals indicates a similar but delayed trajectory compared to neurotypical individuals. *Autism Research: Official Journal of the International Society for Autism Research, 16*(3), 543–557.

Fiorentino, M. (1972). *Reflex testing methods for evaluating CNS development*. Charles C Thomas Publisher.

Hall, J. (2023). *Guyton and Hall textbook of medical physiology* (14th ed.). Elsevier.

Kenney, L., & Comizio, R. (2016). *70 play activities for better thinking, self-regulation, learning & behavior*. PESI Publishing.

Koolwijk, P., de Jonge, E., Mombarg, R., Remmers, T., Van Kann, D., van Aart, I., Savelsbergh, G., & de Vries, S. (2024). Changes in motor competence of 4–8-year-old children: A longitudinal study. *International Journal of Environmental Research and Public Health, 21*(2), 190.

Lane, S., Mailloux, Z., Schoen, S., Bundy, A., May-Benson, T., Parham, L., Smith Roley, S., & Schaaf, R. (2019). Neural foundations of Ayres Sensory Integration®. *Brain Sciences, 9*(7), 153.

Lindner, N., Moeller, K., Dresen, V., Pixner, S., & Lonnemann, J. (2022). Children's spatial language skills predict their verbal number skills: A longitudinal study. *PlOS one, 17*(10), e0277026.

Passarello, N., Tarantino, V., Chirico, A., Menghini, D., Costanzo, F., Sorrentino, P., Fucà, E., Gigliotta, O., Alivernini, F., Oliveri, M., Lucidi, F., Vicari, S., Mandolesi, L., & Turriziani, P. (2022). Sensory processing disorders in children and adolescents: Taking stock of assessment and novel therapeutic tools. *Brain Sciences, 12*(11), 1478.

Schach, S., Braun, D.A. & Lindner, A. (2023). Cross-hemispheric recruitment during action planning with increasing task demand. *Scientific Reports* 13, 15375.

Shonkoff, J. P., & Phillips, D. A. (Eds.). (2000). *From neurons to neighborhoods: The science of early childhood development.* National Academy Press.

Wiener-Vacher, S., Hamilton, D., & Wiener, S. (2013). Vestibular activity and cognitive development in children: Perspectives. *Frontiers in Integrative Neuroscience, 7*, 92.

CHAPTER 4

Using Music Interventions to Strengthen Cognition, Co-regulation, and Self-Regulation

The Pre-K SEND Program

Angelo Molino with Lynne Kenney, United States

Music is not merely an art form that entertains—it is a powerful cognitive tool that shapes how we think, learn, and behave. Research has consistently demonstrated that rhythm, timing, and tempo fundamentally influence neural processing, creating what Thaut et al. et al. (2014) describe as a "temporal scaffold" upon which cognitive functions are built. These musical elements activate multiple brain regions simultaneously, forming what Koelsch (2020) calls "a supramodal network" that enhances memory formation, attention regulation, and executive function. Processing of sound relates to neurological function, cognition, and social relatedness (see Kraus, 2021).

Individuals with stronger rhythmic abilities often demonstrate superior language processing and reading skills, suggesting that our capacity to detect and synchronize with temporal patterns may underlie broader cognitive capabilities (Tierney & Kraus, 2015; Tierney et al., 2021). The relationship between music and cognition is particularly evident in educational settings, where musical interventions have been shown to improve academic performance across domains (Frischen et al., 2019; Jaschke et al., 2018; Miendlarzewska & Trost, 2014).This emerging understanding of music's cognitive impact offers promising avenues for designing learning environments that harness the power of rhythm to optimize information processing, enhance retention, and support behavioral regulation.

THE SYNERGISTIC POWER OF MUSIC AND MOVEMENT IN CHILD DEVELOPMENT

Music and movement together create a powerful developmental framework for children, enhancing multiple domains simultaneously. When rhythmic activities engage a child's body and mind in synchronized patterns, they establish crucial neural connections that support holistic development.

In sensory-motor development, musical activities that incorporate timing and physical movement help children refine their coordination and spatial awareness. As children clap to beats, march to rhythms, or dance with varying tempos, they integrate auditory input with motor responses, strengthening what Tierney and Kraus (2013) call "audio-motor coupling." This synchronization between hearing and movement builds neural pathways that support fine and gross motor skills.

For cognitive development, rhythmic activities create temporal frameworks that help organize thought processes. A decade of research shows that musical training enhances executive functions, including attention, working memory, and cognitive flexibility (Rodriguez-Gomez & Talero-Gutiérrez, 2022). The structured patterns in music provide predictable sequences that help children understand time relationships, anticipate changes, and develop pattern recognition skills that transfer to mathematical and logical reasoning.

Language acquisition benefits tremendously from musical engagement. The prosodic elements of music—rhythm, stress, and intonation—mirror speech patterns, helping children distinguish phonemic sounds and develop phonological awareness. Patel (2011) describes how musical training enhances the neural processing of speech sounds, while synchronized movement to rhythm helps children internalize the temporal aspects of language, supporting both receptive and expressive language skills.

Perhaps most visibly, music-based physical activities foster social development through shared experiences. Group musical games and dance activities teach children to coordinate their actions with peers, building what Cirelli and colleagues (2014) identified as prosocial behaviors through synchronous movement. These shared rhythmic experiences create bonds, teach turn-taking, and develop empathy through collective participation in musical dialogues.

The integration of tempo variations is particularly beneficial, as it helps children modulate their energy levels and develop self-regulation skills. Moving slowly to gentle rhythms can promote calm and focus, whereas faster tempos can channel excess energy productively, teaching children to adjust their arousal levels based on external cues—a crucial skill for emotional regulation and classroom readiness.

When thoughtfully implemented in educational settings, music and movement activities serve as multisensory learning tools that support development across domains, creating enjoyable experiences that naturally motivate children's participation while building essential skills for academic and social success.

Music and Rhythm as Developmental Catalysts for Neurodiverse Children

For neurodiverse children, the relationship among music, rhythm, and development takes on heightened significance, often revealing both unique challenges and remarkable strengths. The neurological differences present in conditions such as ASD, ADHD, developmental coordination disorder, and various learning disabilities create distinct patterns in how these children process and respond to rhythmic stimuli (Lense et al., 2021).

Many neurodiverse children experience unique sensory processing and integration. Music, with its structured temporal framework, can provide predictable patterns that help organize sensory information in ways that verbal instructions alone cannot achieve. Research by Hardy and LaGasse (2013) demonstrates that rhythmic auditory stimulation can significantly improve motor coordination and gait in children with developmental coordination disorders by providing external timing cues that bypass impaired internal timing mechanisms.

The relationship between rhythm perception and cognitive processing is particularly noteworthy in neurodiversity. Children with ADHD, who often struggle with temporal processing and attention regulation, show improved focus and reduced impulsivity when engaged with rhythmic activities. Rhythm-based interventions may help strengthen executive functions by providing temporal structure that supports attention allocation and working memory (Degé & Frischen, 2022; Frischen et al., 2022; Zaatar et al., 2023).

For children with autism spectrum disorder, who may experience challenges in social timing and communication, musical engagement offers a structured yet flexible medium for developing joint attention and social reciprocity. Srinivasan and Bhat (2013) found that rhythmic interpersonal synchronization activities help develop the timing mechanisms crucial for social interaction, allowing children to practice the give-and-take rhythms of communication within a predictable framework. Music interventions are also effective in treating the auditory processing elements of developmental dyslexia in infants (Dondena et al., 2021).

The tempo of musical activities carries particular significance for neurodiverse populations. Children with sensory sensitivities may respond differently to various tempos, with some finding slower, predictable rhythms calming and organizing, while others may need faster tempos to maintain engagement. The individual's response to tempo can provide valuable diagnostic information and therapeutic opportunities, as noted by Thaut and Hoemberg (2014) in their research on neurologic music therapy.

Interestingly, many neurodiverse children demonstrate islands of exceptional ability in rhythm perception or production. Children with dyslexia, while often struggling with language-based temporal processing, sometimes show preserved or enhanced abilities in musical rhythm discrimination (Overy, 2003). Similarly, some autistic individuals display remarkable abilities to perceive and reproduce complex rhythmic patterns, suggesting potential compensatory mechanisms or alternative neural pathways for temporal processing.

The bidirectional relationship between motor timing and cognitive processing becomes evident in music-based interventions. When neurodiverse children engage in structured rhythmic movement, they're not just developing motor coordination—they're simultaneously building cognitive skills related to sequencing, prediction, and pattern recognition (see LaGasse et al., 2024). This integrated approach aligns with the embodied cognition framework described by Maes and Leman (2013), where physical movement shapes cognitive understanding in ways particularly beneficial for those with alternative neural development patterns.

By recognizing the unique ways neurodiverse children respond to and process rhythmic information, educators and therapists can design targeted interventions that leverage individual strengths while supporting areas of challenge, creating more inclusive and effective developmental opportunities.

THE ROLE OF MUSIC THERAPY IN COGNITION AND LEARNING

Music therapy, specifically the Gertrude Orff approach integrated with Orff Schulwerk pedagogy and further refined through Gertrude Orff/Orff-Schulwerk/Multi-Model (G.O./O.S./M.M.) Variations, provides a comprehensive, multisensory pathway for enhancing cognitive, emotional, and social development in preschool children with Special Educational Needs and Disabilities (SEND). Grounded in extensive research and applied practice, this chapter offers a structured and practical framework for embedding these musical interventions effectively within a Pre-K SEND curriculum. The chapter will systematically explore the theoretical foundations, practical methodologies, and evidence-based outcomes associated with music therapy.

Foundations of Music Therapy for SEND Pre-K

Music therapy is a powerful, evidence-based practice that significantly supports key developmental domains crucial for young learners with SEND (Molino, 2023). Specifically, tailored interventions in music therapy effectively enhance cognitive skills, such as attention, memory, and executive functions, enabling children to better engage with their learning environments and daily routines (Kasuya-Ueba et al., 2020). Simultaneously, music therapy nurtures co-regulation by facilitating interactions and emotional synchrony between children and their caregivers or peers. This shared musical experience creates a supportive environment where emotional bonds are strengthened, fostering both social skills and emotional intelligence (Molino, 2024).

Furthermore, music therapy directly contributes to self-regulation development, empowering children to recognize, understand, and manage their emotions effectively. Techniques involving rhythm and melody help young children identify emotional states, express feelings constructively, and build strategies for emotional control and resilience. The G.O./O.S./M.M. model plays an integral role in this developmental journey. This innovative approach seamlessly integrates rhythmic, melodic, and kinesthetic experiences to create holistic and immersive learning opportunities. Children actively participate in movement-based music activities, rhythmic exercises, and melodic explorations that not only stimulate their sensory system, but also anchor learning experiences deeply in their cognitive and emotional frameworks. The comprehensive nature of the G.O./O.S./M.M. model ensures a balanced and inclusive approach to music therapy, promoting meaningful developmental progress and lasting educational benefits.

Enhancing Cognitive Development Through Musical Play

Music engages neural pathways essential for executive functioning, including memory enhancement, sequential thinking, and pattern recognition. The act of listening to and creating music activates multiple areas of the brain simultaneously, fostering improved cognitive abilities, especially during critical periods of early childhood development.

Memory is significantly reinforced through musical play. Songs and melodies provide structured, rhythmic patterns that facilitate memorization and recall, enabling children to encode information more efficiently. For instance, the use of rhythmic chants or simple melodic phrases can help young children remember sequences, instructions, or new vocabulary. Repetitive musical activities not only solidify memory retention, but also encourage the development of auditory discrimination, a key skill for language acquisition.

Sequential thinking, another core executive function, is naturally supported by musical play. Learning to play instruments, singing songs, or engaging in rhythmic movement necessitates an understanding and anticipation of sequences. Children must recognize and predict musical structures, such as rhythm and melody progression, which translates into enhanced cognitive flexibility and improved problem-solving skills. Activities such as following a rhythm or coordinating movements to music reinforce these sequential processing abilities.

Pattern recognition is inherent in musical activities and plays a critical role in cognitive growth. Identifying repeated melodic phrases, rhythmic cycles, or harmonic progressions engages children's brains in active analytical processes. By recognizing these patterns, children build foundational skills necessary for mathematics, reading, and scientific reasoning. Musical play, therefore, provides a playful yet robust framework for sharpening cognitive skills essential for academic success.

Incorporating musical activities into educational contexts creates enriched environments where cognitive abilities flourish. Whether through structured musical lessons, playful improvisations, or rhythmic games, musical engagement supports holistic brain development. Ultimately, musical play serves not merely as entertainment, but as a profound and effective tool for enhancing essential cognitive functions in developing children.

MUSICAL INTERACTION FOR EMOTIONAL CO-REGULATION

Musical interaction, particularly through rhythmic synchronization and emotional mirroring, significantly enhances emotional co-regulation skills, fundamental components in early social-emotional development. Rhythmic synchronization occurs naturally when individuals coordinate their movements or musical responses, such as tapping, clapping, or vocalizing in rhythm together. This synchronization provides young children with sensory and motor feedback, reinforcing their ability to tune into others' emotional states and behavioral cues. Likewise, emotional mirroring in musical interactions facilitates a profound reciprocal connection where caregivers and children reflect each other's emotional expressions and states. By mirroring emotions through musical gestures, melodies, or dynamics, caregivers validate children's feelings, helping them feel understood and emotionally secure.

When children experience repeated musical interactions characterized by these rhythmic and emotional exchanges, their brains gradually build neural connections that underpin social-emotional competencies such as empathy, communication, and self-regulation. These interactions foster a sense of trust and attachment, essential foundations for healthy social relationships. Furthermore, engaging in musical co-regulation offers children opportunities to navigate and manage emotions collaboratively within a safe and supportive environment. In this regard, music serves not merely as entertainment or aesthetic enjoyment, but as a potent developmental tool capable of cultivating critical emotional intelligence skills from an early age.

Self-Regulation Through Musical Improvisation

Improvisation in music therapy is a powerful catalyst for emotional exploration, providing clients with a safe, expressive space to spontaneously engage with and articulate their inner emotional worlds. Through spontaneous musical expression, individuals are invited to explore and express complex emotions and inner states that may be difficult to communicate verbally. This musical improvisation facilitates deep self-awareness and promotes self-regulation by enabling clients to observe, interact with, and ultimately transform their emotional experiences in real time.

Within the therapeutic relationship, reciprocal interaction emerges naturally as clients and therapists engage in musical dialogue. The therapist actively listens, reflects, and responds musically, mirroring or contrasting the client's emotional energy and expression. This reciprocal exchange allows clients to experience immediate feedback, validating their emotional presence and supporting the development of emotional resilience and adaptive coping strategies. Over time, clients begin to internalize these interactions, strengthening their ability to regulate emotional states independently.

Moreover, improvisational music therapy helps clients gain greater mastery over their emotional responses by experimenting with different musical dynamics such as rhythm, tempo, volume, and tonality. Engaging in these spontaneous explorations encourages flexibility, adaptability, and the capacity to tolerate emotional intensity and uncertainty. Through structured yet open-ended improvisational sessions, individuals learn to navigate emotional highs and lows effectively, progressively building confidence in their capacity to manage life's challenges beyond the therapeutic environment.

Ultimately, musical improvisation as a therapeutic intervention serves as a transformative tool for fostering self-regulation, emotional insight, and interpersonal connectivity. By embracing the freedom inherent in improvisation, clients cultivate a profound sense of self-efficacy and emotional intelligence, empowering them to navigate both their inner landscape and external relationships with greater ease and authenticity.

Music for Sensory Processing and Integration

Structured musical experiences effectively address sensory integration issues, assisting children with hypersensitivity and hyposensitivity to adapt to varied sensory inputs. Carefully designed musical activities—such as rhythmic movements, instrumental play, and auditory exercises—provide predictable yet engaging sensory stimuli, creating a secure framework within which children can gradually become comfortable with sensory information they typically find challenging. For children experiencing hypersensitivity, music therapy offers gentle and controlled exposure to sound, rhythm, and vibration, allowing them to build tolerance and progressively reduce anxiety or avoidance behaviors associated with sensory overstimulation.

Conversely, for those with hyposensitivity—often seeking additional sensory input to feel adequately stimulated—structured musical interventions present vibrant and stimulating auditory, tactile, and proprioceptive experiences that satisfy their sensory-seeking behaviors. Instruments such as drums, shakers, and other percussion tools provide direct tactile feedback, encouraging active participation that heightens bodily awareness and refines sensory responsiveness.

Additionally, structured music experiences foster integration across multiple sensory systems. Activities involving coordinated rhythmic movements combined with melodic or harmonic elements facilitate the synchronization of auditory, visual, vestibular, and proprioceptive inputs. Over repeated sessions, children learn to better organize, interpret, and respond appropriately to complex sensory information. Such integrated experiences not only enhance their sensory processing capacities but also improve their overall motor coordination, social engagement, attention span, and emotional regulation.

Ultimately, the purposeful use of structured musical interventions creates a safe and motivating environment in which children can confidently navigate and regulate their sensory experiences. By consistently engaging in these tailored musical activities, they develop essential skills to manage sensory inputs effectively, enabling them to engage more comfortably and successfully in their everyday lives.

LANGUAGE DEVELOPMENT VIA SONG AND MOVEMENT

Music fosters interpersonal connections, enhancing communication, turn-taking, and collaborative skills. Within music therapy settings, carefully guided musical interactions serve as powerful tools for nurturing social competencies, particularly among children who may struggle with traditional forms of social engagement. By participating in group musical activities—such as shared instrument play, rhythmic call-and-response exercises, or group singing—children experience natural opportunities for developing essential social skills in a motivating and nonthreatening environment.

During collaborative musical tasks, participants must practice attentive listening and responsiveness, skills crucial for effective communication. As children engage in rhythmic dialogues or melodic exchanges, they naturally learn the value of turn-taking, recognizing that listening actively is as important as expressing oneself clearly. This reciprocal interaction mirrors everyday social exchanges, reinforcing respectful behavior, patience, and empathy toward peers.

Moreover, structured musical activities require cooperation, shared decision-making, and teamwork. As children participate in activities such as ensemble performances or cooperative improvisation, they experience firsthand the importance of harmonizing their efforts with others to achieve collective goals. Through these shared musical experiences, participants develop stronger social bonds, increased trust, and greater appreciation for diverse perspectives within their peer group.

Over time, regular participation in interactive musical activities enhances children's overall social competence, fostering increased confidence and comfort in interpersonal interactions. As these skills become ingrained, they transfer naturally into everyday social contexts, supporting improved relationships, peer acceptance, and meaningful social integration beyond the therapeutic environment.

MOTOR SKILLS ENHANCEMENT THROUGH RHYTHMIC ACTIVITIES

Rhythm-based activities improve gross and fine motor coordination, essential for overall developmental milestones. Within music therapy, structured rhythmic exercises—such as drumming, clapping, marching, dancing, and instrument play—offer engaging opportunities to refine motor skills through repetitive, synchronized movements. These rhythmic tasks help children develop improved coordination, timing, precision, and balance, facilitating the achievement of crucial physical developmental benchmarks.

Gross motor skills, involving larger body movements and muscular coordination, are effectively enhanced through dynamic rhythmic activities like marching or dance routines set to music. These activities require children to synchronize body movements to an external beat, reinforcing balance, spatial awareness, and body control. Over time, consistent participation strengthens muscular endurance and improves physical agility, promoting confidence and competence in everyday physical activities.

Conversely, fine motor skills—crucial for tasks requiring smaller, precise movements—are refined through activities such as playing small percussion instruments, fingerplays, or rhythmic tapping games. By manipulating instruments, performing rhythmic patterns, or participating in coordinated hand and finger movements set to musical rhythms, children enhance their dexterity, grip strength, and hand-eye coordination. This targeted practice directly translates into improved skills for handwriting, self-care tasks, and other detailed activities critical for independent functioning.

Additionally, rhythmic activities inherently support bilateral coordination, encouraging simultaneous or alternating use of both sides of the body. Such experiences foster efficient communication between the left and right hemispheres of the brain, facilitating motor planning, balance, and coordination (Braun Janzen et al., 2022). Children progressively develop a stronger neurological foundation through repeated rhythmic engagement, which is essential for complex motor sequences. Ultimately, rhythmic musical activities provide an enjoyable and motivating framework for motor skill and cognitive development. Regular participation not only enhances motor abilities but also boosts overall developmental progress, contributing to improved physical independence, self-esteem, and quality of life.

ASSESSING PROGRESS IN MUSIC THERAPY

Effective assessment tools for monitoring progress within music therapy sessions are critical to documenting developmental outcomes. Systematic evaluation within therapeutic practice ensures that interventions remain targeted, relevant, and responsive to each individual's evolving needs. Through the application of structured observational techniques, standardized assessment scales, and qualitative analysis of session recordings, therapists can accurately track clients' progress across emotional, social, cognitive, linguistic, and motor domains.

Structured observational methods, including detailed note-taking and checklists, enable therapists to capture subtle yet significant changes in client behavior, emotional responses, and engagement during sessions. These observations provide ongoing insight into the client's responses to specific musical interventions, highlighting emerging strengths, persistent challenges, and shifting therapeutic needs. Additionally, employing validated assessment tools, such as rating scales specifically designed for music therapy contexts, enhances objectivity and ensures consistency across multiple sessions and different practitioners.

Qualitative analysis of audio and video recordings of therapy sessions further enriches assessment practices. By reviewing session materials, therapists can deeply analyze interactions, identify patterns, and document nuanced developmental gains that may otherwise be overlooked during live observation. These recorded sessions also allow for reflection, peer consultation, and caregiver involvement, offering comprehensive perspectives on the client's therapeutic journey.

Regular assessments empower therapists to refine intervention strategies continuously, ensuring therapy remains effective and goal-oriented. Clear documentation of progress helps validate the benefits of music therapy interventions to stakeholders such as caregivers, educational teams, and healthcare providers, facilitating collaboration and reinforcing the therapeutic value of music therapy.

Ultimately, the thoughtful integration of rigorous assessment practices within music therapy ensures transparency, accountability, and clinical effectiveness, enabling therapists to celebrate successes, adjust interventions thoughtfully, and maximize positive developmental outcomes for every client.

INTEGRATING MUSIC THERAPY WITH FAMILY AND COMMUNITY

Family and community engagement are integral components of successful therapeutic interventions, reinforcing outcomes beyond therapy sessions. When thoughtfully integrated with the client's broader support networks, music therapy can significantly amplify developmental and therapeutic gains, fostering sustained progress in diverse environments such as home, school, and community settings. By actively involving family members in therapy sessions and offering structured guidance on implementing musical strategies at home, therapists strengthen family bonds, enhance mutual understanding, and provide caregivers with practical tools to support their child's continued growth.

Family participation within music therapy sessions enriches the therapeutic experience and cultivates shared enjoyment, emotional intimacy, and improved communication within the family unit. Families can discover new avenues for meaningful connection through structured musical activities such as group singing, cooperative instrument play, or collaborative musical storytelling, fostering resilience and reinforcing the skills and strategies acquired during individual therapeutic interventions.

Additionally, extending music therapy initiatives into community settings—such as schools, community centers, or social groups—broadens the scope of support available to clients. Community-based musical activities facilitate peer interaction, social integration, and increased self-confidence, helping individuals generalize therapeutic progress to real-world contexts. Collaborative events like community concerts, interactive workshops, and inclusive music programs create valuable opportunities for individuals and families to engage with their communities, reducing isolation and promoting a deeper sense of belonging.

Ultimately, therapeutic interventions become more holistic and impactful by embedding music therapy within a broader network of family, classroom, and community engagement. The active participation of families, teachers, and community members ensures that developmental and therapeutic outcomes persist well beyond formal therapy sessions, enabling clients to achieve lasting improvements in emotional well-being, social connectivity, and overall quality of life.

CONCLUSION

Music, rhythm, and movement play a fundamental role in early childhood development, serving as powerful tools that enhance cognitive, physical, social, and emotional growth. During the early years, children's brains are highly receptive to musical experiences, which help strengthen neural pathways associated with language development, cognition, and social relationships. Musical, rhythmic, and movement activities improve gross and fine motor skills, coordination, and body awareness while providing a natural outlet for self-expression and creativity. Beyond individual development, music and movement activities foster social skills through group participation, turn-taking, and collaborative play, while also helping children regulate emotions and develop cultural awareness through exposure to diverse musical traditions. The integration of music, rhythm, and movement into early childhood education creates joyful, multisensory learning experiences that support holistic development and lay the foundation for lifelong appreciation of the arts, making these elements essential components of quality early childhood programs.

REFERENCES

Braun Janzen, T., Koshimori, Y., Richard, N. M., & Thaut, M. H. (2022). Rhythm and music-based interventions in motor rehabilitation: Current evidence and future perspectives. *Frontiers in Human Neuroscience*, *15*, 789467.

Cirelli, L. K., Einarson, K. M., & Trainor, L. J. (2014). Interpersonal synchrony increases prosocial behavior in infants. *Developmental Science*, *17*(6), 1003–1011.

Degé, F., & Frischen, U. (2022). The impact of music training on executive functions in childhood—a systematic review. *Z Erziehungswiss*, *25*, 579–602.

Dondena, C., Riva, V., Molteni, M., Musacchia, G., & Cantiani, C. (2021). Impact of early rhythmic training on language acquisition and electrophysiological functioning underlying auditory processing: Feasibility and preliminary findings in typically developing infants. *Brain Sciences*, *11*(11), 1546.

Frischen, U., Degé, F., & Schwarzer, G. (2022). The relation between rhythm processing and cognitive abilities during child development: The role of prediction. *Frontiers in Psychology*, *13*, 920513.

Frischen, U., Schwarzer, G., & Degé, F. (2019). Comparing the effects of rhythm-based music training and pitch-based music training on executive functions in preschoolers. *Frontiers in Integrative Neuroscience*, *13*, 41.

Hardy, M., & LaGasse, A. (2013). Rhythm, movement, and autism: Using rhythmic rehabilitation research as a model for autism. *Frontiers in Integrative Neuroscience*, *7*(19).

Jaschke, A. C., Honing, H., & Scherder, E.J.A. (2018). Longitudinal analysis of music education on executive functions in primary school children. *Frontiers in Neuroscience*, *12*, 103.

Kasuya-Ueba, Y., Zhao, S., & Toichi, M. (2020). The effect of music intervention on attention in children: Experimental evidence. *Frontiers in Neuroscience*, *14*, 757.

Koelsch, S. (2020). A coordinate-based meta-analysis of music-evoked emotions. *NeuroImage*, *223*, 117350.

Kraus, N. (2021). *Of sound mind: How our brain constructs a meaningful sonic world*. MIT Press.

LaGasse, B., Yoo, G., & Hardy, M. (2024). Rhythm and music for promoting sensorimotor organization in autism: Broader implications for outcomes. *Frontiers in Integrative Neuroscience*, *18*, 1403876.

Lense, M., Ladányi, E., Rabinowitch, T., Trainor, L., & Gordon, R. (2021). Rhythm and timing as vulnerabilities in neurodevelopmental disorders. *Philosophical Transactions of the Royal Society of London. Series B, Biological Sciences*, *376*(1835), 20200327.

Maes, P. J., & Leman, M. (2013). The influence of body movements on children's perception of music with an ambiguous expressive character. *PloS one*, *8*(1), e54682.

Miendlarzewska, E. A., & Trost, W. J. (2014). How musical training affects cognitive development: Rhythm, reward and other modulating variables. *Frontiers in Neuroscience, 7*, 279.

Molino, A. (2023). Music therapy: A look into the world of healing sound. Dorrance Publishing.

Molino, A. (2024). *Music, wellness, and therapy: Integrative approaches for family and community well-being*. Atena Music and Wellness Publishing.

Overy, K. (2003). Dyslexia and music. From timing deficits to musical intervention. *Annals of the New York Academy of Sciences, 999*, 497–505.

Patel A. D. (2011). Why would musical training benefit the neural encoding of speech? The OPERA hypothesis. *Frontiers in Psychology, 2*, 142.

Srinivasan, S., & Bhat, A. (2013). A review of "music and movement" therapies for children with developmental disabilities. *Frontiers in Integrative Neuroscience, 7*, 22.

Thaut, M. H., McIntosh, G. C., & Hoemberg, V. (2014). Neurologic music therapy: From social science to neuroscience. In M. H. Thaut & V. Hoemberg (Eds.), *Handbook of neurologic music therapy* (pp. 1–6). Oxford University Press.

Tierney, A., & Kraus, N. (2013). The ability to move to a beat is linked to the consistency of neural responses to sound. *The Journal of Neuroscience, 33*(38), 14981–14988.

Tierney, A., & Kraus, N. (2015). Neural entrainment to the rhythmic structure of music. *Journal of Cognitive Neuroscience, 27*(2), 400–408.

Zaatar, M., Alhakim, K., Enayeh, M., & Tamer, R. (2023). The transformative power of music: Insights into neuroplasticity, health, and disease. *Brain, Behavior, & Immunity—Health, 35*, 100716.

Part II

WHAT TO DO
(ACADEMIC DEVELOPMENT)

CHAPTER 5

Implementing Cognitive-Physical Activities to Strengthen Executive Function Skills for Better Learning and Behavior

Lynne Kenney with Mike Kuczala, United States

There is such joy in the eyes of a child as they light up in recognition that they just produced a well-timed sequence of coordinative movements. As I write this, I can see the face of a 1st-grade student for whom I was modeling an 8-beat rhythmic movement sequence, only to see her trying so hard, yet experiencing frustration at her inability to tap her hand in time with a beat. "Sonia, let's sit on the yoga ball and do this sequence with our hands," I said. "Tap left, right, left, right, left, left, right, right on your thighs with me. 1, 2, 3, go." She looked at me timidly and began to tap. With a bright smile, she looked up with accomplishment. "I can do it; I can move in time to the beat," Sonia exclaimed. "Yes, you can," I said. "Why?" Sonia lifted one hand in front of her eye, imitating a scientist holding an eyeglass, and responded, "Because the music is within me."

THE SCIENCE OF COGNITIVE-MOTOR MOVEMENT

For over 20 years, a substantial body of research across fields like auditory neuroscience, kinesiology, and physical education has consistently demonstrated that regular physical activity positively impacts both cognitive and motor skill development, highlighting the interconnectedness of physical movement and brain health (Latino & Tafuri, 2024; Luo et al., 2023; Tomporowski et al., 2008).

Advancements in psychophysiology, cognitive science, and kinesiology research have strengthened the neuroscience rationale for the beneficial effect of physical exercise and exercise-related fitness on brain development and cognitive functioning in children and adolescents. There is increasing evidence of the relationship between physical activity, fitness, executive function skills, and academic achievement. The challenge is that less than half of students in the United States get the recommended 60 minutes of moderately vigorous activity daily, and that percentage declines substantially through the teen years (Merlo et al., 2020). Children spend up to 50% of their waking hours on digital devices, and free play outdoors is infrequent (Torjinski et al., 2024). Before, after, and during school is, however, the optimal environment for providing physical activity, play, and movement opportunities to build executive functions and prepare the brain to learn.

Since 2009, I have been implementing cognitive-motor or cognitive-physical activities in clinical practice, in classrooms, and in homes with children and adults ages 3–85. I have also been teaching original patterned, sequential, co-ordinative, rhythmic movements to clinicians, educators, and parents worldwide as part of my CogniSuite Collection of activities. I have written eight cognitive-motor programs based on my theory of Musical Thinking, published by Unhooked Media in 2016. In my work in schools and clinics, I frequently observed that neurotypical children, as well as children with neurodevelopmental differences, benefited from rhythmic songs, beat-based patterned movements, and cognitive-motor games.

Children with attention deficit hyperactivity disorder (ADHD), autism spectrum disorder (ASD), developmental coordination disorder (DCD), and dyslexia present to our clinic—Wellington-Alexander Center—motivated and engaged, yet around 75–80% of our learners experience fine or gross motor delays, difficulty moving in time to a beat, and/or an inability to shift rhythms in sequential movement. As we worked rhythmically, over time, dancing on poly spots, drumming on yoga balls, and stepping in patterns I had used 30 years earlier as a physical education dance instructor, I saw improvements quickly, sometimes within minutes. In 2014, when I started teaching the cognitive-motor activity programs I developed for clinical practice to clinicians and educators internationally, I had several hypotheses, although the research was still in its early stages. The hypotheses were based on observations I made while playing with children, which are now showing some positive evidence in the scientific literature:

- Hypothesis 1: There is a relationship between motor competence and executive function in children (Bao et al., 2024).
- Hypothesis 2: Improving motor rhythm and timing in children leading to better motor coordination may improve executive function and academic achievement (Tao et al., 2025).
- Hypothesis 3: Rhythmic-coordinative movement with progressively and developmentally appropriate increasing cognitive demands is superior to general physical activity in improving executive function skills.

The evidence shows that motor competence and executive functions co-develop throughout childhood and adolescence (Bao et al., 2024). There is emerging evidence that improvements in motor competence may have cognitive benefits in these populations (Bao et al., 2024).

Deficits in rhythm or timing are shown to be associated with many aspects of neural development, learning, and behavior (Lense et al., 2021). Poor motor production in association with a rhythm or beat may be a sign of diminished perception and communication between key parts of the brain. Variations in fine and gross motor control, rhythm, tempo, and timing have been consistently reported in the literature across several diagnostic groups, including ADHD, developmental dyslexia, reading, and speech-language deficits (Corriveau et al., 2007; Gordon et al., 2015; Schaefer & Overy, 2015; Zelaznik & Goffman, 2010).

Children with speech language delays, ADHD, and developmental dyslexia have also been observed in studies to have impaired motor production to auditory cues. Auditory discrimination and auditory memory are both critical for learning. A child must hear, discriminate, and respond to auditory information throughout the learning process.

Corriveau and Goswami (2009) reported that "Tapping in synchrony with a beat has been described as the simplest rhythmic act that humans perform" (p. 119). Yet we know that many children with neurodevelopmental challenges cannot tap to a beat; they have poor rhythm, and they exhibit difficulty matching gross motor output to both rhythm and beat. Like the researchers, we observe the presence of subtle impairments in the neural mechanisms for the perception and expression of rhythm and timing, which affect normal language, motor, and cognitive development. The questions relevant to those of us who play rhythmic coordinative activities with children are threefold:

1. How does repeated rhythmic patterned motor practice improve the neural mechanisms underlying executive function, self-regulation, and learning?
2. How can we apply current neuroscience to determine which types of cognitive-motor activity will benefit which clinical presentations?
3. How can we automate the delivery of brief cognitive-motor activities to improve equity of access in high-need communities?

Aiming for Automaticity

When we consider brain anatomy, we recognize the importance of the integration of the cortical and subcortical structures of the brain in learning and behavior. We need to keep in mind that the higher-level cognitive systems rest on the subcortical structures, including the limbic system, brainstem, and cerebellum. Proper integration is needed for high-quality learning. As the phylogenetically older of the brain systems, the cerebellum and brainstem precede the prefrontal cortex in the automaticity of learning and behavior. Both are stored in and mediated by the cerebellum. In fact, when we teach a new skill to a child, such as how to read simple phonics, at the point where that skill is so well known that it is automatized, the prefrontal cortex fires much less often because less information needs to be processed by the cognitive control system. Further, working memory is less taxed when skills are automated, freeing up the prefrontal cortex to process more difficult scaffolded information. The layering of behavior and learning begins with automaticity. I observe that when gross motor rhythm is well established before the introduction of a new behavioral or academic skill, the gross motor rhythm exists as a platform on which the more highly scaffolded cognitive skills can rest.

Cognitively Engaging Physical Activity

Since the publication of *70 Play Activities for Better Thinking, Self-Regulation, Learning, and Behavior* (Kenney & Comizio, 2016), the research has grown in meaningful directions. We have evidence that a variety of movement programs, such as tai chi, yoga, quadrato, and exergaming, engage executive functions in the brain—improving health, cognition, and fitness (Jarraya et al., 2019; Kolovelonis & Goudas, 2023; Kong et al., 2019; Tomporowski et al., 2011).

Research on "cognitively challenging physical movement" explores how physical activities that require mental engagement, like self-regulation, response inhibition, problem-solving, decision-making, and processing, can significantly improve cognitive functions, particularly executive function skills, compared to standard physical activity. By stimulating the same neural networks used for cognitive tasks in the brain, rhythmic and cognitively demanding exercises have positive impacts on memory, attention, and processing speed. It has been shown that cognitively challenging physical movement may help enhance executive functioning for students at risk of poor cognition (Kolovelonis et al., 2022; Watson et al., 2017), and research shows that we improve executive function skills by engaging the neural networks involved in attention, memory, and self-control (Garcia-Madruga et al., 2016).

Children who are physically fit generally outperform their peers academically, socially, and behaviorally (Donnelly & Lambourne, 2011; Garcia-Hermoso et al., 2021; Vasilopoulos & Ellefson, 2021). Many fit children show higher rates of self-esteem, confidence, social engagement, and financial earning potential. Yet not all physical activity is alike. Rhythmic-coordinative activity with cognitive demands shows the highest potential for strengthening the executive function skills that underlie learning (Wang et al., 2024; Williams & Berthelsen, 2019).

HOW DOES RHYTHMIC MOVEMENT WITH COGNITIVE DEMANDS STRENGTHEN COGNITION?

Research indicates that engaging in rhythmic and cognitively demanding exercises can positively influence memory, attention, and processing speed by stimulating the same neural networks used for cognitive tasks in the brain, essentially "training" these networks through physical activity.

- **Brain Regions Involved:** Studies have shown that areas like the prefrontal cortex, hippocampus, and parietal lobe, which support cognitive functions, are particularly activated during rhythmic exercise (Symanski et al., 2022).
- **Cognitive Demands:** Incorporating cognitive challenges within physical activity, like following complex dance steps or reacting to changing visual or auditory cues, further stimulates the neural networks responsible for attention, decision-making, and working memory (Bell et al., 2025; Foster Vander Elst et al., 2023).
- **Neural Activation:** When performing rhythmic exercises, like dancing or drumming, specific brain regions associated with cognitive functions like planning, coordination, and memory are activated, leading to potential improvements in those areas (Bruchhage et al., 2020).
- **Neuroplasticity:** Exercise is known to promote neuroplasticity, the brain's ability to adapt and form new neural connections, which can enhance cognitive function over time (Jing et al., 2024).

EXAMPLES OF ACTIVITIES

Dance Classes: Various dance styles, especially those with intricate choreography, can provide a good cognitive-motor workout. Recently, I went back to my aerobic dance roots and started ballroom dancesport. The cognitive and cardiovascular benefits were immediately palpable, resulting in my referring our patients with ADHD and dyslexia to dancesport classes.

Martial Arts: Practicing techniques that require quick reactions and strategic thinking can improve attention and processing speed.

Music-Based Cognitive-Motor Exercise: Engaging in activities like drumming or singing along to music can stimulate the brain's auditory processing and memory networks.

Tai Chi: The slow, deliberate movements with a focus on balance and coordination can stimulate cognitive functions as well as provide a heightened sense of mind-body awareness.

ACTIVATING NETWORKS

One way to activate these brain networks is to exercise in patterned sequences of coordinative-rhythmic beat-based movement. While the research is ongoing, it appears that by engaging in rhythmic-coordinative movement, which requires thought, we engage attention, planning, working memory, cognitive flexibility, response inhibition, self-regulation, and creativity, which are among the executive function skills that precede learning. By implementing brief beat-based rhythmic coordinative movement, you can create thoughtful motor activities with cognitive elements to help your students alert their attention and exercise their memory, cognitive flexibility, and response inhibition.

Next, we will explore the underlying theory of Musical Thinking so that you understand the basic tenets of our cognitive-motor work. Then, we will practice some cognitive-motor activities you can use in your family, school, clinic, or work life to engage self-regulation, attention, working memory, response inhibition, and cognitive flexibility in yourself and your children.

MUSICAL THINKING

In an era where children learn academic content earlier than in the past, the ability to creatively problem-solve with cognitive flexibility, focused attention, and self-control has never been more important. Having worked with thousands of children on developing and applying executive function skills, I have found that when we teach children how they think, not simply what to think, they become empowered learners.

Early in my work as a psychologist in schools and clinics, I heard students told to alter their behavior with words like, "Just slow down," "Think it out," and "Use your creative problem-solving skills," only to see the children look up bewilderedly. It struck me that we often tell children what to do without telling them how to do it. This results in children who become disorganized thinkers, using trial and error to try to meet the expectations of teachers, parents, and those whom they love. To empower the children to become more masterful over their thoughts and actions, we began to make the cognitive processes that underlie thinking "transparent" to the students by providing explicit instruction regarding what executive function skills are, how to develop them, and when and how to use them.

Over the years, I developed a cognitive empowerment strategy called Musical Thinking that allowed me to talk with the children about how their brains learn in a manner that was fun, engaging, and based on cognitive science. Musical Thinking evolved rather naturally while I was tutoring math and reading at a local elementary school. I observed that the children with math and reading difficulties had "output" challenges. They seemed to know what they wanted to write or say, but their oral pace was inconsistent, their approach to tasks was disorganized, and their overall tempo, rhythm, and timing were poor. When we incorporated rhythmic movement into our lessons, the children improved dramatically.

Musical Thinking has many elements within the theory. What is most relevant to this chapter is that we naturally leverage the musicality within our brains and bodies to teach children how to exert better control over their thoughts and actions by teaching them the "felt-sense" of slowing down. Introducing musical notes to children through movement allows them to experience what it feels like to move:

- Slow (50–85 Beats per Minute)
- Quick (85–120 Beats per Minute)
- Fast (120–160 Beats per Minute)

When children have metacognitive awareness of the speed, pace, tempo, and timing of their words and actions, they are better able to participate in the back-and-forth volley in a conversation, move at a more modulated pace as they transition from activity to activity, and create enough space between their urges and their actions that they speak and act in a more goal-directed manner.

The Tenets of Musical Thinking

Cognitive Skill Coaching: By making cognitive skills "transparent" and easy to understand, children are empowered to better manage their thoughts, feelings, urges, and actions.

Brain-Body Connection: Musical and rhythmic movement activities can enhance neural connectivity and cognitive processing.

Rhythmic-Coordinative Training: Regular engagement with rhythm, tempo, and timing exercises helps improve executive function skills, including self-regulation, attention, working memory, planning, and cognitive flexibility.

Cross-Modal Learning: Combining auditory (music), kinesthetic (movement), and visual learning pathways creates stronger neural networks than single-modality approaches.

Sequential Processing: Cognitive-motor activities that involve patterns and sequences with increasing cognitive demands help strengthen cognitive sequencing abilities that transfer to academic tasks.

Social-Emotional Development: Group musical activities foster social skills, emotional regulation, social cohesion, and cooperative learning.

Academic Integration: Musical thinking strategies can be incorporated into academic content to improve the encoding, retrieval, retention, and processing of information.

COGNISUITE

The broad array of rhythmic-coordinative cognitive patterns, songs, and dance sequences I have created for children in grades Pre-K–8th grade live in what I call the CogniSuite Collection. When I teach internationally, I choose activities from the collection, depending on the needs of the population with whom I am working. All of my programs are based on Musical Thinking and are applied similarly and systematically across all the activities in the CogniSuite Collection. For this chapter, I present a sampling of activities for use in your classroom, clinic, or home.

In my clinical work, cognitive-motor movement is a class of movement in which one thinks while one moves. We model for our students that there is a fraction that looks like this:

$$\frac{C \; +-}{M \; +-}$$

We can "turn up" either the cognitive or motor elements of any movement such that there is a slight yet detectable increase in either cognitive or motor complexity. We incrementally increase (or decrease) the cognitive or motor demands with intention as the patterns become more automated.

The Importance of Rhythm and Timing in Development

Rhythm and timing play a crucial role in developing cognitive skills, motor coordination, and fine motor skills in children. This connection among rhythm, timing, and motor coordination has been studied across various fields, including kinesiology, neuroscience, auditory neuroscience, developmental psychology, and education.

Cognitive Skills. The link between rhythm timing and cognitive development is established by studies that have shown that children who engage in rhythmic activities tend to have better cognitive skills, including self-regulation, attention, memory, cognitive flexibility, and problem-solving abilities (Miendlarzewska & Trost, 2014). The rhythmic patterns present in music, for example, can help improve a child's ability to process and remember academic information (see Bonacina et al., 2019; Frischen et al., 2022).

Cross-Modal Integration. Rhythm and timing involve the integration of visual, auditory, and kinesthetic sensory inputs. This cross-modal integration enhances the brain's ability to process the coordinate information from different sensory channels. As a result, children who engage in rhythm-based activities are better equipped to integrate sensory cues and appropriately respond to various stimuli (see Bharathi et al., 2019).

Educational Impact. Rhythm and timing activities have been shown to be related to reading prosody, grammar, and early math (see Lundetrae & Thomson, 2017). Children with better rhythm have been shown to learn with greater ease. Using rhythmic patterns to teach math concepts or language skills not only makes learning more engaging, but also makes learning more effective.

Gross and Fine Motor Skills. Rhythm and timing activities often involve a combination of gross motor skills, larger movements involving multiple muscle groups, and fine motor skills with smaller, more precise hand movements. The ability to synchronize movements with rhythm is fundamental to children's ability to pull to a stand, walk, run, skip, and gallop. As an example, dancing involves both whole-body coordination and intricate footwork at the same time; writing requires planning, visual tracking, core strength, and shoulder stability. Engaging in rhythm-based activities encourages the development of a wide range of motor skills, contributing to the foundational skills associated with learning.

Neurological Development. Research suggests that rhythm and timing activities can have a positive effect on the neurological development in children (Fiveash et al., 2023; Frischen et al., 2022). Engaging in activities that require rhythmic coordination, such as clapping to a beat, dancing, and moving rhythmically, helps strengthen neural connections in the brain, particularly in the areas related to cognition, motor control, and coordination (Kenney & Comizio, 2016). These activities enhance the communication between different brain regions responsible for attention, planning, previewing, and task initiation.

THE SEQUENCE IS THE SECRET

Moving rhythmically to the sequenced patterns for the varied activities in our programs is a core feature of my work. *Cognitive sequencing* is the ability to perceive, represent, and execute a set of actions that follow a particular order. This ability underlies planning, problem-solving, speech, language, reading, and math. When children are able to sequence their thoughts, actions, words, procedures, and approaches to tasks, learning and behavior are managed with greater ease. Sequencing plays a significant role in both reading and math, as it helps to develop and enhance important cognitive skills needed for learning. Here are a few examples of when sequencing is important:

Reading: In reading, sequencing refers to the ability to understand, follow, and apply the order of tasks needed to encode, decode, read fluently, and comprehend what is read.

- **Phonics:** Mapping phonemes to graphemes requires sound, alphabetic, and sequencing knowledge.
- **Contextual Understanding:** Sequencing enables readers to grasp the context of a story or informational text. By following the sequence of events or ideas, readers can interpret the meaning and significance of each element within the larger context.
- **Comprehension:** Sequencing helps readers understand the logical progression of a story or text. It allows them to make connections between events, identify cause-and-effect relationships, and comprehend the text's overall meaning.
- **Storytelling Skills:** Sequencing is essential for effective storytelling. When retelling a story or summarizing a text, individuals need to organize the events in a logical sequence, ensuring that the narrative flows coherently.

Math: In mathematics, sequencing involves arranging numbers, operations, or steps in the correct order. Here's why sequencing is important:

- **Numeracy:** Cardinality, ordinality, number decomposition, and order of operation all require sequencing ability.
- **Problem-Solving:** Many math problems require a step-by-step approach. Sequencing helps students understand the order in which operations must be performed to arrive at the correct solution. For example, understanding the correct order of operations is essential when solving equations.
- **Mathematical Reasoning:** Sequencing assists in developing logical thinking and mathematical reasoning skills. It helps students identify patterns, make predictions, and understand mathematical relationships by recognizing the sequence of numbers or operations involved.
- **Algorithmic Thinking:** Sequencing is fundamental in algorithmic thinking, which is an essential skill in computer science and problem-solving. Algorithms require a precise sequence of steps to achieve a desired outcome.

Overall, sequencing is important because it promotes literacy, numeracy, comprehension, logical thinking, problem-solving, and the ability to communicate ideas effectively. We tell our students, "The sequence is the secret." When students can approach language, reading, and numeracy with sequencing in mind, they are more efficient in both reading and math.

In the following sections, I introduce some rhythmic patterned work from the CogniSuite Collection for your use in the classroom, clinic, and home. First, let's improve our self-regulation skills with a few Think-Ups.

The QR code below will bring you to a printable version of all Think-Ups for Chapter 5. This material may also be accessed under the "Downloads" tab at https://www.tcpress.com/move-more-learn-more-9780807784051.

THINK-UPS

We often think of people as having five senses: sight, hearing, smell, touch, and taste. Yet there are two other senses that are central to self-regulation and calming. They are the *vestibular* sense, which is responsible for balance and perception of body positioning in space, and the *proprioceptive* sense, which relays information about body awareness and joint pressure to the brain. (See Chapter 3 to learn more about the vestibular sense and proprioception.)

To help students manage their internal energy to attain and maintain an "alert state of calm," we engage the vestibular and proprioceptive systems to help with self-regulation. Think-Ups are slow, rhythmic activities requiring a person to hold their body weight as they move, engaging cognition and proprioception. With Think-Ups, we do a variety of heavy work activities using Musical Thinking. Occupational therapists often use heavy work to help organize and connect the brain and body through the reticular activating system. Heavy work describes movements that create a pushing, holding, or pulling feeling in the muscles and joints in the body. When one pushes, pulls, or holds heavy objects (such as a weighted ball) or one's own body weight in space, the vestibular and proprioceptive systems of the brain and body become engaged. The exertion associated with heavy work stimulates endorphins, neurotransmitters, increased blood flow, and increased oxygenation, all beneficial for the brain. When heavy work is done slowly and rhythmically, it can be calming to the sensory and central nervous systems of the body. For students who need to self-regulate, 2 to 3 minutes of Think-Ups can be very helpful.

Think-Up #1: Rhythmic Wall-Sit

Action: Rhythmic Wall-Sits are an excellent way to alert the brain before an academic task.
Why: Rhythmic Wall-Sits involve the whole body, oxygenating the brain with the lower body, where 80% of one's large muscles reside. The rhythmicity adds cognitive demands, stimulating focus attention, memory, and response inhibition.
How: Sit against the wall, with your thighs parallel to the floor.
Count to 8 slowly out loud.
For the next 8 counts, tap your knees with your hands, right, left, right, left, right, left, right, left.
Excellent!
Now, for the last 8 counts, tap your toes, keeping your heel on the ground. This is just a toe-tap, while you are still in a wall-sit.
Ready!
Tap—right, left, right, left, right, left, right, left.
Stand up and shake it out!
Super! You have the foundational timing down; now let's turn up the cognition.

Think-Up #2: Rhythmic Supermans

Supermans are an excellent activity for circle time, as well as beneficial right before you do an academic activity at home or in the clinic. You all have done a good old-fashioned superman. Laying on your belly with your arms reaching tall in front of you and your legs outstretched, usually you lift your upper or lower body. When we do this rhythmically in 4/4/ time, it sounds like this:

In Superman position, we will count in 4/4 time, two measures, so that's 8 beats.

For Superman 1 (Upper Body), we do this:

Practice:

Lift your right arm, place it down.
Lift your left arm, place it down.
Lift both arms, place them down.

It sounds like:

Right up, down.
Left up, down.
Both up, down.

Now, in tempo:

Lift your right arm on beat 1, hold on beats 2 and 3, down on beat 4.
Lift your left arm on beat 1, hold on beats 2 and 3, down on beat 4.
Lift both arms on beat 1, hold on beats 2 and 3, down on beat 4.

For Superman 2 (Lower Body), we do this:

Practice:

Lift your right leg (3 inches above the ground), place it down.
Lift your left leg (3 inches above the ground), place it down.
Lift both legs (3 inches above the ground), place them down.

It sounds like:

Right up, down.
Left up, down.
Both up, down.

Now, in tempo:

Lift your right leg on beat 1, hold on beats 2 and 3, down on beat 4.
Lift your left leg on beat 1, hold on beats 2 and 3, down on beat 4.
Lift both legs on beat 1, hold on beats 2 and 3, down on beat 4.
Fabulous! Let's turn up the motor cognition.

Think-Up #3: Stand-Squat-Hold

You are familiar with a squat: You tighten your core muscles, sit down, and then you stand up. A squat is usually down 2 counts, up 2 counts. A squat is slow and controlled.

We are going to do squats in tempo with timing.

Practice: Stand tall, with your shoulders strong yet relaxed. Sit down into a squat slowly: 2 counts down, hold for 4 counts, rise to a stand in 2 counts.

It sounds like:

Sit, hold, rise.

In tempo:

Complete one series, then stand and shake your body out. Then prepare for the next series. We do this series three times, at a slow tempo, about 60 beats per minute.

THE BENEFITS OF HEAVY WORK

Heavy work provides proprioceptive input to the muscles and joints to help calm, organize, and regulate the body. The exertion that comes with heavy work can also help decrease anxiety and impulsivity. Heavy work can help students develop better awareness of where their body is in space. Stationary heavy work can help ground the body, providing a sense of stability and calm. Coordinative rhythmic heavy work engages executive functions, including but not limited to attention, memory, cognitive flexibility, response inhibition, processing speed, and self-regulation. Thoughtful, heavy work can engage focused attention.

The rhythmic activities in Think-Ups can teach children important classroom skills, including following instructions, making decisions, problem-solving, teamwork, and self-regulation. Practicing these actions through physical activity helps children develop executive function skills such as attention control, working memory, cognitive flexibility, and inhibitory control. Recent evidence suggests that adding developmentally appropriate cognitive demands to patterned movement stimulates executive function and the precursor skills to reading and math (Kolovelonis & Goudas, 2023; Paschen et al., 2019).

Tips for Engaging Children in Cognitive-Physical Activity

Be a Role Model: Participate in physical activities with your children to set a positive example.

Encourage Social Interaction: Invite friends or neighbors to join in, making activities more fun and socially engaging.

Be Inclusive: Children vary in their cognitive-motor abilities. When students have difficulty following along, make time to adapt the activities in the moment and work with them individually to increase opportunities to practice in a cooperative manner.

Let Them Teach: As soon as your students understand how to move in time on the beat together, let them stand in the front and lead. We have had students make up moves and patterns, to their delight. I even published one of their moves, "The Crane," in our Cognitivities® program published by Fit and Fun Playscapes.

Choose activities that children enjoy and vary them to keep things interesting. Remember, safety first. Ensure that all activities are age-appropriate and that children use proper equipment and wear suitable gear. By incorporating a mix of these activities, you can help children develop physical fitness, coordination, social skills, and a lifelong love for staying active.

COGNITIVE-PHYSICAL ACTIVITY IN YOUR CLASSROOM

The classroom is an optimal setting for students to develop and practice the precursor skills that precede learning. These skills include core strength, balance, weight shift, motor rhythm, motor timing, and visual-spatial and object-perceptual skills. Due to a variety of factors, including less opportunity for physical activity throughout the day, more seated classroom time, and fewer foundational motor experiences (swinging, climbing trees, jumping rope, building forts, and kicking the can in the alley), children's fundamental motor skills are on the decline (Brian et al., 2019; Hardy et al., 2013).

Children climb, run, skip, jump, push, pull, and move in different planes far less than they did 20 years ago. A recent study reported that 77% of a sample of children ages 3–5 years from across the United States were at or below the 25th percentile, with approximately 30% of children demonstrating profound developmental delays (<5th percentile) in their gross motor skills (Brian et al.,

2019). Deficits such as these in foundational motor skills have consequences for cognition and achievement (Alesi et al., 2018).

In our rhythmic-movement collection, we begin movements in the vertical and horizontal planes. As beat competency and coordination improve, we move to cross-midline and diagonal planes of movement.

In kinesiology, physical therapy, and occupational therapy, planes of motion have been identified to note where the body is moving. The three planes of motion include coronal (frontal), sagittal (longitudinal), and transverse (axial) planes (Marz et al., 2020). These planes involve moving side-to-side, front and back, on the diagonal, or rotationally. I speak with children in our clinical practice about "moving through the planes, fluidly and in time with the beat." Qualitatively, I can stand in front of a child and ask them to mirror my movements through the vertical, horizontal, and diagonal quadrants in the coronal, sagittal, and transverse planes and learn a lot about their awareness of their body in space, their balance, weight shift, and beat competency.

The simplest movements are within the vertical and horizontal planes. Any movement that keeps the body centered on the sagittal axis of the body would be vertical; this could also include a clap at the body's midline or a two-handed thigh pat. Horizontal movements include heels, alternating forward or step side-to-side, as these moves require a shift in weight that takes one off the vertical axis. Young children, ages 3–4, move well within the vertical plane. As children develop, they can begin to move within the horizontal plane, shifting their body weight right and left, or forward and back. To help you see this, you can imagine a 3-year-old participating in clapping songs or reaching above their bodies. You can also imagine a 5–6-year-old, stepping or stomping to a beat. By the time children are 7–9 years of age, they can reach on a diagonal, with a weight shift, or movement in rotational patterns (see the rotational patterns work of Crispiani and Palmieri in Chapter 8).

Understanding the planes of movement in kinesiology helps you—whether a teacher, clinician, or parent—recognize when children exhibit deficits in spatial awareness, body awareness, and coordination. More than once, I have observed a teacher call a child "clumsy" or accuse the child of intentionally falling down for attention when it was clear to me that they were not motorically prepared to show coordinated, fluid movement outside of the vertical plane. The QR code below will direct you to a printable version of all motor skills activities for Chapter 5. This material may also be accessed under the "Downloads" tab at https://www.tcpress.com/move-more-learn-more-9780807784051.

MOTOR SKILL ACTIVITIES ENHANCE COGNITION AND LEARNING

Advances in neuroscience have resulted in substantial progress in linking physical activity to cognitive performance, brain structure, and function (Donnelly et al., 2016). Research shows that the motor skill development associated with consistent participation in physical education/activity can improve academic performance, cognition, visual-perceptual skills, attention, memory, and problem-solving skills (de Greeff et al., 2018; Fernandes et al., 2016; Greco et al., 2023; Shi & Feng, 2022). Wick et al. (2021) conducted a strength-dominated kindergarten-based exercise program aiming to increase physical fitness and cognitive performance in healthy children aged 4–6 years. They found that a 10-week strength-dominated exercise program resulted in larger gains in jump performance and trended toward improved attentional span in preschool children compared with active control children who followed the regular kindergarten curriculum.

In previous chapters you have learned some foundational motor movements, including rocking, rolling on diagonals, and counting to the beat. The next section turns up the cognition a bit, incorporating broader movement throughout the planes identified in kinesiology and physical therapy to practice rhythm, tempo, timing, and cognition in your classroom, home, or practice.

Activity #1: Little Jane Fonda

Action: Have you ever been in a Zumba® class? You know how you do different dance steps to the music. Well, in Little Jane Fonda, we choose an energetic song and two different motor moves, such as sidestep and heels up. Then we do each move for 8 counts, then 4 counts, and then 2 counts. This is a great way to wake up our brains and bodies so that we are alert and ready to learn.
Why: The developmental progressive patterns require attention, memory, cognitive flexibility, and response inhibition.
How: Have you ever seen a Zumba class? Well, this is Zumba for our brains. Get ready to pay attention because your feet are going to get fancy.
    Begin to sidestep, right, left for 8 counts.
    Now, lift alternating heels 8 counts.
    Repeat.
    Switch to sidestep, right, left for 4 counts.
    Now, lift alternating heels 4 counts.
    Repeat.
    Switch to sidestep, right, left for 2 counts.
    Now, lift alternating heels 2 counts.
    Repeat four times.

We did it! Look at us alert our brains by moving and thinking at the same time!

Activity #2: *Big* Ball Bounce

Action: Children bounce a *big* yoga ball in unison with the teacher, instructor, or peers. The purpose of this activity is to teach children how to move in time on the beat while pausing.

Why: The ability to inhibit a motor or verbal response is closely tied to learning, social, and academic achievement. The "pause" or "rest" in our activities is central to practicing executive function skills such as impulse control and response inhibition. Waiting, counting, or breathing through the pause provides children the experience of the "felt-sense" of slowing down. Take that moment to teach them to "pause or rest" before they initiate the skill again. Enjoy that pause yourself. We all need to pause and breathe.

How: In *big* Ball Bounce we hold the yoga ball or playground ball with two hands at chest level. Then we bounce the ball down on the vertical path for 3 counts, then we hold 1 2 3 4.

    Count 1: Hold the ball with two hands.
    Count 2: Push the ball in a vertical path toward the ground.
    Count 3: Catch the ball with both hands.

Hold the ball for 4 counts, 4, 5, 6, 7, 8.
Again.

    Count 1: Hold the ball with two hands.
    Count 2: Push the ball in a vertical path toward the ground.
    Count 3: Catch the ball with both hands.

Hold the ball for 4 counts, 4, 5, 6, 7, 8.
You've got this! Let's turn up the cognition by changing the beats.

    Count 1: Push the ball in a vertical path toward the ground.
    Count 2: Hold.
    Count 3: Push the ball in a vertical path toward the ground.
    Count 4: Hold.

Again, two more sequences.
Way to go!

Activity #3: 1–2 Cha, Cha, Cha

Action: Teach how to move in 4/4 and 3/4 time. Teach your students how to move fluidly in 4/4 time with the beat. Moving in 4/4 time, four beats to a measure, activates the natural musicality in the human body, supporting skill development. Then turn up the motor-cognition by adding a 3-count cha, cha, cha!

Why: We live in a decimal society that is great for math, measurement, and science, yet it is not as beneficial to cognition and movement. We walk in 4/4 time, we dance in 4/4 and ¾ time, and we even learn languages in 4/4 time.

How: Have your students stand up and model stepping 1–2, right, left for 8 beats. Now, step right foot on 1 left foot on 2 right foot on 3.
Left foot on 1 right foot on 2 left foot on 3.
Go back to stepping right left for 8 counts.
Great, you are getting the rhythm. Let's turn up the cognition.

> Now it sounds like:
> Right 1, left 2
> Right 1, left 2, right 3
> Left 1, right 2
> Left 1, right 2, left 3
> Or
> Right, left
> Cha, cha, cha
> Left, right
> Cha, cha, cha

You can do this with partners, in circles, in squares, or even during transitions to centers or in and out of the classroom to the lunchroom or recess.

Families, you can do this as you move toward the car to go to school or out of the bathroom to head to bed.

Nothing like a 1, 2, cha, cha, cha to bring a smile to a child's face!

Activity #4: Knee Up Down

Action: Knee Up Down combines 4 counts with a 3-count action, requiring both attention and inhibition. This might take a bit of practice, but once you get it, the kids are gonna love it!

Why: Switching from 4/4 time to a 3-count movement with a pause requires thought. When children do Knee Up Down, they practice sustained attention and response inhibition.

How: We're going to do a sequence that has a little pause in it. "Wait a moment," that's gonna be interesting.
Begin with alternating heels in front.
We usually do this pattern for four rhythmic sets to alert attention.

> Right 2, 3, 4.
> Left 2, 3, 4.
> The next move is right heel forward, knee up, place it down by the left foot like an Irish step dancer; repeat on the left side.

Activity #5: Dynamic Balance

Action: Dynamic balance refers to the ability to maintain postural control and stability while the body is in motion or experiencing external forces, such as during walking, turning, lifting, or reaching.
Why: In this activity, students practice core strength and postural control while they lift alternating legs behind their bodies.
How: Okay, let's challenge both our thinking and our motor skills. I want us to count together out loud, 1, 2, 3, 4. Let's do it again: 1, 2, 3, 4. Great.
Now the next time we reach beat 4 we are going to lift our right leg a few inches off the ground, straight back, behind your body. Hold that move for 4 beats. Ready, count 1, 2, 3, lift (hold 2, 3) and put your leg down on beat 4. Excellent.
Now, with our left leg. Count 1, 2, 3, lift (hold 2, 3), down.
Easy or hard? You tell me?
All right, now we are going to do the entire sequence twice. This will take some concentration. Are you all ready to focus?

> 1, 2, 3. Let's *focus*.
> Count out loud 1, 2, 3, lift right leg (hold 2, 3), down.
> Count out loud 1, 2, 3 lift left leg (hold 2, 3), down.
> Again!
> Count out loud 1, 2, 3; lift right leg (hold 2, 3), down.
> Count out loud 1, 2, 3; lift left leg (hold 2, 3), down.

If you wish to add variations to dynamic balance, have your students move forward in a lunge on beat 4 and then back to center. You can even teach your students to Walk Forward 2, 3, Lunge (hold 2, 3), Up, Walk Back 2, 3, Lunge (hold 2, 3), Up (return to ready position). There are so many variations here; use your creativity!
Wow! That took a lot of focus. Good work!
Now our brains and bodies are primed for our next activity.

Activity #6: Use Rhythm to Teach Basic Sports Actions

Action: Teach a motor activity such as a soccer kick or bouncing a playground ball in 4/4 time.
Why: When children learn new motor skills, it is easier if they do so in rhythmic time. You can teach a student how to bounce a ball, hit a ball with a racquet, or kick a ball, all in rhythm. The cool thing is that once your students become used to moving rhythmically, then they can change things up. The rhythm is simply the scaffold the body relies on to learn the skill.
How: Soccer—If you teach a foundational soccer kick, do so in time.

Kids, we are going to learn how to kick a soccer ball. When we think about the steps, they include: Stand on your nondominant leg (balance), swing your dominant leg back (dynamic balance), and follow through to kick the ball. It sounds like:
1. Stand (balance).
2. Extend leg back.
3. Swing the leg through to kick the ball.

See, it's as easy as 1, 2, 3, then rest.
Let's try each step together.
Count 1: Balance on your nondominant leg.
Count 2: Extend your dominant leg back.
Count 3: Swing your dominant leg through to kick the ball.
Count 4: Rest.

A Few Quick Tips

1. When children are learning to move in time with rhythm, it helps for them to count and say what they are doing out loud together as a team. This action leads to better social cohesion. It also activates biological entrainment, which supports the students who may be having difficulty moving and speaking in synchronization.
2. Feel free to slow down. If moving (quickly) at 100–120 beats per minute is a challenge, encourage the students to perform the movements (slowly) at half-time, 50–85 beats per minute, until they get experienced with tempo, timing, and rhythm.
3. Have fun with this process; it can be new to students. Encourage them to use their creativity; perhaps on beat 4, they choose a new movement together, like a Superman position or a Clap/Clap, increasing the cognitive demands of the activities while feeling empowered and playful.
4. Use your knowledge. You are experienced teachers. Change things up. Add rhythm to other activities you do. All you need is 2–3 minutes of rhythmic coordinative movement at a time to prime your students' brains for learning.

YOU'RE A COGNITIVE SCIENTIST!

I so enjoy supporting our learners as *cognitive scientists*. Here is some *meta-messaging* for you to use in your good work.

- When we listen for the beat, we are using our attention engines.
- When we focus on the pattern, we are activating our neurons.
- When we think about what is next, we are using the cognitive skill called planning.

- We are cognitive scientists coaching our brains to move to the beat. Sequences require us to move with intention; this builds our brains.
- When we have to wait a moment before we do the next action or say the next word, we are using the cognitive skill called self-control. That's good for all of us.
- When we learn how to move slowly, we can make more intentional choices throughout our day.
- We enjoy making patterns; thinking sequentially develops our planning skills.
- When we move together as one, we are using our brains and bodies in synchrony.
- When we are able to imagine what is next, we are exercising our memory.

CONCLUSION

Research shows that children are currently behind in foundational motor competencies, including vestibular abilities, proprioceptive awareness, motor rhythm, tempo, and timing (Brian et al., 2019). When you incorporate what the body biologically knows well, rhythm and timing as well as motor and cognitive skills develop with greater ease. Importantly, you, as an educator, parent, or clinician, contribute in a meaningful way to the skills that underlie your students' academic achievement as well as their physical competencies. These approaches can support students in connecting with others and reconnecting with their bodies in ways that enhance their wider health and greater awareness of their sense of self and embodied cognition.

REFERENCES

Alesi, M., Pecoraro, D., & Pepi, A. (2018). Executive functions in kindergarten children at risk for developmental coordination disorder. *European Journal of Special Needs Education*, *34*, 285–296.

Bao, R., Wade, L., Leahy, A. A., Owen, K. B., Hillman, C. H., Jaakkola, T., & Lubans, D. R. (2024). Associations between motor competence and executive functions in children and adolescents: A systematic review and meta-analysis. *Sports Medicine (Auckland, N.Z.)*, *54*(8), 2141–2156.

Bell, M., Gonzalez, Y., Weinstein, A., Ciosek, D., Wang, Y., & Yoon, G. (2025). I got rhythm and executive function, memory, and more: The Automated Test of Embodied Cognition (ATEC). *Brain Sciences*, *15*, 299.

Bharathi, G., Jayaramayya, K., Balasubramanian, V., & Vellingiri, B. (2019). The potential role of rhythmic entrainment and music therapy intervention for individuals with autism spectrum disorders. *Journal of Exercise Rehabilitation*, *15*(2), 180–186.

Bonacina, S., Krizman, J., White-Schwoch, T., Nicol, T., & Kraus, N. (2019). How rhythmic skills relate and develop in school-age children. *Global Pediatric Health, 6,* 2333794X19852045.

Brian, A., Pennell, A., Taunton, S., Starrett, A., Howard-Shaughnessy, C., Goodway, J. D., Wadsworth, D., Rudisill, M., & Stodden, D. (2019). Motor competence levels and developmental delay in early childhood: A multicenter cross-sectional study conducted in the USA. *Sports Medicine (Auckland, N.Z.), 49*(10), 1609–1618.

Bruchhage, M., Amad, A., Draper, S., Seidman, J., Lacerda, L., Laguna, P., Lowry, R., Wheeler, J., Robertson, A., Dell'Acqua, F., Smith, M., & Williams, S. (2020). Drum training induces long-term plasticity in the cerebellum and connected cortical thickness. *Scientific Reports, 10*(1), 10116.

Corriveau, K. H., & Goswami, U. (2009). Rhythmic motor entrainment in children with speech and language impairments: Tapping to the beat. *Cortex: A Journal Devoted to the Study of the Nervous System and Behavior, 45*(1), 119–130.

Corriveau, K., Pasquini, E., & Goswami, U. (2007). Basic auditory processing skills and specific language impairment: A new look at an old hypothesis. *Journal of Speech, Language, and Hearing Research, 50*(3), 647–666.

de Greeff, J. W., Bosker, R. J., Oosterlaan, J., Visscher, C., & Hartman, E. (2018). Effects of physical activity on executive functions, attention and academic performance in preadolescent children: A meta-analysis. *Journal of Science and Medicine in Sport, 21*(5), 501–507.

Donnelly, J., Hillman, C., Castelli, D., Etnier, J., Lee, S., Tomporowski, P., Lambourne, K., & Szabo-Reed, A. (2016). Physical activity, fitness, cognitive function, and academic achievement in children: A systematic review. *Medicine and Science in Sports and Exercise, 48*(6), 1197–1222.

Donnelly, J., & Lambourne, K. (2011). Classroom-based physical activity, cognition, and academic achievement. *Preventive Medicine, 52* (Suppl 1), S36–S42.

Fernandes, V. R., Ribeiro, M. L., Melo, T., de Tarso Maciel-Pinheiro, P., Guimarães, T. T., Araújo, N. B., Ribeiro, S., & Deslandes, A. C. (2016). Motor coordination correlates with academic achievement and cognitive function in children. *Frontiers in Psychology, 7,* 318.

Fiveash, A., Ferreri, L., Bouwer, F. L., Kösem, A., Moghimi, S., Ravignani, A., Keller, P. E., & Tillmann, B. (2023). Can rhythm-mediated reward boost learning, memory, and social connection? Perspectives for future research. *Neuroscience and Biobehavioral Reviews, 149,* 105153.

Foster Vander Elst, O., Foster, N., Vuust, P., Keller, P., & Kringelbach, M. (2023). The neuroscience of dance: A conceptual framework and systematic review. *Neuroscience and Biobehavioral Reviews, 150,* 105197.

Frischen, U., Degé, F., & Schwarzer, G. (2022). The relation between rhythm processing and cognitive abilities during child development: The role of prediction. *Frontiers in Psychology, 13,* 920513.

García-Hermoso, A., Ramírez-Vélez, R., Lubans, D. R., & Izquierdo, M. (2021). Effects of physical education interventions on cognition and academic performance outcomes in children and adolescents: A systematic review and meta-analysis. *British Journal of Sports Medicine, 55*(21), 1224–1232.

García-Madruga, J. A., Gómez-Veiga, I., & Vila, J. Ó. (2016). Executive functions and the improvement of thinking abilities: The intervention in reading comprehension. *Frontiers in Psychology, 7*, 58.

Gordon, R. L., Fehd, H. M., & McCandliss, B. D. (2015). Does music training enhance literacy skills? A meta-analysis. *Frontiers in Psychology, 6*, 1777.

Greco, G., Poli, L., Carvutto, R., Patti, A., Fischetti, F., & Cataldi, S. (2023). Effects of a complex physical activity program on children's arithmetic problem solving and arithmetic reasoning abilities. *European Journal of Investigation in Health, Psychology and Education, 13*(1), 141–150.

Hardy, L. L., Barnett, L., Espinel, P., & Okely, A. D. (2013). Thirteen-year trends in child and adolescent fundamental movement skills: 1997–2010. *Medicine and Science in Sports and Exercise, 45*(10), 1965–1970.

Jarraya, S., Wagner, M., Jarraya, M., & Engel, F. A. (2019). 12 weeks of kindergarten-based yoga practice increases visual attention, visual-motor precision and decreases behavior of inattention and hyperactivity in 5-year-old children. *Frontiers in Psychology, 10*, 796.

Jing, J., Jia, S., & Yang, C. (2024). Physical activity promotes brain development through serotonin during early childhood. *Neuroscience, 554*, 34–42.

Kenney, L., & Comizio, R. (2016). *70 play activities for better thinking, self-regulation, learning & behavior*. PESI Publishing.

Kolovelonis, A., & Goudas, M. (2023). The effects of cognitively challenging physical activity games versus health-related fitness activities on students' executive functions and situational interest in physical education: A group-randomized controlled trial. *European Journal of Investigation in Health, Psychology and Education, 13*(5), 796–809.

Kolovelonis, A., Pesce, C., & Goudas, M. (2022). The effects of a cognitively challenging physical activity intervention on school children's executive functions and motivational regulations. *International Journal of Environmental Research and Public Health, 19*(19), 12742.

Kong, J., Wilson, G., Park, J., Pereira, K., Walpole, C., & Yeung, A. (2019). Treating depression with tai chi: State of the art and future perspectives. *Frontiers in Psychiatry, 10*, 237.

Latino, F., & Tafuri, F. (2024). Physical activity and cognitive functioning. *Medicina (Kaunas, Lithuania), 60*(2), 216.

Lense, M., Ladányi, E., Rabinowitch, T., Trainor, L., & Gordon, R. (2021). Rhythm and timing as vulnerabilities in neurodevelopmental disorders. *Philosophical Transactions of the Royal Society of London. Series B, Biological Sciences, 376*(1835), 20200327.

Lundetræ, K., & Thomson, J. M. (2017). Rhythm production at school entry as a predictor of poor reading and spelling at the end of first grade. *Reading and Writing, 31*(1), 215–237.

Luo, X., Herold, F., Ludyga, S., Gerber, M., Kamijo, K., Pontifex, M., Hillman, C., Alderman, B., Müller, N., Kramer, A., Ishihara, T., Song, W., & Zou, L. (2023). Association of physical activity and fitness with executive function among preschoolers. *International Journal of Clinical and Health Psychology, 23*(4), 100400.

Marz, A., Kamatchi, G., D'Silva, J., Prabhakaran, K., Chandra, R., & Isekeije, S. (2020). *Anatomy and physiology laboratory manual for nursing and allied health*. VIVA Open Publishing.

Merlo, C., Jones, S., Michael, S., Chen, T., Sliwa, S., Lee, S., Brener, N., Lee, S., & Park, S. (2020). Dietary and physical activity behaviors among high school students—youth risk behavior survey, United States, 2019. *MMWR Supplements, 69*(1), 64–76.

Miendlarzewska, E. A., & Trost, W. J. (2014). How musical training affects cognitive development: Rhythm, reward and other modulating variables. *Frontiers in Neuroscience, 7,* 279.

Paschen, L., Lehmann, T., Kehne, M., & Baumeister, J. (2019). Effects of acute physical exercise with low and high cognitive demands on executive functions in children: A systematic review. *Pediatric Exercise Science, 31*(3), 267–281.

Schaefer, R. S., & Overy, K. (2015). Motor responses to a steady beat. *Annals of the New York Academy of Sciences, 1337,* 40–44.

Shi, P., & Feng, X. (2022). Motor skills and cognitive benefits in children and adolescents: Relationship, mechanism and perspectives. *Frontiers in Psychology, 13,* 1017825.

Symanski, C., Bladon, J., Kullberg, E., Miller, P., & Jadhav, S. (2022). Rhythmic coordination and ensemble dynamics in the hippocampal-prefrontal network during odor-place associative memory and decision making. *eLife, 11,* e79545.

Tao, Y., Zhang, Y., Qian, H., & Cao, Z. (2025). Long term effects of physical activity types on executive functions in school aged children. *Scientific Reports, 15,* 30303.

Tomporowski, P., Davis, C., Miller, P., & Naglieri, J. (2008). Exercise and children's intelligence, cognition, and academic achievement. *Educational Psychology Review, 20*(2), 111–131.

Tomporowski, P., Lambourne, K., & Okumura, M. (2011). Physical activity interventions and children's mental function: An introduction and overview. *Preventive Medicine, 52*(Suppl 1), S3–S9.

Torjinski, M., Cliff, D., & Horwood, S. (2024). Associations between nature exposure, screen use, and parent-child relations: A scoping review. *Systematic Reviews, 13*(1), 305.

Vasilopoulos, F., & Ellefson, M. (2021). Investigation of the associations between physical activity, self-regulation, and educational outcomes in childhood. *PloS one, 16*(5), e0250984.

Wang, S., Yang, A., Wei, X., Qian, R., Chen, Y., Bi, W., Hu, B., & Wen, C. (2024). Influence of rhythmic-movement activity intervention on hot executive function of 5- to 6-year-old children. *Frontiers in Psychology, 15,* 1291353.

Watson, A., Timperio, A., Brown, H., Best, K., & Hesketh, K. D. (2017). Effect of classroom-based physical activity interventions on academic and physical activity outcomes: A systematic review and meta-analysis. *The International Journal of Behavioral Nutrition and Physical Activity, 14*(1), 114.

Wick, K., Kriemler, S., & Granacher, U. (2021). Effects of a strength-dominated exercise program on physical fitness and cognitive performance in preschool children. *Journal of Strength and Conditioning Research, 35*(4), 983–990.

Williams, K., & Berthelsen, D. (2019). Implementation of a rhythm and movement intervention to support self-regulation skills of preschool-aged children in disadvantaged communities. *Psychology of Music, 47,* 800–820.

Zelaznik, H. N., & Goffman, L. (2010). Generalized motor abilities and timing behavior in children with specific language impairment. *Journal of Speech, Language, and Hearing Research, 53*(2), 383–393.

CHAPTER 6

Using Movement and Music to Enhance Language and Reading Skills in Young Children

Stacy Fretheim, United States

The purpose of language is to connect us—to give shape and allow us to share our thoughts and internal imaginations with others. Language acts as the bridge between our inner world and the external world that enables us to express ideas, share our perspectives, and foster understanding. The ability to understand and express ourselves with language also allows for the development of empathy and deeper relationships. This empowers individuals to express their own unique experiences while also participating in the collective human experience—sharing dreams, solving problems, and creating meaning together.

EARLY LANGUAGE DEVELOPMENT

Watching a baby progress from the ability to only process sound as a newborn to being able to communicate verbally and nonverbally in a matter of months is a breathtaking journey to observe as it unfolds. It is like watching a symphony come to life where every sound, word, and gesture work together to transform internal ideas into meaningful expressions.

Language development in young children is a dynamic process influenced by biological and environmental factors. Children develop language through a combination of innate abilities, interaction with their caregivers, and exposure to linguistic stimuli.

Language development in children is heavily influenced by the quantity and quality of the language stimuli they receive, particularly in their early years. High-quality language interactions—including shared book reading, face-to-face engaging conversations, and joint attention activities—support stronger vocabulary, grammar, and overall linguistic skills. Hart and Risley (1995) found that children exposed to rich and varied language from their caregivers demonstrated superior language skills compared to children with limited exposure. These differences often reflect socioeconomic disparities, where children in lower-income households may receive fewer words per hour than their peers in higher-income households.

This gap in early language exposure can lead to cumulative effects over time, often referred to as the "Matthew Effect," a term popularized by Stanovich (1986). The Matthew Effect in language and literacy development refers to the concept that children with strong early language skills tend to accumulate more linguistic knowledge over time ("the rich get richer"), while children with weaker skills fall further behind ("the poor get poorer"). These differences are compounded as children progress through school, where a strong foundation in language is necessary for academic success. Without intervention, children with weaker early language skills may struggle to catch up, as limited vocabulary and linguistic knowledge hinder their ability to fully engage in learning opportunities.

Early intervention and exposure to high-quality language experiences are essential to mitigating language development delays or disorder. An understanding of how language development occurs can certainly help prepare parents, teachers, and therapists to provide the best possible intervention. A summary of the elements of language development are described below.

Early Perception, Cooing, and Babbling

From birth, infants are capable of recognizing speech sounds and distinguishing phonemes across languages, a process known as *phonetic discrimination*. This ability narrows as they focus on the language or languages spoken in their environment, a phenomenon referred to as *perceptual narrowing* (Kuhl, 2004). From a very young age, babies experiment with sounds and begin to develop the foundational skills for communication. Around 6 to 8 weeks, they produce cooing sounds, such as "ooo" and "ahh," as they explore their vocal cords. By 4 to 10 months, babbling emerges, which involves the production of repetitive consonant-vowel combinations like "ba-ba" or "da-da." Babbling is considered a precursor to speech and supports the development of motor control necessary for articulation (Oller, 2000). Babbling also helps facilitate social interaction and communication. Through these interactions, babies are learning the back-and-forth nature of communication, such as turn-taking skills. Infants who exhibit typical babbling patterns are more likely to show typical language development as they get older. Conversely, delays in babbling can sometimes, but not always, indicate potential speech or language difficulties. Witnessing a "conversation" between a babbling infant and their caregiver is a beautiful sight.

It is worth noting that there is a distinct rhythmic nature to the exchange. These rhythmic patterns in babbling introduce infants to the prosodic features of language, such as pitch, stress, and timing. These features are critical for understanding and producing meaningful speech. Variations in rhythm and intonation during babbling help infants learn how to convey emotions or intentions through speech (Jusczyk, 1997). For example, a baby might use rising inflection at the end of a string of sounds to indicate a questioning tone. Furthermore, the rhythmic nature of babbling is associated with early phonological awareness, which is a clear predictor of vocabulary growth and literacy skills. Babies who exhibit more complex and rhythmic babbling are often those who develop larger vocabularies and stronger phonological skills later in childhood (Iverson & Wozniak, 2007; Lee et al., 2018).

Vocabulary Development

Vocabulary acquisition begins with a child's first words, typically spoken around 12 months. By 18 to 24 months, children often experience a "vocabulary explosion," learning several new words each day (Bloom, 2000). For example, during this period, a child might learn the word "dog" after seeing one in the park, then rapidly expand their understanding by associating the word with pictures of dogs in books or hearing it spoken during playtime. This rapid mapping of new words highlights the brain's capacity for integrating auditory and visual stimuli to build a robust vocabulary. Fast mapping, the ability to learn new words after limited exposure, plays a critical role in this rapid vocabulary expansion (Tomasello, 2003).

Prior to making semantic associations, children perceive arbitrary strings of phonemes. Over time, these phonemes are mapped to specific word associations through repeated exposure and interaction. This process of phoneme mapping is crucial for building a foundation for vocabulary and language acquisition (Werker & Tees, 1984).

Early Syntax Skills

By age of 2, toddlers start combining words into simple two-word phrases such as "want milk" or "go park." These early combinations demonstrate an emerging grasp of syntax, or the rules governing word order (Brown, 1973). Over the next year, sentences become more complex, though they often resemble "telegraphic speech," consisting of only essential content words like "Mommy go store." As their language skills advance, they begin to include grammatical markers, such as plurals, past tense, and pronouns (Clark, 2003). By age 3, their sentences are longer and more grammatically accurate, reflecting significant growth in their understanding of language structure.

As children progress to the preschool years, between 3 and 5 years old, their language skills continue to blossom. Vocabulary continues to expand, and they master increasingly complex sentence structures, such as those involving compound and complex sentences. Pragmatic language skills also develop during this time, enabling children to adjust their speech based on social context. They learn to take turns in conversations, use polite forms of communication, and engage in storytelling (Snow & Dickinson, 1991).

Overall, language development is a cumulative process, where each stage builds upon the last. From the first cooing sounds to sophisticated sentence construction, children rely on rich social interactions and responsive caregivers to guide them through this journey. These early experiences lay the foundation for their ability to communicate effectively and navigate the complexities of language in their social world (Adlof & Hogan, 2018).

IMPORTANCE OF FACE-TO-FACE INTERACTIONS AND EARLY LANGUAGE DEVELOPMENT

From the moment they are born, infants begin their journey of language development. Newborns are remarkably attuned to the sounds of human speech, displaying the ability to perceive and differentiate phonemes in any language in the world. This innate ability allows infants to develop phonemic representations—mental images of sounds—that form the building blocks for future language development (Kuhl, 2004). Over time, as they are exposed to one's native language through interactions with caregivers, infants start to associate these sounds with meaning, laying the groundwork for vocabulary acquisition and semantic understanding.

Research indicates that an infant's visual eye gaze (i.e., visual attention) evolves during the first year of life (Lewkowicz & Hansen-Tift, 2012). At first, the baby focuses visual attention on the caregiver's eyes. This shifts as the baby gets older, and between 6 and 10 months, the baby will shift more of its visual attention to the caregiver's mouth region. This shift is thought to support language development as the visual features of the phonemes are processed alongside the auditory features of the phoneme.

As infants grow older, this focus transitions toward a more balanced attention to both the eyes and mouth of their communicative partner. By doing so, babies continue to refine their understanding of speech sounds while also beginning to interpret emotional and social cues. This shift supports the integration of linguistic and cognitive skills, enabling infants to decode the complexity of spoken language and social interactions simultaneously. This focus on the mouth helps them link visual cues with auditory input, which is crucial for speech sound development and the formation of phonemic representations (Lewkowicz & Hansen-Tift, 2012). This attention to the visual feature of sounds as it pertains to the development of phonemic representations will become particularly important as the child becomes school-age and is ready to learn how to read and spell.

As mentioned previously, between the ages of 1 and 2 years, children begin to experiment with combining sounds into simple words and phrases. Through face-to-face interactions, where they can observe their communicative partner's facial expressions and mouth movements, children refine their ability to produce speech sounds and learn basic rules of syntax.

By the age of 4 or 5, most children are able to communicate using "adult-like" sentence patterns, incorporating complex syntax and expanding their vocabulary rapidly (Brown, 1973). This progression is supported by the interplay of phonological processing—the ability to recognize and manipulate the sound structure of language—and pragmatics, which governs the social use of language. Research highlights that children's ability to process and organize sounds during early development directly influences their later success in language and literacy acquisition (Adlof & Hogan, 2018; Kuhl, 2004; Eunice Kennedy Shriver National Institute of Child Health and Human Development, 2000).

This attunement to speech sounds is preparing the young child to develop a strong capacity to understand language as well as to expressively communicate. Research shows that phonology is the first language system to develop alongside pragmatics, providing the framework for receptive and expressive language. Accurate perception of speech sounds enables children to build phonemic representations that are essential for understanding and producing language. These representations influence the acquisition of vocabulary and syntax, ultimately supporting both comprehension and communication (Kuhl, 2004; National Reading Panel, 2000). Pragmatics, on the other hand, ensures that children learn the appropriate contexts for communication, such as turn-taking in conversations or interpreting nonverbal cues. Together, these elements form the bedrock of language development, enabling children to navigate both the linguistic and social aspects of communication.

It is through repetitive face-to-face interactions that babies are "bathed" in language. Babies do not just babble one syllable and jump right into words; they say these repetitive strings over and over and over again. Coupled with interactions where they can also see their caregiver's face, the brain is able to wire these features together. Through this process, the baby is able to build strong phonemic representations, putting them on the path toward becoming a strong reader. This aligns with the principle that "what fires together, wires together" (Hebb, 1949, p. 62), emphasizing the importance of engaging multiple senses—seeing, feeling, hearing, and experiencing—to strengthen neurological pathways for improved language processing and learning.

ORAL LANGUAGE PROVIDES THE PATHWAY TO LITERACY

Oral language is the foundation of literacy, serving as the essential pathway through which reading and writing skills are developed. Without strong oral language skills, most children will be hard-pressed when it comes to learning the code of how we represent our language on paper. Research has shown that oral language development serves as the foundation for literacy, directly influencing a child's ability to decode written text and comprehend what they read (Snow et al., 1998). Oral language lays the groundwork for literacy by supporting vocabulary acquisition, syntactic understanding, and phonological awareness—skills that are essential for reading success.

Children who have challenges with language development, particularly phonological processing, require explicit and structured intervention to lay down this important skill in order for them to continue down the path toward literacy. This requires first raising an individual's awareness of the different sensory features of a phoneme—putting together what the sound feels like inside their mouth (tactile kinesthetic feedback) and what the mouth looks like when making a phoneme (visual feedback), alongside what the phoneme sounds like (auditory feedback). These three features of a phoneme need to be integrated to comprise a strong phonemic representation. Once the phonemes are better perceived, steps need to take place to foster the development of phonological awareness—how sentences are made up of words and how those words can be broken into syllables.

To help illustrate the concept of a phonemic representation, imagine a stoplight. A stoplight is a commonly used and effective analogy to explain the neural flow from sensory inputs—such as auditory, visual, and kinesthetic stimuli—and phonemic representations. The green light symbolizes optimal neural flow, where the input is clear, consistent, and repeated, and the neural system is highly responsive, enabling distinct and accurate mapping. A yellow light indicates compromised flow, which may result from unclear, inconsistent, delayed, or infrequent stimuli, or from issues with neural responsiveness, such as misaligned neurons. In this case, phonemic maps become vague and indistinct. Finally, the red light represents a complete lack of stimulation or neural responsiveness, such as in cases of deafness or the absence of neurons in language-related areas to process the input. Ideally, we strive for all lights to be on green, a goal that should be strongly considered when designing treatment or intervention plans to optimize phonemic processing and language outcomes.

The image found through the QR code shows a schematic that highlights the components essential for the mapping of phoneme representations and typical phonological development. It also illustrates how working memory and rapid naming rely on phoneme representations for efficient functioning. Together, these components are critical for the normal processing and production of speech, collectively referred to as phonological processing (Alexander & Slinger-Constant, 2004). This material may also be accessed under the "Downloads" tab at https://www.tcpress.com/move-more-learn-more-9780807784051.

Ultimately, one needs awareness of the individual phonemes within a word, which is known as *phonemic awareness*. Phonemic awareness is one of the nonnegotiable prerequisite skills for becoming a skilled reader. The findings of the National Reading Panel (2000) emphasized the critical role of phonemic awareness, phonics, fluency, vocabulary, and comprehension in reading instruction. Phonemic awareness and phonics were identified as foundational skills for learning to read, with strong evidence supporting explicit instruction in these areas. The panel highlighted the importance of systematic and multisensory approaches to teaching phonemic awareness, such as integrating activities that involve auditory, visual, and kinesthetic feedback. These findings underscore the necessity of interventions that engage children in interactive and meaningful learning experiences, aligning closely with the practices discussed in this chapter.

THE IMPORTANCE OF MOVEMENT AND MUSIC IN LANGUAGE DEVELOPMENT

It is critically important to provide multiple repetitions of stimuli when building stronger phonological skills. By themselves, phonemes (i.e., speech sounds) are inherently boring. As such, a traditional "sit and get" educational model will be ineffective with most children very quickly. A more impactful approach incorporates movement, rhythm, music, and play to engage children effectively.

Not only does incorporating music and movement into language therapy make it much more engaging and enjoyable, but it also activates multiple areas of the brain simultaneously, creating and strengthening connections that support language acquisition and literacy skills. Research demonstrates that engaging in rhythmic activities and purposeful movement enhances phonological awareness, vocabulary, syntax, and listening skills (Gromko, 2005; Schön et al., 2004). This multisensory stimulation promotes auditory discrimination, memory retention, and motor coordination—skills that are essential for successful reading and writing.

For example, rhythmic activities such as clapping to syllables, stomping to beats, or singing songs with rhyming words provide children with a structured and engaging way to break down the components of spoken language. These activities help children build accurate phonemic representations—the mental images of sounds—which are critical for recognizing, segmenting, and blending phonemes in both oral and written language (Schön et al., 2004).

Furthermore, research has shown that musical activities involving rhythm and repetition are particularly beneficial for children at risk for language delays. For instance, drumming along to the syllables in words like "ba-na-na" or "po-ta-to" reinforces the internal structure of words while engaging motor and auditory systems. A study by Patel (2008) highlights how rhythm in music parallels the prosody of speech—the stress, pitch, and timing patterns—helping children not only perceive but also replicate speech sounds more accurately.

This multisensory approach to language therapy ensures that children are actively engaged while building foundational skills. By combining movement, rhythm, and sound, children strengthen neural pathways that support decoding written text, comprehending what they read, and expressing their thoughts fluently in both speech and writing. The QR code below will bring you to a printable version of all activities for Chapter 6. This material may also be accessed under the "Downloads" tab at https://www.tcpress.com/move-more-learn-more-9780807784051.

BUILDING PHONOLOGICAL SKILLS THROUGH MUSIC AND MOVEMENT

Phonemic awareness refers to the ability to focus on and manipulate individual phonemes, the smallest units of sound in a language. It is a critical component of language and literacy development, serving as the foundation for learning to read and write. For instance, children who can identify and isolate the sounds in words (e.g., recognizing that "cat" consists of /k/, /a/, and /t/) are better prepared to understand how letters correspond to sounds, a skill essential for decoding written text. Additionally, phonemic awareness supports spelling and writing by helping children segment and blend phonemes into words.

As mentioned previously, phonemic awareness is a nonnegotiable prerequisite skill that supports one's ability to build literacy skills. While it is conceivable to build phonemic awareness without the addition of music and movement, anyone who has the privilege of working with young children will tell you that engagement is the cornerstone of all learning. As therapists, educators, or clinicians, it is important to try and channel our inner entertainer (so to speak) in order to be interesting enough to attract and maintain the attention of the beautiful children we serve. Music and movement are the perfect tools to use to gain their attention.

Specific to building phonemic awareness, activities such as clapping to syllables or engaging in rhythmic chants provide children with the tools to discern patterns in speech and predict linguistic structures. Clapping, marching, or tapping out the syllables in words like "butterfly" ("but-ter-fly") allows children to connect the auditory and physical aspects of language while internalizing the rhythmic patterns of speech. This rhythmic engagement helps bridge the gap between oral and written language by reinforcing the sequential nature of sounds, a fundamental skill for decoding words. Similarly, singing songs with rhyming patterns often accompanied by hand gestures, such as "Twinkle, Twinkle, Little Star" or "I'm a Little Teapot," enhances children's ability to perceive and replicate sound patterns. These activities not only make the learning process enjoyable, but also prepare children for the structured rhythm of written text (Anvari et al., 2002; Gromko, 2005).

Musical training has been shown to enhance phonological processing abilities, foundational for language and literacy development (Schön et al., 2004; Gromko, 2005). For example, children who engage in music lessons often display improved auditory discrimination, which helps them identify and differentiate phonemes more accurately.

Videos for the following three sample activities may be accessed using the QR code below or under the "Downloads" tab at https://www.tcpress.com/move-more-learn-more-9780807784051.

Sample Activity for Building Phonemic Representations

Target: Child will discover the multisensory feature of the short vowel sound /ɑ/ as in the word "hot."

Sample Script

Adult: I'm going to say a sound and I want you to repeat it to me. Are you ready? The sound is /ɑ/.
Child: /ɑ/
Adult: Great! We matched the same sound. Look in the mirror and see what you notice when you say the sound /ɑ/.
Child: I notice my mouth is open.
Adult: I noticed the same thing. What do you feel your mouth doing when you say /ɑ/?
Child: I feel my jaw open, and it is relaxed. My tongue is just hanging out in the bottom of my mouth.
Adult: That's what I feel too! Let's compare how this feels different from the other sound we discovered earlier, /i/ (as in "eat"). To help us see the

difference, I have a song for us to sing called "If All the Raindrops." I will sing the song first and then we can sing it together. (The adult should then sing the song "If All the Raindrops" by Pete Seeger.)
Adult: Now let's change the lyrics a little bit and instead of saying /a/ (as in "hot") when we try to catch the candy rain, let's say / ē / (as in "feet").
Now repeat the song and say the / ē / sound instead of /o/ when trying to catch the lemon drops, then ask which one would catch more lemon drops, /o/ or /ē/. Ask, why that may be? Go back and forth saying /ē/ and /o/ (or any other vowel) and pretend to catch the delicious candy.

This activity helps one be able to better perceive the contrasts between vowel sounds. You can repeat the song with a vowel of your choosing. Be sure to question back to how that feels different from another vowel.

Sample Activity for Building Phonemic Awareness—Phoneme Segmentation

Target: Child will segment words with CVC, VCC, CCV, and CCVC, CVCC, and CCVCC syllable structures into the individual phonemes that comprise the word.
Set up: Place five poly spots on the ground that are all different colors.
Directions: Children hop on a poly spot for each sound in a word like "map" (/m/ /a/ /p/) or a longer word like "sleeps" (/s/ /l/ / ē / /p/ /s/). This type of movement-based activity makes abstract concepts more concrete and engaging, facilitating deeper learning. Alternatively, you can have the children march in place, once per sound, or tap the sounds with their hands on the table or on their body.

Comment on the length of the word (e.g., "Wow! We hopped five times for the word 'sleeps' but only two times for the word 'it.'"). Below is a list of words organized by number of phonemes that can be used as the stimuli for the hopping game. When first playing the game, start with words that have up to three sounds, then progress to words that contain consonant blends (e.g., "stops").

Stimuli Words to Hop Out:
1. Phoneme:
   - I
   - Oh (/ō/)
2. Phonemes:
   - me (/m/ /ē/)
   - no (/n/ /ō/)
   - go (/g/ /ō/)
   - hi (/h/ /ī/)
3. Phonemes:
   - cat (/k/ /a/ /t/)

- dog (/d/ /o/ /g/)
- mom (/m/ /o/ /m/)
- dad (/d/ /a/ /d/)
- sun (/s/ /u/ /n/)
- bug (/b/ /u/ /g/)
- top (/t/ /o/ /p/)
- hat (/h/ /a/ /t/)

4. Phonemes:
   - frog (/f/ /r/ /o/ /g/)
   - clap (/k/ /l/ /a/ /p/)
   - play (/p/ /l/ /ā/ /y/)
   - stop (/s/ /t/ /o/ /p/)
   - drum (/d/ /r/ /u/ /m/)
   - nest (/n/ /e/ /s/ /t/)

5. Phonemes:
   - spider (/s/ /p/ /ī/ /d/ /er/)
   - stand (/s/ /t/ /a/ /n/ /d/)
   - trunk (/t/ /r/ /u/ /n/ /k/)
   - plant (/p/ /l/ /a/ /n/ /t/)
   - sweet (/s/ /w/ /ē/ /t/)

Sample Activity for Building Phonemic Awareness—Phoneme Blending

Target: Child will blend phonemes to form words with CVC, VCC, CCV, and CCVC, CVCC, and CCVCC syllable structures.

Set up: Sit or stand across from the child or children so that they can see your mouth.

Directions: Tell the children that you have some words that have been "broken" into parts, and you need their help to fix them back into a whole word. Place one hand in front of your body and say the sounds within the word, chopping the air as you say each phoneme. For example, if the target word is "sweeps," you would say /s/ /w/ /ē/ /p/ /s/ as you chop the air in front of your chest.

After saying each sound, glide your hand across to connect the sounds into a whole word. Alternatively, you could tap the sounds down your arm, starting near your shoulder and moving toward your wrist. After saying each sound, move your hand back to the starting point and have it slide down the arm as you say the complete word. Listed below are words arranged by the number of phonemes in the word.

A video supplement showing each English phonene without a more lengthy explanation is available using the QR code below. This material may also be accessed under the "Downloads" tab at https://www.tcpress.com/move-more-learn-more-9780807784051.

Using Movement and Music to Enhance Language and Reading Skills in Young Children   103

1. Phoneme:
    - A (the letter name)
    - Oh (/ō/)
2. Phonemes:
    - it (/i/ /t/)
    - up (/u/ /p/)
    - on (/o/ /n/)
    - in (/i/ /n/)
3. Phonemes:
    - bed (/b/ /e/ /d/)
    - pig (/p/ /i/ /g/)
    - cup (/k/ /u/ /p/)
    - car (/k/ /ar/)
    - fish (/f/ /i/ /sh/)
    - fan (/f/ /a/ /n/)
    - bag (/b/ /a/ /g/)
4. Phonemes:
    - star (/s/ /t/ /ar/)
    - slide (/s/ /l/ /ī/ /d/)
    - skip (/s/ /k/ /i/ /p/)
    - hand (/h/ /a/ /n/ /d/)
    - milk (/m/ /i/ /l/ /k/)
    - jump (/j/ /u/ /m/ /p/)
5. Phonemes:
    - grass (/g/ /r/ /a/ /s/ /s/)
    - snack (/s/ /n/ /a/ /k/)
    - clown (/k/ /l/ /ow/ /n/)
    - crunch (/k/ /r/ /u/ /n/ /ch/)
    - float (/f/ /l/ /ō/ /t/)

VOCABULARY AND SYNTAX THROUGH MUSIC AND MOVEMENT

Music offers a rich and engaging way to introduce new vocabulary and complex sentence structures. Songs provide a context for learning words and phrases, making them memorable through repetition and melody. For example, singing "The Itsy-Bitsy Spider" introduces words like "spout," "washed," and "climbed," along with their syntactic relationships. The accompanying hand gestures, such as moving fingers to mimic a spider climbing or hands sweeping downward to represent the rain, enhance engagement and provide a multisensory experience. These gestures help children connect physical actions to the words, reinforcing comprehension of abstract concepts like "spout" and "washed." Repeating these lyrics and gestures helps children internalize language structures and expand their vocabulary while simultaneously building motor coordination and spatial awareness (Paquette & Rieg, 2008).

Moreover, music enhances memory and recall, enabling children to retain and use new words in meaningful contexts. For instance, a song like "Old MacDonald Had a Farm" helps children learn and recall animal names and associated sounds ("cow" and "moo"). Repetition of the lyrics reinforces vocabulary, while the predictable structure encourages attention to word order and grammatical rules ("With a moo-moo here and a moo-moo there"). Singing songs like this in a group setting further supports syntax development as children internalize patterns of language and begin to construct sentences that mirror these structures (Gordon et al., 2015).

OVERVIEW OF THE ALEXANDER INTEGRATED METHOD (AIM)

At Wellington-Alexander Center (WAC), we use the Alexander Integrated Method (AIM), which was developed by Ann Alexander, MD, a developmental pediatrician, along with her team. Dr. Alexander recognized the need for a literacy approach that aligns with how the brain naturally develops language and reading skills. Rather than rushing into reading and spelling before foundational skills are in place, AIM ensures that students first build the strong phonological and phonemic awareness necessary for literacy success.

This structured method focuses on strengthening oral language as the critical first step, ensuring that students can hear, distinguish, and manipulate sounds before moving on to connecting them with written symbols. The program follows a carefully sequenced progression, beginning with the most accessible sounds and gradually introducing more complex phonemes, syllables, and spelling patterns. Multisensory tools help reinforce learning, making abstract concepts more concrete.

Once students develop a solid awareness of sounds, they transition to phoneme-to-grapheme mapping, learning how spoken language translates into written form. This phase introduces phonics rules, syllable structures, and strategies for breaking down words, ensuring that students can read and spell with confidence. As they progress, they apply these skills to increasingly complex texts, moving from controlled practice to real-world reading and writing.

AIM is structured as an intensive intervention, with daily sessions designed to build fluency and automaticity. After this initial phase, students transition to a period of guided practice where they apply their skills in broader literacy contexts in other environments (in the classroom, at home, etc.), reinforcing long-term success. Rooted in a neurodevelopmental framework, AIM is designed to support the brain's natural progression in learning language and literacy. By prioritizing foundational skills before introducing higher-level reading demands, the program provides a systematic, evidence-based approach to literacy that effectively supports struggling readers, including those with dyslexia.

A Typical Day of Intensive Intervention

To help illustrate the concepts described in this chapter, I thought it would be helpful to describe what intensive intervention looks like where I serve so many beautiful children at the WAC.

At the center, the children participate in intensive intervention programs consisting of four language and literacy-focused sessions and one occupational therapy (OT) session each day, 5 days a week, for approximately 6 to 8 weeks. Each day involves 5 hours of intervention, during which the child rotates through different clinicians every hour. This rotation helps maintain their alertness and arousal levels by introducing built-in novelty, especially as the subject matter—building sounds and sound awareness for phonological processing can be inherently less engaging, necessitating the need to incorporate as much movement and music as possible to "gamify" the process.

In an intensive setting, such as a language and literacy intervention program, children rotate through sessions with different clinicians. Yet each clinician follows the exact same scope and sequence and methodology. These sessions integrate movement and music into targeted activities to ensure engagement and effectiveness. Between each session, children participate in brief movement breaks or activities designed to regulate alertness and prepare them for the next task.

All clinicians focusing on language and literacy adhere to the same theoretical framework and are highly trained in the methodology employed. The variety of clinician personalities enhances engagement, as children benefit from diverse interactions while still experiencing frequent repetition of stimuli. This prevents monotony and ensures dynamic, engaging learning experiences.

For example, a child might begin with an activity that builds phonological awareness where they practice word chains. Using manipulatives like blocks or tokens, the child touches and says each phoneme in a word (e.g., "cat" as /k/ /a/ /t/). The clinician models the rhythm and pacing of this activity using a sing-songy approach, helping the child internalize the cadence of language. As the word chain progresses to "cap" and "tap," the child builds connections between sounds and their representations, reinforcing their understanding of sound-symbol relationships.

Later, the child might reinforce the development of phonemic awareness in music-focused activities where they sing songs that emphasize rhyming patterns and syllables. For instance, clapping along to "Bingo" ("There was a farmer had a dog . . .") reinforces syllable segmentation and helps the child recognize how sounds combine to form words. Songs like "Down by the Bay" can further enhance rhyming skills by encouraging children to predict and create their own rhyming words, fostering both creativity and phonemic awareness. These engaging activities integrate rhythm and melody to strengthen oral language skills while laying a robust foundation for reading success.

At the start of each session, children receive a verbal and written plan outlining the activities for that session, providing a clear preview of what to expect. Break times are scheduled but flexible, allowing for adjustments based on the child's needs. Activities are carefully designed to reinforce phonemic awareness, phoneme-to-grapheme mapping, phonics skills, reading fluency, and reading comprehension. The methodology employed is highly multisensory, which inherently boosts engagement by incorporating elements of discovery and modeling rather than relying solely on a didactic approach.

Through the guidance provided by an occupational therapist, clinicians may use deep pressure or brushing protocols to address sensory integration challenges. Opportunities for heavy work and movement breaks are integrated into sessions, promoting sensory regulation and focus. Additionally, games are used as a fun and engaging way to develop cognitive and social skills. For example, playing Uno reinforces fine motor skills, manual dexterity, turn-taking, strategic planning, initiation, adaptive strategy shifts, and sportsmanship, all of which contribute to overall learning readiness.

Recognizing that expecting a child to sit still for a full 50-minute to 1-hour session is unrealistic, sessions incorporate movement into activities rather than treating it solely as a break.

Between sessions, children also participate in group breaks that offer opportunities to socialize with peers, engage in both structured and unstructured play, and practice social communication skills. These breaks are designed to support the development of interpersonal skills and provide a balanced approach to intensive intervention.

Preparing the Brain for Learning

Integrating movement and music into daily routines prepares the brain for learning by increasing alertness and engagement. Rhythmic clapping or a short song can serve as a warm-up activity, helping children transition into focused learning tasks. These activities also provide sensory input that regulates arousal levels, ensuring that children are in an optimal state for absorbing new information.

CONCLUSION

Movement and music are not merely enhancements to traditional teaching methods; they are essential components of effective language and literacy instruction. By combining rhythm, physical activity, and play, educators and therapists can create engaging, multisensory experiences that build foundational skills and strengthen neurological connections. These approaches can be implemented in both structured therapy settings and everyday classroom environments, making them versatile tools for supporting children's language and literacy growth. When movement and music are integrated into learning, children develop not only the skills they need to succeed academically but also the confidence and enthusiasm to explore the world of language and literacy.

REFERENCES

Adlof, S., & Hogan, T. (2018). Understanding dyslexia in the context of developmental language disorders. *Language, Speech, and Hearing Services in Schools*, 49(4), 762–773.

Alexander, A., & Slinger-Constant, A. (2004). Current status of treatments for dyslexia: Critical review. *Journal of Child Neurology*, 19(10), 744–758.

Anvari, S., Trainor, L., Woodside, J., & Levy, B. (2002). Relations among musical skills, phonological processing, and early reading ability in preschool children. *Journal of Experimental Child Psychology*, 83(2), 111–130.

Bloom, P. (2000). *How children learn the meanings of words*. MIT Press.

Brown, R. (1973). *A first language: The early stages*. Harvard University Press.

Clark, E. (2003). *First language acquisition*. Cambridge University Press.

Eunice Kennedy Shriver National Institute of Child Health and Human Development, NIH, DHHS. (2000). *Report of the National Reading Panel: Teaching children to read: Reports of the subgroups* (Reference Only) (00-4754). U.S. Government Printing Office.

Gordon, R., Fehd, H., & McCandliss, B. (2015). Does music training enhance literacy skills? A meta-analysis. *Frontiers in Psychology*, 6, 1777.

Gromko, J. (2005). The effect of music instruction on phonemic awareness in beginning readers. *Journal of Research in Music Education*, 53(3), 199–209.

Hart, B., & Risley, T. (1995). *Meaningful differences in the everyday experience of young American children*. P.H. Brookes.

Hebb, D. (1949). *The organisation of behaviour*. John Wiley & Sons.

Iverson, J., & Wozniak, R. (2007). Variation in vocal-motor development in infant siblings of children with autism. *Journal of Autism and Developmental Disorders*, 37(1), 158–170.

Jusczyk, P. (1997). *The discovery of spoken language*. MIT Press.

Kuhl, P. K. (2004). Early language acquisition: cracking the speech code. *Nature reviews. Neuroscience*, 5(11), 831–843.

Lee, C. C., Jhang, Y., Relyea, G., Chen, L. M., & Oller, D. K. (2018). Babbling development as seen in canonical babbling ratios: A naturalistic evaluation of all-day recordings. *Infant Behavior & Development, 50,* 140–153.

Lewkowicz, D., & Hansen-Tift, A. (2012). Infants deploy selective attention to the mouth of a talking face when learning speech. *Proceedings of the National Academy of Sciences, 109*(5), 1431–1436.

Oller, D. (2000). *The emergence of the speech capacity.* Lawrence Erlbaum Associates.

Paquette, K., & Rieg, S. (2008). Using music to support the literacy development of young English language learners. *Early Childhood Education Journal, 36*(3), 227–232.

Patel, A. (2008). *Music, language, and the brain.* Oxford University Press.

Piek, J., Dawson, L., Smith, L., & Gasson, N. (2008). The role of early fine and gross motor development on later motor and cognitive ability. *Human Movement Science, 27*(5), 668–681.

Schön, D., Magne, C., & Besson, M. (2004). The music of speech: Music training facilitates pitch processing in both music and language. *Psychophysiology, 41*(3), 341–349.

Snow, C., & Dickinson, D. (1991). *Language development and early literacy: Bridging home and school.* Harvard Educational Review.

Snow, C., Burns, M., & Griffin, P. (eds.) (1998). *Preventing reading difficulties in young children.* National Academy Press.

Stanovich, K. (1986). Matthew effects in reading: Some consequences of individual differences in the acquisition of literacy. *Reading Research Quarterly, 21*(4), 360–407.

Tomasello, M. (2003). *Constructing a language: A usage-based theory of language acquisition.* Harvard University Press.

Werker, J., & Tees, R. (1984). Cross-language speech perception: Evidence for perceptual reorganization during the first year of life. *Infant Behavior and Development, 7*(1), 49–63.

CHAPTER 7

Handwriting and Movement
Addressing Delays and Difficulties

Mary Mountstephen, UK

In this chapter, I propose that the development of secure motor skills is crucial to the development of cognitive skills and will provide the reader with an overview of how this applies to handwriting. I will reference key international research and practice, drawing on a cognitive-motor paradigm and my own work as a practitioner, researcher, and trainer. This chapter will reference research-led interventions and the role that targeted training for practitioners in movement skills can have. Since there are known links between fine and gross motor skills and learning difficulties, I propose shifting the dynamics of the classroom toward a cognitive-motor paradigm. When we recognize and appreciate that motor activities underpin and support cognitive activities and academic achievement, we implement movement not simply as brain breaks. We move with intention to build the neural pathways associated with learning and cognition. Adopting a cognitive-motor paradigm allows learning to take place more effectively.

This chapter will identify some key themes in the development of early writing skills, with references to learning differences such as dyslexia, with recommended activities to support daily functioning. We will also connect to discussions about the significance of shifting the dynamics of the classroom toward a cognitive-motor paradigm, with associated training for classroom practitioners. The chapter provides examples of activities that can be integrated into class, group, or individual sessions, the related research, and indicators for further reading, resources, and training. I mainly reference research and practice in the UK, Europe, and Asia. The body of work is also based on background reading, collaborations, and projects that span over 20 years.

I am a dyslexia specialist practitioner, researcher, and trainer working internationally in the early years, primary, special, and independent sectors. My professional life has been devoted to acquiring skills and knowledge to more effectively meet the needs of early years and primary school children. My vision is to contribute to international learning communities that are skilled in observation, analysis, and interventions within a cognitive-motor paradigm that places active learning at the very heart of their ethos.

A multisensory, multidisciplinary approach, with a focus on the early identification of barriers to learning, has been a prominent feature of my professional career. I've been fortunate to work with recognized experts and develop innovative partnerships. This approach has also informed the development of assessment and intervention protocols for addressing the needs of many children in my private practice.

SPECIFIC LEARNING DIFFERENCES (SpLD)

The Helen Arkell Dyslexia Charity defines Specific Learning Differences (SpLDs) as a neurodevelopmental disorder that may affect an individual's ability to receive, process, and recall information. It is a difference or difficulty with particular aspects of learning. The term SpLD is used to denote a range of learning difficulties. The most common include:

- Dyslexia
- Dyspraxia or Developmental Coordination Disorder (DCD)
- Dyscalculia
- Dysgraphia

In this chapter, the focus is on aspects of dyslexia, as well as other learning differences that impact young children's progress in school and wider daily functioning. This is not the place to debate the confusion around the very concept of dyslexia or indeed to describe it in depth (reference Chapter 6 on early language development). Key issues that will be concentrated on here include those aspects of the learning and performance profile that may benefit from a cognitive-motor program, recognizing that this approach is inclusive in terms of neurodiversity and adaptable to the needs of most children.

The professionalism of the teacher is acknowledged, and, as such, the activities in this chapter are guidelines rather than prescriptive and dogmatic. When teachers use this approach, it can, or may, assist in the identification of those in their classrooms who are underachieving, have developmental delays, and/or have unidentified learning challenges.

There is a growing body of evidence-based research linking early motor problems with physical, social, and cognitive difficulties (Zeng et al., 2017). Other chapters in this book will refer, for example, to the role of neonatal reflexes, auditory processing, and rhythm. This chapter focuses on research and practice in early years and primary schools and reflects the work of independent specialists working in the fields of dyslexia, dyspraxia, and associated difficulties (SpLD).

Writing as a specialist teacher who has always placed movement at the center of the learning process, I've frequently presented internationally on the need to focus on the motor foundations of learning. We can use movement not only to support cognition, but also as an assessment tool to identify possible barriers to progress (Leisman et al., 2016). This is why we also need to upskill our physical education instructors to identify those students who are unable, for example, to carry out static and dynamic balances with the expected levels of competence. This informed part of my doctoral research, as it is my belief that schools are undervaluing the ways in which stronger connections between physical education sessions and the classroom can enhance learning for all students, and particularly those at risk of underachieving.

CORE DIFFICULTIES: DYSLEXIA

Table 7.1 is a brief overview, focusing on some of those aspects that may be identified as benefiting from the activities outlined later in the chapter. Further information about dyslexia can be found in the references.

SCHOOL READINESS

Children with dysgraphia, dyspraxia, dyslexia, and other learning differences often have difficulties with fine and gross motor skills that can impact their classroom competence. Their earliest handwriting experiences can often be frustrating. Dysgraphia requires fluid communication between several distinct brain regions; therefore, it does not respond positively to conventional interventions (Chung et al., 2020; Portwood, 2003). It has been my experience that the earlier we act at a whole class level, the easier it is to identify those children who are beginning to struggle with skills such as mark making and early writing through active daily classroom routines that benefit the whole class. The activities outlined later in this chapter are based on my many years of research and experience working as a practitioner, trainer, and consultant internationally.

It's a win-win strategy! Kids get to move and have fun, and the teacher spots those who might need more targeted interventions by closely observing how children move.

Historically, many children entered the school system at least minimally prepared to function independently, having had access to outside play, climbing, spinning, etc. (gross motor skills) and social interactions such as play group activities, puzzles, and games with other children and family members (fine motor skills).

The pandemic further exacerbated already existing challenges concerns that predate COVID-19 (Soan & Hutton, 2021). As we have shown, more

Table 7.1. Dyslexia Core Difficulties

Difficulty/Challenge	Observations
Literacy difficulties that are persistent even when the student is appropriately well taught. There is often a mismatch between literacy abilities and verbal strengths.	There are often associated weaknesses in sequencing, fluency, and fluidity in reading aloud and in other aspects of learning. Motor activities may contribute to a multisensory support program for the development of these skills.
Processing difficulties: Poor short-term and working memory. Difficulties with recall of complex auditory instructions.	Learning in the classroom often relies heavily on rapid responses and the ability to manipulate information and instructions. Motor activities can provide a welcome release from classroom pressures, and allow "recovery time" as well as provide curricular enrichment support.
Difficulties in recalling sequences of events and organizing information.	Regularly practiced motor activities follow predictable routines that can also be used to support learning, such as the development of vocabulary, sequences (days of the week, months of the year, rhythms and rhymes, math). They engage the learners in active sensory learning.
Motor coordination: Some children with dyslexia may also display motor difficulties such as those associated with dyspraxia (Reid, 2020). Handwriting can often be compromised.	Multisensory activities, teaching, and learning are well-founded principles. Motor activities can contribute to an inclusive ethos when the teacher/practitioner is alert to observation and differentiation.
Automaticity: Children with a dyslexic profile often need far more repetitions for learning to become secure and easily accessed.	Students benefit from structured, explicit, cumulative, consistently applied programs. Motor activities can support the development of gross and fine motor skills that underpin many skills such as handwriting.

digital screen time and less hanging on trees, playing piano, knitting, sewing, crocheting, and so forth have diminished opportunities to practice fine motor skills daily. Many young children are currently entering school without the necessary levels of cognitive-motor development, independence, expressive and receptive language, and social communication skills. Economic and social disadvantage may also compound a child's early development and exert a significant long-term impact on the achievement of potential.

Young children today often experience limited spatial, physical, social, and interactional skill development opportunities, as well as fewer activities to develop the skills needed for manual dexterity. Unfortunately, they may be more likely to be seated and swiping or passively watching mobile devices.

Difficulties with movement and coordination are known to significantly affect participation and learning and have an impact on self-esteem and general health. However, many of these difficulties and delays can be addressed through adaptations to the curriculum, environment, daily classroom routines, and whole school ethos.

Cheung et al. (2020) identify five domains of school readiness:

- Physical health and motor development
- Socio-emotional development
- Cognition and general knowledge
- Language development
- Approaches to learning

They propose that there is a "growing body of research" supporting strong relationships among the motor, cognitive, and socioemotional domains and that the theory of embedded cognition proposes that fine motor, gross motor, and cognitive skills form a complex, multilayered, embodied structure that is activated as children interact with their environment. Cognitive processes are deeply rooted in the child's physical interactions, and children need different places and spaces where they can refine and practice their gross and fine motor skills. Post COVID-19, this has become even more of an issue as children need to catch up on missed activities and experiences (Musgrave et al., 2024). With much emphasis being placed on "core" subjects such as literacy and numeracy, it remains fundamental that early well-structured movement experiences be incorporated to contribute to the wider cognitive-motor development of young children.

The challenge is to support early years and primary practitioners with professional development that provides the knowledge and skills required to plan and deliver cognitive-motor activities confidently and consistently. The training should link this to the child's holistic development, classroom performance, emotional regulation, and social interaction, as well as outline a reasoned rationale for leadership teams regarding the value of this approach as a low-cost, high-value intervention to support learning needs. The author refers to "holistic development" as a way of seeing the child as a whole person whose areas of development intertwine and interact with each other. A cognitive motor–based curriculum, when well planned, enables practitioners and teachers to maximize the benefits that can be derived from the learning process, as well as provide deeper insights into individual learning profiles.

It is truly time for children to move more, based on sound research-led evidence. This revolution should nurture the development of flexible, independent, confident, and physically competent learners and facilitate classroom practices that can also contribute to the early identification of learning delays and differences such as dyslexia (SpLD). Despite substantive research showing that motor competencies support learning and academic achievement, classroom teacher/practitioner knowledge about motor skill development is still not well-known in general education (Ramos-Campo & Clemente-Suárez, 2024). These are combined with pressures on raising academic standards and reductions in the time scheduled for free play and recess.

Less time is often available or prioritized for consolidating movement competencies that support balance, posture, and coordination and that underpin effective classroom learning, academic achievement, cognition, social connections, and behavior. In the drive to raise standards, the focus is frequently on delivering the curriculum, regardless of the developmental maturity of the individual child.

The intention here is to ignite a spark of excitement in the reader and to propose the potential for recalibrating the ways in which settings can develop and implement a shift toward a dynamic, movement-based curriculum based on the understanding of the following:

- The complex relationship among motor skills, cognitive skills, and classroom performance;
- How informed and rigorous observation of balance, coordination, posture, and movement can support the identification of difficulties and delays and thus contribute to earlier intervention;
- Key elements of research from a range of international sources and practices, spanning the fields of academia, education, physical education, and occupational therapy.

Action Points

Let's get practical. What 3–5 changes would provide significantly more floor space for motor activities if you reorganized the classroom and looked at more effective use of storage? Brainstorm with a colleague. What three actions could you take to include more cognitive-motor activities in your setting, and how might you measure the impact?

EARLY YEARS AND PRIMARY PRACTICE

Over 50 years ago, Marianne Frostig's book *Movement Education: Theory and Practice* outlined her program for teaching movement skills and developing creative movement. The following concept resonated with me in terms of the professional role of educators:

> To achieve goals, in the academic setting, the teacher must not regard their job as a mechanical one. To be most effective, one must know the goals towards which

one works in movement education and base one's choice of exercises and activities on what is known about children's needs and growth. Educators must adapt their activities to the particular situation and, in doing so, consider all aspects of human development. (Frostig, 1970)

Frostig also recognized the role of movement in developing self-awareness and creativity; supporting self-concept as well as social and emotional development; and working as part of a group. By acknowledging and drawing on the inspiring history of advocates of movement-based learning, in partnership with the emerging research, teachers and practitioners can begin to address the balance between children's largely passive experiences in an increasingly digital world and active, embodied learning.

Research From Physical Education

While recognizing the "compelling evidence" concerning the positive educational value of physical activity and sport, Pickup and Price (2015) maintain that it appears to be regarded as relatively low status, with often limited investment in time, resources, and professional development opportunities. Although there has been some progress over the last 10 years, recent research indicates, for example, that primary school teachers in England continue to feel ill-prepared to teach physical education (P.E.) curriculum.

When working on my EdD in the period 2016–2021, I studied research on the perspectives of physical education specialists and classroom teachers in early years settings and primary schools in relation to primary physical education. My findings were in line with those of Pickup and Price (2015) and with my own anecdotal evidence in relation to a number of schools that I worked with. A significant number of teachers and practitioners in the U.K. report that there is still a lack of curricular leadership to ensure a positive and progressive whole-school vision. Also, perceived weaknesses also exist in initial teacher training and continuing professional development. Requests for my training indicate that this is perceived as an international concern.

Implications

The work of Schott and Klotzbier in Meeusen et al. (2018) references studies that motor and cognitive development are "more closely related than previously assumed," and they cite additional references linking fine motor skills, nonverbal intelligence, and executive functioning. Evidence compiled by Tomporowski et al. (2015) indicates that physical activity performed in close proximity to information may enhance learning in a number of ways.

If we want to look at the ways that children develop fine motor skills such as handwriting, it is necessary to understand how motor skill development can be integrated more effectively into daily classroom practice. Handwriting is a high-level skill that is dependent on complex sensory and motor elements, including adequate muscle tone, and balance for postural stability, bilateral integration, coordination, and manual dexterity (Christmas & Van de Weyer, 2020).

Would it be appropriate for closer collaborations between physical education (P.E.) specialists and classroom practitioners to also contribute more effectively to classroom performance? Might more effective relationships between classroom teachers and P.E. specialists provide the potential to improve classroom performance and physical competencies? By focusing more precisely on developmental skill acquisition, based on targeted observations and effective communication protocols, there is the potential to create a holistic approach to learning development.

While this does ideally require a whole school commitment to change, the many eminent contributors to this publication provide a treasure chest of knowledge, expertise, and experience that can inspire changes at many levels.

Action Points

- Is there a designated P.E. lead in your school, and are they included in dyslexia/SpLD professional development training?
- What training is available in your area or online to support the development of your knowledge?
- Join me on one of my online training sessions to learn and interact with other professionals internationally.

OBSERVATIONS/NOTICING

To implement the activities in this chapter successfully, it is essential to develop the skills of observing how children move and behave. It requires practitioners to be alert to the gross and fine motor skills of their students and to acknowledge that these are as significant as their cognitive skills.

The process of motor skill observation and analysis demands focused attention, an awareness of the critical features, and an understanding of the inclusive management of the process (Haywood & Getchell, 2014). It is a disciplined and systematic process that needs practice to identify the appropriate support, interventions, and extensions that may be required. In my experience, this process is more effective when the school has developed a culture that emphasizes collaborative teaching partnerships, where staff can support one another, based on a clearly understood and strongly embedded structure.

Haywood and Getchell (2014) cite Barrett (1979) and outline the three principles proposed to underpin the process of motor skill observation and analysis:

1. **Analysis:** The observer needs to be aware of the developmental sequences of the skill and the characteristics of the proficient performance.
2. **Planning:** Prompt sheets or checklists support effective observations, planning, and monitoring of progress.
3. **Positioning in observation and activities:** The observer should be aware of the importance of dynamic, responsive positioning (seated beside, standing beside, standing behind) to establish more precisely how the child performs the task and whether this differs in sitting and standing, for example.
   - Where do children need to be positioned in activities so that they can observe your movements and you can observe them?
   - Would it be more appropriate to split the class into smaller groups, depending on the number of children in the class? If so, what will the rest of the class be doing at this time?
   - What adaptations might be required for those children requiring differentiation that reflects inclusivity and neurodiversity?

The units are designed to complement your curriculum demands, with minimum distraction and time implications. Observations may provide unanticipated information. Some children appear to be functioning well academically, but their cognitive-motor performance can prompt concern about more subtle or unanticipated learning challenges. Recent studies suggest that motor and cognitive development are more closely related than previously assumed, and motor and cognitive functions appear to be even more strongly connected in children with motor and/or cognitive impairment (Schott & Klotzbier, 2018). Findings by Schott and Klotzbier (2018) indicate interesting links between physical education lessons and cognitively challenging sessions.

CROSSING MIDLINE

Crossing midline can be defined as the ability to move hand, foot, and eye(s) across the center of the body, so that, for example, a child is able to write across the body from left to right.

Children with midline crossing and laterality problems may have difficulties with a number of activities, including aspects of handwriting such as these:

- Writing across the body from left to right
- Difficulties drawing or copying shapes such as diagonals

Additionally, if their postural stability and balance skills are insecure, the early development of handwriting skills is likely to be compromised.

According to Griffin (2019), hand dominance is developed between 2 and a half and 6 years of age, although opinions differ on this. She maintains that a child may need further assessment from an occupational therapist if they are not showing some signs of hand preference by the age of 5, and if they are not crossing the midline with their hands.

Action Point

Identify a child in your setting who may be causing some concern in relation to hand dominance and laterality (who does not have a neurological condition or significant developmental delays). Griffin suggests observing them over a period of a week, noting which hand they use for a range of common tasks and activities such as reaching, grasping, turning, manipulating, climbing and pushing heavy objects.

Preparing a checklist in advance (see Figure 7.1.) helps to standardize repeated observations. Make a list of up to 10 situations to observe, with an additional 3–5 rows that can be used to make additional notes or to record more situations.

Figure 7.1. Sample Form

Child's name: Class: Dates of observations:	Observer:			
Situation	Rt	Left	Both	Notes
Observations and actions:				

The QR code below will bring you to a printable PDF version of Figure 7.1. This material may also be accessed under the "Downloads" tab at https://www.tcpress.com/move-more-learn-more-9780807784051.

HANDWRITING RESEARCH

Handwriting is a complex skill that develops dependent on gross and fine motor skills, as well as many other factors such as visual perceptual skills. Poor handwriting may impede academic progress and achievement, although assistive technology has been beneficial in providing increasingly sophisticated alternatives. Students who struggle to develop an appropriate, fluid, legible handwriting style, or whose handwriting is slow and laborious, are at risk of later underachievement and of being underestimated in terms of what they are capable of (Kohli et al., 2018).

Early handwriting experiences can shape the development of a lifelong skill that has a multitude of benefits (note-taking, creativity, personal communications, and many more). For those interested in exploring this topic in greater depth, there are eminent research articles that cite the benefits of actual handwriting as opposed to the use of assistive technology (Hu & Young, 2024).

At the same time, early years practitioners and teachers often face pressures to meet curricular targets with insufficient training in understanding the developmental sequences that underpin early readiness for handwriting confidence and competence.

Please note that the following information is not intended as a substitute for professional clinical guidance. It is offered as information based on my professional experience as an educator, not a clinician.

The columns in Table 7.2. should be read vertically.

SAMPLE ACTIVITIES

The following activities can contribute to the development of a movement culture in the school setting that sees adults participating, observing, and nurturing the building blocks of movement that underpin not only motor competence but also social interaction and communication skills, an increase in self-confidence, motivation, and retention of information (Musgrave et al., 2024).

Table 7.2. Handwriting: Potential Key Issues for Consideration

Motor	Cognitive	Social & Emotional
Immature posture, balance, and coordination	Distractible	Frustration at slowness
Overflow movements (see retained reflexes)	Switches off during literacy activities that involve letter formation and writing	Loss of self-esteem and possible aggression
Pencil grip issues	Mismatch to perceived early ability	Emotional about any writing requirements
Letter formation	Underachieving	School refusal
Speed of writing	Verbal strengths don't match written output	Avoidance of writing activities
Child writing with head resting on hands	Child staring out the window	Young child looking frustrated

These activities support physical development and contribute to the recommended amount of time that children should be engaged in physical activity. At the same time, they provide valuable insights to inform the planning and differentiation required for effective implementation of the curriculum. Through my training courses, teachers, practitioners, other professionals, and the public can acquire the knowledge and skills to apply, adapt, and extend activities that build the foundation for later competencies in the areas of

- Gross and fine motor skills
- Balance and timed activities
- Visuospatial abilities
- Visual-motor integration
- Visual-perceptual skills

Please note that these are identified as sample activities rather than stages, as it is essential that the teacher's professional expertise remains in charge of the process, dependent on their observations and knowledge of the individual.

The units can also contribute very effectively to the development of a wide range of vocabulary and creative exercises relating to

- Body parts (arms, legs, shoulders)
- Movement terms (fast, slow, reach, stretch)
- Analogies (like a tiger, snail, lizard)

They also underpin learning across the curriculum when the approach is embedded as foundational to the school's approach to learning.

Remember, what works for one teacher or class will not necessarily work for another.

Consider flexibility in location and the timing of activities (the beginning of the day, early afternoon, etc.). Experiment with short sessions at different speeds, dependent on whether the intention is to stimulate or calm the participants.

It is not necessary to carry out all the activities sequentially, and they can be spaced throughout the day. Floor-based activities can be integrated into P.E. lessons.

NOTE: The person leading the activities should always be an active participant if appropriate. Please adhere to all relevant health and safety guidelines and risk assessment protocols and seek advice from the special needs coordinator about any relevant accommodations, such as difficulties with balance and coordination.

General Floor-Based Activities

- Parachute activities
- Rolling in a straight line, rolling from one marker to another, rolling with a partner
- Rolling over different surfaces
- Commando crawling
- Crawling at different speeds and in different ways
- Working with a partner and in a small group

Sample Seated Activities

- Finger-tapping and clapping sequences with eyes open and closed
- Both hands rotate from palm up to palm down, with eyes open/closed
- Hands alternate: one palm faces up and one faces down
- Crossing midline activities with bean bags
- Table press-ups/push-ups

Sample Standing Activities

- Balancing
- Breathing activities
- Simple yoga poses
- Copying an adult's pose
- Bouncing rhythmically on heels
- Adding on tapping or clapping rhythms

Sample Moving Activities

- Moving at different speeds
- Marching activities
- Marching and pausing
- Tiptoe walking
- Legs crossing over the midline walking

The QR code below will bring you to a printable version of all activities for Chapter 7. This also leads to Table 7.3, which shares a few examples of Early Movements, Young Minds™ activities, and Table 7.4, which shares a sample unit from Early Movements, Young Minds™. This material may also be accessed under the "Downloads" tab at https://www.tcpress.com/move-more-learn-more-9780807784051.

EARLY MOVEMENTS, YOUNG MINDS™

Table 7.3 shares a few examples of Early Movements, Young Minds™ activities. Table 7.4. shares a sample unit from Early Movements, Young Minds™.

CONCLUSION

The intention of this chapter was to draw on some international elements of research and practice and to make links between motor skills and cognition, highlighting the many benefits of integrating a cognitive-motor approach into daily practice. This approach has the benefits of being inclusive and supports a multisensory approach to over-learning, automaticity, and the development of executive functions. By linking curricular targets and concepts to motor activities, the individuals benefit from the potential advantages of improvements in coordination, balance, active cognitive input, and increased levels of concentration and engagement.

When teachers and practitioners are empowered, through training, to draw on their creativity and professionalism to devise, adapt, and develop activities that support skillful motor performance, they are aiding the development of core executive functions such as working memory and cognitive flexibility, as well as higher-level executive functions such as planning, reasoning, and problem-solving (Pesce et al., 2018).

Table 7.3. Examples of Early Movements, Young Minds™ Activities

Orientation	Activity Overview	Notes/Materials Needed
Floor-based	Instructions: The adult can demonstrate this movement or show a video clip of it in action. Verbal instructions should be kept to a minimum. It is not a taught movement. Action: Commando crawl for a short distance, using arms and legs, depending on the individual child's ability. Differentiate the activity, if necessary, by considering different surfaces to make the activity more accessible.	Ensure the floor is smooth and clean. Gym mats may be appropriate. Be aware of potential sensory issues.
Tips	Ensure the surface is easy to glide along. Avoid the temptation to teach the movement. Model it.	
Seated	Large circular movements in the air with alternating arms, eyes following the hand. Include clockwise and counterclockwise movements.	
Tips	Consider holding a small soft toy, pinching and releasing fingers closed fists/open palms in rhythmic pattern.	Soft toys
Standing	Stand with arms by the side of the body. Breathe in and bring arms overhead, counting to 4. Hold arms overhead, count to 4, lower arms, count to 6. Shake out 4 times.	Define the area by standing behind the table, or on a carpet square. The longer outbreathe is a calming movement.
Tips	Consider using calm music (e.g., forest or sea sounds) with no lyrics to support the activity. Avoid verbal instruction. Model the activity and always participate with the group.	
Moving	Marching on the spot 8 times, with arms swinging.	
Tips	Experiment with rhythm and patterns such as 1, 2, 3, clap. Model good posture.	

This is an exciting area of research that recognizes the centrality of movement, motor skills, and cognitive development in young children, in addition to its role as a potential for highlighting the early identification and support for learning differences such as dyslexia. Research studies are improving the understanding of the processes that underpin learning, although it is prudent to exercise some caution in adopting approaches without sufficient understanding of the basic concepts. This chapter proposes an active approach to

Table 7.4. Sample Unit: Early Movements, Young Minds™

Orientation	Activity	Notes
Floor-based	Commando crawling for a short distance, depending on the individual child's ability. Look for improvements in fluidity and involvement of upper and lower limbs. Some children will find this quite challenging. Slow, deliberate crawling is an alternative.	Ensure the floor is smooth and clean. Gym mats may be appropriate. The surface needs to facilitate smooth movement.
Seated	Large movements across the midline, at eye level, moving left to right: Curved path Straight line Experiment	Add on singing rhymes. Recite the days of the week. Add on a stick or pencil and "conduct" the orchestra.
Standing	Stand with arms at shoulder level, facing forward, feet close together. Arms cross, with palms facing the floor. Work toward alternating arms on top. Shrug shoulders several times to release tension. Aim for slow, fluid movement. This can also be integrated into P.E. sessions or be made into a playground activity.	Define the area by standing behind the table, or on a carpet square if indoors. Be alert to those individuals whose arms droop down quickly and adjust the move to a lower level if necessary.
Moving	Heel/toe walking forward along a short line on the ground. Aim for good balance and control, with an adult modeling the activity.	Look for good posture. Provide a focal point for children to look at to avoid looking at their feet. Observe arm movements and be alert to potential loss of balance. Recommended as a small-group activity with a supervising adult.

learning, and the references cited provide a significant body of evidence that supports children having access to progressive, consistent, well-planned activities, by practitioners who are skilled and confident, and alert to the needs of those children at risk of learning differences or delays.

REFERENCES

Cheung, W. C., Meadan, H., & Shen, S. (2020). Motor, cognitive, and socioemotional skills among children with disabilities over time. *The Journal of Special Education*, 55(2), 79–89.

Christmas, J., & Van de Weyer, R. (2020). *Hands on dyspraxia: Developmental coordination disorder* (2nd ed.). Routledge.

Chung, P. J., Patel, D. R., & Nizami, I. (2020). Disorder of written expression and dysgraphia: Definition, diagnosis, and management. *Translational Pediatrics, 9*(Suppl 1), S46–S54.

Frostig, M. (1970). *Movement education: Theory and practice*. Follett Educational Corp.

Griffin, K. (2019). *Supporting pencil grasp development*. Book Printing UK.

Haywood, K., & Getchell, N. (2014). *Life span motor development*. Human Kinetics.

Hu, C., & Young, L. (2024). *Why writing by hand is better for memory and learning*. Scientific American.

Kohli, A., Sharma, S., & Padhy, S. K. (2018). Specific learning disabilities: Issues that remain unanswered. *Indian Journal of Psychological Medicine, 40*(5), 399–405.

Leisman, G., Moustafa, A. A., & Shafir, T. (2016). Thinking, walking, talking: Integratory motor and cognitive brain function. *Frontiers in Public Health, 4*, 94.

Meeusen, R., Schaefer, S., Tomporowski, P., & Bailey, R. (2018). *Physical activity and educational attainment*. Routledge.

Musgrave, J., Dorrian, J., Josephidou, J., Langdown, B., & Rodriguez, L. (2024). *Promoting physical development and activity in early childhood*. Routledge.

Pesce, C., Faigenbaum, A., Goudas, M., &Tomporowski, P. (2018). Coupling our plough of thoughtful moving to the star of children's right to play. In R. Meeusen, S. Schaefer, P. Tomporowski, & R. Bailey (Eds.), *Physical activity and educational achievement* (pp. 1–359). Routledge.

Pickup, I., & Price, L. (2015). *Teaching physical education in the primary school*. Bloomsbury.

Portwood, M. (2003). *Dyslexia and physical education*. David Fulton.

Ramos-Campo, D. J., & Clemente-Suárez, V. J. (2024). The correlation between motor skill proficiency and academic performance in high school students. *Behavioral Sciences (Basel, Switzerland), 14*(7), 592.

Reid, G. (2020). *Dyslexia and inclusion*. Routledge.

Schott, N., & Klotzbier, T. (2018). The motor-cognitive connection: Indicator of future developmental success in children and adolescents. In R. Meeusen, S. Schaefer, P. Tomporowski, & R. P. Bailey (Eds.), *Physical activity and educational attainment* (pp. 111–129). Routledge.

Soan, S., & Hutton, E. (2021). *Universal approaches to supporting children's physical and cognitive development in the early years*. Speechmark.

Tomporowski, P., & Pendleton, D. (2017). Varieties of learning and developmental theories of memory. In P. Tomporowski, D. M. Pendleton, & B. A. McCullick (Eds.), *Physical Activity and Educational Achievement* (1st ed., pp. 31-43). Routledge.

Zeng, N., Ayyub, M., Sun, H., Wen, X., Xiang, P., & Gao, Z. (2017). *Effects of physical activity on motor skills and cognitive development in early childhood: A systematic review*. BioMed Research International, 2760716.

# CHAPTER 8

Activity Gym and Cross-Body Activities for Children

Piero Crispiani and Eleonora Palmieri, Italy

The Crispiani Method has been developed by Professor Piero Crispiani and Dr. Eleonora Palmieri in Italy (University of Macerata) and is based on the Praxis-Motor Theory (PMT) (Crispiani, 2016). The cognitive-motor method improves reading and processing fluency in children with dyslexia, dyspraxia, dysgraphia, and dyscalculia through a dynamic combination of word reading and rapid coordinated movement. The program has also been used to support students with autism spectrum disorders. The Crispiani Method is used globally in schools and clinics, and by families at home.

Dr. Palmieri has established her own independent school to support neurodiverse students. The school is an innovative multidisciplinary setting incorporating outdoor activities, dance, movement, and academic skill development. Drawing on her previous role as a clinical director focused on interventions such as Champion Pressing, the school provides special intensive cognitive-motor and academic training practices.

Professor Crispiani, Dr. Palmieri, and their team have also been instrumental in raising the profile of the links between cognitive and motor development and drawing on historical European pedagogical theory and practice.

NEUROACTIVATION

Neuroactivation refers to the process by which neurons become active and generate electrical impulses within the nervous system. Relevant to the Crispiani Method and Activity Gym, neuroactivation involves actively stimulating neuronal pathway growth in the brain through systematic and intensive cognitive-motor movement exercises. These exercises are developmentally progressive and adaptable based on the skill sets presented by each individual. In the Crispiani Method, neuroactivation aims to functionally reorganize the brain to support an individual's ability to achieve academic, social, and behavioral goals that stem from enhanced neurological processes.

In the Crispiani Method, there are several programs: the Individual Habilitation Treatment Program (TAI), Cognitive Motor Training (CMT), and Activity Gym, which together build fundamental reactive processes that develop the brain and promote prosocial behavior (Crispiani, 2019). Cognition (organizational cognitive processes) and intensive motor skills represent the path to strengthening general functionality by exercising human actions in different contexts. Their synergistic interaction generates cognitive and motor actions that prompt and coordinate the activation of intentional and targeted neuromotor processes, characterized by at least four capacities: (a) startup readiness (incipit); (b) cognitive-motor coordination; (c) the implementation of self-regulation; and (d) cognitive-motor consistency (fluency). What follows is one of the distinct programs in the Crispiani Method, Activity Gym, a series of rapid movements aimed at creating what Crispiani and Palmieri refer to as a "neurostorm," an intense activation of neurons through rapid coordinative motor movements.

ACTIVITY GYM

Activity Gym is a professional practice consisting of an intensive series of cognitive-motor activation that is useful in developing and enhancing human functions at different ages and in the presence of multiple states of personal efficiency (Crispiani & Palmieri, 2020). Activity Gym is applied across all ages and levels of competency in a variety of clinical diagnoses, including but not limited to ASD, ADHD, dyslexia, dyscalculia, and changes associated with aging. With reference to both developmental disorders and functional changes related to aging, Activity Gym enlivens the brain, activating cognitive-motor connections related to learning and adaptive living skills. The neuromotor patterns in Activity Gym involve cognitive stimulation and coordinative movements requiring thought when moving.

The intensity and speed of movement in Activity Gym differ from other internationally recognized cognitive-motor programs, as they emphasize the swift stimulation of motor cognition through coordinated movements combined with auditory cues that stimulate the brain's motor and language centers.

Activity Gym is flexible in that it can be applied in individual, dyadic, and group settings in educational, clinical, and medically rehabilitative contexts, with a broad range of both developmental and medical conditions.

The Five Physio Praxis Vectors

Activity gym's intensity is based on five important **Physio Praxis Vectors**: Incipit, Fluidity, Cross Patterns, Rotator Patterns, and Reverse Patterns (Crispiani & Palmieri, 2020).

1. **Incipit:** Incipit refers to the speed with which one initiates a verbal or motor action. In neurodevelopmental disorders, there is often a delay in starting a response to visual, auditory, or motor stimuli. When children are slow to initiate motor and language responses, they may also struggle to organize their thoughts, words, and actions. This slowness in starting, executing, and completing actions, particularly in initiation, can be easily recognized across various activities, from motor to cognitive, and may be associated with a lack of lateral dominance and dyspraxia, indicating potential neuronal cortical disorders.
2. **Fluidity:** Fluidity describes the smoothness, efficiency, and ease of movement. It reflects how well a person can perform a motor skill, and it's often associated with practice and the ability to make movements automatically. In the Crispiani Method, fluidity refers to the consistency and smoothness of movement, often in conjunction with changing rhythm, tempo, and timing of movements. The Crispiani Method uses activities such as moving in response to a verbal or physical gesture to increase coherence and coordination between the brain and the body.
3. **Cross Patterns:** Cross patterns are a core feature of Activity Gym. Students practice sequences of cross-motor patterns and sequences involving unilateral and bilateral movements. Unilateral movements refer to any movement that engages one side of the body at a time. This contrasts with bilateral movements, where both sides of the body (or both limbs) are used simultaneously. In Activity Gym, patterns and sequences combine the movement of upper and lower limbs, with cross-touching of the ears, head, shoulders, and arms. This takes place in both stationary and dynamic movement with rapid changes in directionality and space.
4. **Rotator Patterns:** Rotator patterns involve rotating the limbs around the body's vertical and horizontal axes. They can be performed in a stationary position or dynamically in space. Rotator patterns improve motor planning, coordination, and awareness of one's positioning in space.
5. **Reverse Patterns:** Reverse patterns increase both cognitive and motor demands as the students practice cross-motor patterns while walking backward. In the Crispiani Method, reverse patterns are usually done facing the teacher or instructor, facilitating an increase in spatial organization and praxis, the ability to plan and execute skilled, fluid movements.

The five Physio Praxis Vectors (5VFP) stimulate fundamental neuro-coordinative functions, including lateral patterns, hemispheric dominance, orientation in space and time, and response time, specifically, when initiating a movement. What follows are examples of activities in Activity Gym.

Practical Elements of Activity Gym

The first actions in Activity Gym are designed to orient the child to the comfort and flexibility of the setting. Individual needs are foremost as the teacher, instructor, or clinician introduces a movement series involving repetition. The clinician welcomes the child and asks them to repeat a series of actions. The actions include walking in place, backward and forward, or on diagonals with cueing from the clinician. These are rapid movements done in concert with the clinician. The aim is to establish rapport and familiarize the student with motor movement that requires executive function skills; no corrections in timing or tempo are made.

General Instructions. The therapist/teacher/parent stands in front of the individual or group and acts as a model. Because Activity Gym involves intense, rapid activity, the educator must be quick and dynamic, inviting the student to participate by mirroring and responding to the instructor's actions. The therapist uses the dynamics of Succession, Automation, and Fluidity (SAF) throughout Activity Gym.

Duration. Activity Gym is a practice that extends across several phases of progressively demanding cognitive-motor sessions with a maximum duration of 10 minutes per lesson. In school, it can be done in 2–3-minute segments throughout the day. One can also use it at home before a cognitive task, such as homework, activities of daily living, or transitions to and from school, sport, or music class. Activity Gym is flexible and personalized based on the student's needs.

The QR code below will bring you to a printable version of all activities for Chapter 8. This material may also be accessed under the "Downloads" tab at https://www.tcpress.com/move-more-learn-more-9780807784051.

Activity #1: Move Freely

Overview

The first section of Activity Gym consists of arranging the individual or group in front of the therapist and asking the students to walk freely, maintaining a certain distance between each other, encouraging freedom of natural movement.

Benefits

Move Freely engages the students in practicing attention, working memory, previewing, and planning as they respond to the instructor's verbal cues. Students experience the fluidity of the cross-pattern movements while walking. Recognizing their position in space relative to others and the speed at which they are moving is strengthened while increasing cognitive-motor demands, including rotations and reverse walking.

Instructions

In this activity, the therapist asks students to walk, make turns, stomp their feet, and walk back and forth without moving too far away from the other participants, practicing the initial spatial-temporal organization in the dyad or group. The sequences of the basic motor patterns are repeated with a progressive increase in speed and rhythm.

Example Language:

Walk With Me
"Walk with me."
"Now, backward, walk with me."
"Now walk and stop, walk again and stop."
"Perfecto."

Turn With Me
"Now walk, come on, follow me."
"Now stop on the spot."
"Walk with me."
"Turn to your right."
"Now, turn to your left."

Stomp Your Feet
"Now walk, come on, follow me."
"Now stop on the spot."
"Stomp your right foot."
"Walk with me."
"Stomp your left foot."
"Perfecto."

Tip: Move Freely orients students to a foundation element of Activity Gym, following and mirroring the instructor. If a student makes a mistake, they are not corrected; they are encouraged to try again and keep going.

Activity #2: Rapid Responding

Overview

In Rapid Responding, the group is in front of the clinician and continues to walk on the spot (in place) without stopping. The instructor is the model and gives verbal input and gestural output. Each verbal input (word) is associated with a gestural output (gesture). The verbal stimuli have no meaning other than associating a word (any word) with a specific motor gesture. First, the student or group, walking on the spot, observes the gesture without reproducing it and says the corresponding word fluently. Next, the student(s) repeat the word and the gesture. The therapist alternates the gestural output, rhythm, and speed.

Benefits

In this activity, the sequences are performed by combining the increase in repetitions with a progressive increase in speed. The gestures are alternated, and the speed of the gesture is increased to make the verbal output more fluid. Rapid Responding improves the onset of a movement to a stimulus. In Italian, this is called the *incipit*. Incipit refers to a readiness to act, in Italian terms, a preparedness, that results in increased speed of initiating an action.

Rapid Responding increases verbal planning, initiation, and responding. Rapid Responding also provides opportunities for the student(s) to practice focused attention, sustained attention, response inhibition, processing speed, motor planning, motor initiation, motor fluency, and coordination.

Instructions

Ask the students to stand up and look at the instructor. Tell them, "We are going to play a word game. We will move quickly, so listen carefully."

Part I:

"Come on, follow me."
"Walk on the spot." (In place.)
"Now repeat after me, one word at a time."
"Ready?"
"Go."
"Lunch."
"Job."
"Gong."
"Job."
"Gong."

"Lunch."
"Very nice."

Part II:

"Now, when I say 'Lunch,' you reach your arm forward and point your finger."
"When I say 'Job,' you reach your arm out to your right side and point your finger."
"When I say 'Gong,' you reach your arm up above your body and point your finger."
"With each gesture you say the matching word."
"We are playing this game quickly. I will randomly change the words."

Tip: In Activity Gym, the primary goal is to increase verbal and motor initiation (incipit). If a student misses a cue or responds incorrectly, the instructor does not stop to correct the student. Over time, the student improves in their response time and accuracy.

Activity #3: I Clap, You Move Your Feet

Overview

The I Clap, You Move Your Feet activity aims to improve motor fluency in the student.

Benefits

Gross motor coordination, response inhibition, attention, planning, and motor fluency
The student(s) move on from the previous activity by watching the instructor walk in place, modeling various clapping patterns. Integrating both slow and fast rhythms, the student(s) clap their hands and tap their feet, following along in time with the instructor. The sequences of patterns increase cognitive and motor demands, progressively speeding up execution and changing the rhythm.

Instructions

"Now, we are going to clap our hands and tap our feet. Follow me and repeat the rhythm I make."
"I am going to change the rhythms. Sometimes we will move slowly, other times we will move quickly, do as I do."
"Do your best and have fun."

Tip: The aim of this activity is fluency. If students fall off the beat or make a mistake, the clinician does not stop. The student(s) is encouraged to continue and do their best.

Activity #4: Cross Patterns

Overview

In Cross Patterns, the instructor introduces more advanced movements that require action across the vertical, horizontal, and medial planes of movement. The instructor guides the student(s) in the execution of sequences of cross motor patterns in front of themselves and across the midline of the body.

Benefits

Cross patterns are known in science to stimulate both sides of the brain, leading to better coherence and coordination. Cross patterns require previewing, planning, focused attention, sustained attention, response inhibition, rhythm, tempo, timing, and motor coordination.

Instructions

In Cross Patterns, there is an increase in cognitive and motor demands. The developmentally progressive sequences are performed by combining the increase in repetitions (from 1 to 4) with a progressive increase in speed in the four phases of each exercise. On a constant basic motor platform (walking on the spot, forward and backward, or in rotation around the body's vertical axis, etc.), the sequences are performed in progressive repetition from one to four times. All the patterns are repeated and may vary based on the instructor's observations. Platforms can vary from a flat surface to a slanted surface and even a moving surface like a balance board or trampoline.

CHART OF ACTIONS

Part I

Phase 1:

Arms Up

"Right arm up to the left." (Thrust the arm up and down, four times in tempo and rhythm.)
"Left arm up to the right." (Thrust the arm up and down, four times in tempo and rhythm.)

Leg Out

"Right leg to the left." (Tap the right leg in front of the left leg, 1–4 times.)
"Left leg to the right." (Tap the left leg in front of the right leg, 1–4 times.)

Phase 2: Punch on a Diagonal

"Right arm above the head from right to left." (Reach right arm up and across, in a punching motion, across the diagonal 1–4 times.)
"Left arm above the head from left to right." (Reach left arm up and across, in a punching motion, across the diagonal 1–4 times.)

Opposites

"Right arm above the head to the left." (Right arm above the head from left to right; reach right arm up and across, in a punching motion, across the diagonal 1–4 times.)
"Left arm above the head to the right." (Left arm above the head from right to left; reach left arm up and across, in a punching motion, across the diagonal 1–4 times.)

Phase 3: Arm and Leg Reach

"Right arm and right leg reach out to the left." (Lift your right arm and your right leg, punch at midline across the body 1–4 times.)
"Left arm and leg reach out to the right." (Lift your left arm and your left leg, punch at midline across the body 1–4 times.)

Opposites

"Right arm to the left and left leg to the right." (Lift your right arm and your left leg, punch at midline across the body 1–4 times.)
"Left arm to the right and right leg to the left." (Lift your left arm and your right leg, punch at midline across the body 1–4 times.)

Part II

Phase 4: Add Hand Claps

Add hand claps, right (1, 2, 3, or 4 times to the right side of the body)
Add hand claps, left (1, 2, 3, or 4 times to the right side of the body)
Add hand claps alternating right and left side of the body (1, 2, 3, or 4 times, alternating sides)

> Cross patterns in Activity Gym can get quite complex. The key is for the teacher, instructor, or clinician to vary the number of repetitions and speed of movements depending on the cognitive-motor competency of the student(s).

Tips: The instructor supports, models, and guides the student(s) in the cross-motor patterns, encouraging, smiling, and making fun and motivating what could otherwise be pretty tricky.

Activity #5: Rotator Patterns

Overview

Rotator patterns involve complex multiplane movements in Activity Gym. Similar to cross patterns, sequences including rotator patterns vary in speed and difficulty based on the observations of the instructor.

Benefits

Rotator patterns demand focused attention, sustained focus, and cognitive shifts. They also involve self-regulation, response inhibition, and cognitive flexibility. This series of activities enhances rhythm perception, spatial-temporal orientation, fluidity, laterality, visual-spatial skills, motor and mental rotations, and dynamic coordination. Rotator patterns are cross hemispheric (see Ocklenburg & Guo, 2024).

In Rotator Patterns, the developmentally progressive sequences are performed by combining an increase in repetitions (from 1 to 4) with a progressive increase in speed across the four phases of each exercise. On a consistent motor platform (walking on the spot, forward and backward, or rotating around the body's vertical axis, etc.), the sequences are executed in progressive repetition from one to four times. All the patterns are repeated and may vary based on the instructor's observations. The patterns are across the midline and circular; thus, they are called rotator patterns. Platforms can range from a flat surface to a slanted surface and even include a moving surface like a balance board or trampoline.

Instructions

"We are going to do a series of patterns that will increase in speed with changes in rhythm. This can be tricky, so pay close attention."

CHART OF ACTIONS

Phase 1: Drawing Circles in the Air

"Lift your right arm up in front of you and draw a circle in the air, above your head, with your finger crossing the midline of your body."
"Draw one small circle, then one large circle."

"Now, draw two small circles, one after the other; now draw two big circles, one after the other."

"Now, alternate, draw one small circle, then one big circle, four times in a row. Keep your pace constant and your circles the same size."

Phase 2: Make Circles by Crossing Your Feet

Cross-Step Practice

"Lift your right foot up in front of you and cross it over your left foot; return to a neutral, two-foot position."

"Left your left foot up in front of you and cross it over your right foot; return to a neutral, two-foot position."

Phase 3: Making Circles

"Lift your right foot up in front of you and cross-step over your left foot."
"Continuing crossing while you make a circle on the ground."
"Lift your left foot up in front of you and cross step over your right foot."
"Continuing crossing while you make a circle on the ground."

Phase 4: Make Two Circles

"Lift your right foot up in front of you and cross step over your left foot."
"Continuing crossing while you make two circles on the ground."
"Lift your left foot up in front of you and cross step over your right foot."
"Continuing crossing while you make two circles on the ground."

Phase 5: Make Alternating Circles—Small

"Now, focus on staying balanced, in the center of your body."
"Left your right foot and make a small circle."
"Lift your left foot and make a small circle."
"Lift your right foot and make two small circles."
"Lift your left foot and make two small circles."

Phase 6: Make Alternating Circles—Big

"Again, focus on staying balanced, in the center of your body."
"Left your right foot and make a large circle."
"Lift your left foot and make a large circle."
"Lift your right foot and make two large circles."
"Lift your left foot and make two large circles."

Phase 7: Rapid Alternating Circles—Both Sides of the Body

"Now, we will maintain our balance while we increase the speed of our circles and alternate legs quickly."

"Left your right foot and make a small circle."
"Lift your left foot and make a small circle."
"Lift your right foot and make two small circles."
"Lift your left foot and make two small circles."
"Left your right foot and make a large circle."
"Lift your left foot and make a large circle."
"Lift your right foot and make two large circles."
"Lift your left foot and make two large circles."
"Now, make small circles quickly, right foot, left foot, right foot, left foot, four times in a row."
"Do you think we can do three circles? Wow! Now that's tricky."

Phase 8: Rapid Alternating Circles—Both Sides of the Body in Threes

"Make three small circles with your right foot."
"Make three small circles with your left foot."
"Make three large circles with your right foot."
"Make three large circles with your left foot."
"Way to go! Great work!"

Tips: Rotator patterns demand a higher level of auditory, visual, cognitive, and motor processing. The student is stepping with one foot over the other foot in a criss-cross step. Take your time modeling and practicing with students. Create a joyful atmosphere where your students can grow and thrive.

Activity #6: Reverse Patterns

Overview

Reverse Patterns include walking forward and backward with quick turns and rotations. The basic patterns of the reverse pattern are walking and running backward, always crossing their arms. The sequences of patterns are performed by combining the backward walking and addition of cognitive-verbal elements such as naming the days of the week, naming objects found in different rooms of a home, or skip counting.

Benefits

Reverse Patterns utilize procedural memory, spatial-temporal organization, fluidity, and a variety of executive function skills not limited to previewing, planning, self-regulation, response inhibition, attention, and cognitive flexibility.

Instructions

"Now we will move, backward and forward, responding to my gestures and words. The basic movement we will build upon is walking backward, crossing your arms, low behind your hips."

"As we walk backward, I will ask you questions or tell you to recite things like the days of the week."

"Try to make your movements smooth and at the established tempo."

The instructor asks the students to walk backward, crossing their arms behind them, like a scissor arm cross, with long, strong arms. Once they have reached a certain distance, the group and the therapist/teacher, without stopping, rotate 180 degrees to begin the reverse pattern.

Verbal cues include but are not limited to:

"While you walk, name animals you find in the sea."

"Say one animal as you right foot touches the ground."

"If you are thinking and choosing an animal, it's fine to skip a beat; just keep walking."

"Only name animals when your right foot touches the ground."

"Now we will switch feet."

"As you walk backward, when your left foot strikes the ground, name something you would find in a living room."

"Very good!"

"This is tricky, but you are doing a great job!"

Walking backward continues, rotating 180 degrees to begin the next pass, until the instructor says "Stop."

The variety of verbal cues in Reverse Patterns is broad and flexible.

Tips: Reverse Patterns are the most advanced actions in Activity Gym. Students love this activity. Consider having cards with different categories on them and let your students choose a card to determine the cognitive category: Days of the week; Name the states in the United States; Name the regions in Italy; Name animals with four legs; Name things you find in a living room.

FUNCTIONAL RESULTS AND EXPECTED OUTCOMES

The effectiveness of Activity Gym is its dynamic and intensive nature. The progressive increase in cognitive-motor demands in concert with the speed of the movements excites the neurons in the brain, creating what the authors call a "neurostorm" (Crispiani & Palmieri, 2020). As you have read in other chapters, there is research evidence that the brain in neurodevelopmentally involved children can have diminished communication and coherence between neuronal hubs in the brain. Activity Gym enlivens the brain, improving neural connections through cognitive-motor movement.

Intensity in cognitive-motor practices is essential for both general behavior as well as specific conditions, such as sports, dance, group play, environmental stress, emotional changes, and the demand for quick actions. This intensity also applies to multitasking, which can involve dual tasks and may extend to overlapping four or five action sequences.

Intensive performance is achieved through the adoption or pursuit of various training traits: acceleration of movement initiation (incipit); prompt self-regulation (self-correction, response inhibition); executive fluidity (consistency, absence of pauses); sequencing, prediction; and dynamic practice (Crispiani, 2016).

The activities that comprise Cognitive Motor Training enable global neuroactivation across all ages and in relation to various developmental and age-related conditions. Their translation into behaviors and lifestyle regimens, often characterized by high stress, induces processes of biopsychic adaptation. This is particularly evident given the rapid pace of life to which new generations are exposed, revealing both their unpreparedness and the potential for necessary epigenetic adaptation processes.

Activity Gym tends to generate neurophysiological automaticity that is fluid and automatic in terms of tempo, time, speed, and space. The simultaneous activation of coordinated and consistent cognitive and motor functions is the strength behind reorganizing interhemispheric communication, coherence between brain hemispheres, fluidity, automaticity, and speed, leading to more effective cognition. Working in reciprocity (both sides of the body) and parallelism (one side of the body) with cognitive cues to develop smooth, automated, coordinative movement leads to more effective cognition and behavior. The increased fluidity (readiness incipit—to initiate action, the right speed, agile self-correction, perseverance, etc.), together with the global approach to real learning (words, sentences, gestures, numbers, shapes, etc.), allows the integration cognition and movement to increase response time, processing speed, and cognition. The Crispiani Method approach in its entirety guides the actions of all people with neurounique conditions toward more adaptive functionality.

The most important qualitative indicator is cognitive-motor fluidity, not speed. Speed is the factor that creates the neurostorm, leading to reorganization of the brain.

Activity Gym enhances the fluidity of executive functions by improving self-regulation, response inhibition, and self-control, enabling a shift in dynamics from slow and precipitous to smooth, consistent, and automatic.

CONCLUSION

This chapter introduced some of the basic concepts that underpin the use of cognitive-motor sequences in the Crispiani Method to support individuals with a range of challenges. It outlined a conceptual framework with professional practices that have been developed and refined over many years, drawing on the skills and knowledge of expert practitioners (educators, therapists, teachers, pedagogues, psychologists) and supporting research and literature. Its authors are recognized as international experts in this field and have developed ongoing support and professional development programs that have been implemented in many settings.

The Crispiani programs have proven very successful in Europe and have been implemented in a variety of settings where skills can be developed, beginning with basal motricity, which activates, maintains, and regulates central neurological activity, the organization of neural circuits, and self-regulation. It is an intensive method that combines modulated cognitive-motor sequences with language, perception, and thought, requiring dedication and stamina from the practitioner.

In Europe, our practices are defined as Ecological-Dynamic, encouraging neuromotor and neurocognitive activity, with particular reference to the fluidity and efficiency of interhemispheric exchange, while strengthening executive dysfunction. Activity Gym tends to accelerate improvements in neuroplasticity, which are reflected in learning, language, academic achievement, social skill competency, and motor coordination. The intensity, appropriate pressure, and consistency of the work are the origins of enhancing neurological patterns in the brain. Direct observations regarding the benefits of Activity Gym and the Ecological-Dynamic practices of the Crispiani Method enhance executive function skills, resulting in better academic readiness and improvements in graphomotor skills, reading, and comprehension.

REFERENCES

Crispiani, P. (2016). *Il Metodo Crispiani. Clinica della dislessia e disprassia*. Istituto Itard, Ancona (Italy).

Crispiani, P. (2019). *Ippocrate pedagogico. Manuale professionale di pedagogia speciale, della abilitazione e riabilitazione*. Istituto Itard, Ancona (Italy).

Crispiani, P., & Palmieri, E., (2020). *Champion pressing*. Special intensive practices of cognitive motor training. Istituto Itard, Ancona (Italy).

Ocklenburg, S., & Guo, Z. V. (2024). Cross-hemispheric communication: Insights on lateralized brain functions. *Neuron, 112*(8), 1222–1234.

CHAPTER 9

The Kinesthetic Classroom
Teaching and Learning Through Movement

Mike Kuczala, United States

During the early 2000s, I was regularly teaching graduate courses on brain-compatible methods. At the same time, I was becoming aware of some pioneers who were writing, creating, and speaking regarding the use of movement in the teaching and learning process. Included in this list would be Eric Jensen, author of one of my personal favorite books, *Learning With the Body in Mind* (Jensen, 2000). Others such as Jean Moize (formerly Jean Blaydes Madigan and creator of Action Based Learning along with Cindy Hess), Carla Hannaford (author of *Smart Moves*), and Paul and Gail Dennison (creators of Brain Gym) became my north stars as I had no idea how this would change the course of my life and career.

I began using their techniques in my courses, not so much as part of the curriculum but for movement breaks during the course. Adults need to move, too, especially in an intensive time format within an 8 a.m. to 5 p.m. day. I had no idea of the reaction I would receive. The participants (classroom teachers) loved all the movement! They began using the activities with their own students, and the joyful reports when they returned to my class were empowering:

- "My students loved these activities!"
- "Classroom management was much improved!"
- "My class became more attentive and efficient!"

I was astonished! Reports of this success started showing up in participants' final class projects, and it was not even part of the curriculum. The tip of the iceberg was bringing in Jean Moize to speak to our graduate instructors on the importance of movement in learning. My life would never be the same.

I connected with one of our dynamic graduate instructors, Traci Lengel, who was using some of the same techniques in her courses. After creating a health and wellness graduate course together, we embarked on what was not only a new course, but a mission. "The Kinesthetic Classroom: Teaching and

Learning Through Movement" became, and still is, one of the most popular graduate courses in the 35-year history of Regional Training Center. I assume that it remains unique in graduate course offerings anywhere. The book (Lengel & Kuczala, 2010) would come out a few short years later and became a Corwin bestseller.

It is not lost on me how difficult a decision it was for Corwin to publish this book. Using movement in classrooms was a relatively new concept, but our editor believed in it and pushed on our behalf. It was a good decision for us all!

In a fairly short period of time, the education ecosystem has gone from endorsing very little movement to understanding its importance, with some schools and districts giving full-throated approval. Though we have come a long way, kids still sit far too long in classrooms globally.

A BRIEF OVERVIEW OF THE RESEARCH THAT INFLUENCED THE KINESTHETIC CLASSROOM

In the early 2000s, research regarding movement in the teaching and learning process was not very prevalent. By now, movement has become a well-established and researched classroom support, but it did not happen overnight. One of the major influences during our early interest in this topic was the teacher action research that was coming out of the MEd program at Gratz College in Melrose Park, Pennsylvania. In 2009, 17 of the 250 pieces of action research that came from the graduating class were focused on the impact of movement on the teaching and learning process, which was strongly positive. Traci and I specifically wrote the following in *The Kinesthetic Classroom: Teaching and Learning Through Movement*:

> Nearly all studies commented on the positive effect of movement on motivation levels and the creation of a more enjoyable classroom environment. More specifically, Burr (2009) found a high correlation between kinesthetic activities and increased spelling assessment scores in the second-grade classroom. Gibbs (2009) identified improved comprehension and authentic use of Spanish in the high school Spanish classroom using bodily-kinesthetic activities. Harding (2009) cited a dramatic increase in all students in the degree of attending through performing gross motor activities before structured academic lessons in the early intervention program. Wood (2009) found that students were able to retain information in greater amounts and more easily if movement activities were used in lessons in the seventh-grade classroom. Adams (2009) found that kinesthetic activities helped raise benchmark scores, create class enthusiasm, and enhance the overall academic experience in the eighth-grade classroom. Hubbard (2009) discovered that using movement-oriented activities with students who had suffered traumatic brain injury created a positive

> impact on students' understanding of number concepts and enabled them to compute simple addition problems more easily. Her research was some of the first of its kind. (Lengel & Kuczala, 2010, pp. 22, 23)

Clearly, taken as a whole, this grouping of teacher action research pieces shows that using movement can increase motivation, create better learning states and classroom environments, raise test scores, make content more easily recalled, and increase levels of student participation and attention.

By the time *Ready, Set, Go! The Kinesthetic Classroom 2.0* was published in 2018, the research supporting movement was much more robust. By 2010, the U.S. Department of Health and Human Services Centers for Disease Control had released their report that solidified physical activity in America's schools and classrooms. *The Association Between School-Based Physical Activity, Including Physical Education, and Academic Performance* was critical to "synthesize the scientific literature that has examined the association between school-based physical activity, including physical education, and academic performance, including indicators of cognitive skills and attitudes, academic behaviors, and academic achievement" (USCDC, 2010).

Other studies influenced our work, including research from the University of Kansas that showed that physically active academic lessons of moderate intensity improved overall performance on a standardized test (Donnelly & Lambourne, 2011), and a study of 153 Finnish children between the ages of 6 and 8 that showed the boys who spent the most time sitting and the least amount of time moving had poorer reading skills than the rest of the group, which was also found in the math skills of the youngest boys (Brage et al., 2016).

Many years later, when I provide professional development to teachers, the piece of research I tend to highlight is that classroom-based physical activity has an estimated effect size of an impressive 1.51 in the United States (Erwin et al., 2012). While physical activity interventions generally have a positive influence on learning in young children, the magnitude of the effect varies depending on the specific type and dose of interventions, the learning domain, and individual characteristics. I also cite, "breaking up lesson time with physical activity offers a promising strategy to improve on-task behavior" (Watson et al., 2017). Taken as a whole, the research is clear in suggesting that classroom-based physical activity is essential in all classrooms.

THE ORIGINAL AND REVISED FRAMEWORKS IN THE KINESTHETIC CLASSROOM

In the original Kinesthetic Classroom graduate course and book, Traci and I created a framework for using movement thoughtfully and purposefully. We wanted to give teachers a systematic way of incorporating movement rather than it being a haphazard attempt that may not be successful. The original framework consisted of six purposes and could be used in any order depending on the needs of the classroom. It included the following:

- **Purpose 1:** Prepare the brain (for learning), which includes both crossing the midline and vestibular system development activities. Currently, when I do professional development, I include executive function support through rhythmic, coordinative, and beat-based physical activity.
- **Purpose 2:** Provide brain breaks, including singular, paired, and small-group activities for refocusing attention, creating blood and oxygen flow around the brain and body, increasing positive classroom emotions and fun, and providing the brain with an important break in dealing with the great amount of content demanded of students.
- **Purpose 3:** Support exercise and fitness. Deciding whether to include this was difficult for us. Ultimately, we decided to include it because physically fit students generally do better academically than their counterparts, and the rates of obesity, pre-diabetes, and diabetes in school-age students continue to be alarming. This includes 1-to-5-minute exercise activities that teachers can use in the classroom to not only demonstrate that a student's fitness life is critical to their academic life, but also to provide activities that stimulate the brain and body much the way brain breaks do.
- **Purpose 4:** Develop class cohesion to not only provide a safe home for the mind but also an emotional environment that stimulates intellectual achievement. These group activities build community, teamwork, communication, and group decision-making, and they can provide increased alertness, blood flow, and fun with other classmates.
- **Purpose 5:** Review content that provides an emotionally safer way to review in small groups and large class environments while also providing a way to incorporate movement while still working on academic content. It is much different than traditional ways of reviewing content. I am certainly not against more traditional methods, but I think these activities should be included more often than they are currently. They are fun and engaging and can provide the teacher with immediate feedback on what might need to be reviewed with more attention and detail. They can also provide more sensory information than is normally used, making the content more memorable.
- **Purpose 6:** Teach content to provide an alternate way to engage information and creative thinking than is normally used. The brain prefers more implicit channels to remember things often through emotions and physicality than the more explicit channels normally

employed in schools. I am not at all against the explicit channels such as lecture, note-taking, listening, discussion, and so forth; it's just that when appropriate, teachers might try using the body to learn concepts when applicable. When doing this, it is possible to engage environmental or episodic memory as well.

In the follow-up book, *Ready, Set, Go! The Kinesthetic Classroom 2.0* (2017), we made several adjustments to the framework. Though the labels for each part of the framework would remain the same, Traci and I shifted the order of the purposes and integrated them with new labels. The new framework would be approached this way (Kuczala & Lengel, 2017):

- **Part 1: Take Your Position—Become a Kinesthetic Educator:** Essentially, this created a mindset of gaining knowledge about using movement and creating a philosophy about how it would best be used in individual classrooms.
- **Part 2: Ready: Develop Strategies and Build Comfort:** As teachers use movement to improve the classroom environment, classroom management, and academic achievement, more comfort becomes a natural outcome. Teachers sometimes fear lack of control or comfort using movement strategies, but as they soon learn them, the benefits far outweigh any drawbacks they may encounter. Two of the purposes are listed in this section: Along with devising a plan, only one of the six purposes is included in this section: Creating Cohesion. We moved this to the beginning of the framework because creating the right environment for movement is crucial to its use. Reduced stress in classrooms has numerous benefits, as it creates class cohesion and encourages students to help one another.
- **Part 3: Set: Energize the Brain and Make Connections:** Included in this part of the updated framework are (1) Preparing the Brain, (2) Brain Breaks, and (3) Fitness Challenges. As this section is self-explanatory, this is where the real movement begins to occur. As mentioned earlier, preparing the brain can support vestibular system development and executive function. Brain breaks (also called brain boosts and brain energizers) provide a sometimes much-needed break from the content as the brain continues to process the recently learned content and provide more blood and oxygen flow around the brain and body to increase alertness. Finally, fitness challenges provide many of the same benefits as brain breaks and begin to show students how critical their fitness life is to their academic life.
- **Part 4: Go: Energize the Brain and Make Connections:** Included here are reviewing content and teaching content. Both areas provide more creativity to teaching and learning as well as giving students

more sensory-oriented and nontraditional ways of engaging with content. Using the body to learn and review can be more favored by the brain than using traditional methods, giving way to more learning opportunities and processing content.

In thinking about classroom movement in the context of this book, specifically about early childhood, not all parts of either framework may be appropriate. Discussion of and/or use of fitness activities at the earliest might be appropriate in middle to late elementary school. Also, much of this book deals with preparing the brain to learn, which would render a discussion in this chapter as repetitive information. In that light, I would like to offer just a few Kinesthetic Classroom activities from only the areas of providing brain breaks, creating class cohesion, reviewing content, and teaching content. While the Kinesthetic Classroom books were written for kindergarten through grade 12, the following activities are appropriate for early childhood.

CLASSROOM APPLICATIONS

The following activities for use in early childhood learning experiences and based on the framework described above were originally written in *The Kinesthetic Classroom: Teaching and Learning Through Movement* and *Ready, Set, Go: The Kinesthetic Classroom 2.0*. They are reprinted in this chapter with permission from the publisher.

Providing Brain Breaks

1. **Show Your Size.** Have students move around the room. The teacher will call out one of three sizes, "small," "medium," or "tall." Students will squat to show small, stand normal for medium, and stretch as high as they can for tall. Students keep moving until another size is called. The educator can shake things up by saying different sizes and allowing participants to react (super small, Empire State Building, caveman, etc.).

2. **Body Writing.** Have students stand up and get into their personal space. Instruct students to do the following:
    - Write their last name in the air with the top of their head.
    - Write their favorite animal in the air with their right elbow.
    - Write their best friend's name in the air with their left elbow.
    - Write what they had for breakfast with their right hip.
    - Finally, if they could have any dessert they wanted, what would it be? Write it with your left hip.

The educator can change these questions to fit their students' interests. If students are too young to spell, they can use various body parts to draw things like a cloud, the sun, a dog or cat, a bike, or whatever you choose.

Creating Class Cohesion

1. Name Pass. Have students gather around one another to make a small, tight circle with their chairs. Students will sit as close as possible while still maintaining a level of comfort. To start the game, one student will hold a ball, say their name loudly, and pass the ball to the right. Everyone will do this at least one or two times, with the goal of teaching everyone each other's name. Once all the names are spoken, the game begins! Now, the person with the ball must say the name of the person to whom they are passing the ball. If the name is not said correctly, the ball should not be passed. If a whistle is sounded, the ball should quickly switch directions. The goal is to get rid of the ball as soon as you get it. Once students feel some success, more balls should be added to the game. All balls will be traveling in the same direction. The goal of the game is not to be stuck with two more balls. The better your students' skill level, the more balls you can enter into the game. If a participant is caught with more than one ball, they are out of the game (if the teacher chooses to play this as an elimination game). If you do not want to eliminate students from the game, you can invite everyone back after so many rounds. When the participants reenter the game, the instructor will direct them to find new seats next to different players (new names to learn). Having students change seats throughout the game is important so that all students can learn many names.

2. Duck and Point. Participants form a circle with the teacher standing in the center. The teacher spins around slowly and eventually stops and points at a student and says, "Duck." That person ducks to the ground. The people on the right and left of the person who ducked have to race to point at one another. The person who points the fastest wins that round and takes the teacher's place in the center of the circle. (The game can also be played where the person who loses is out for one or two rounds and later reenters the game.) Continue by playing as many rounds as time allows. This can also easily be turned into a name game.

Reviewing Content

1. Cardio Review. This activity can be used for reviewing multiple-choice questions. Choose a cardiovascular exercise for answers A, B, C, and D (e.g., walking in place, jogging in place, jumping jacks, knee bends). Present the class with a review question. Allow them to answer by performing the cardiovascular exercise that represents their choice. It will be easy to see which students know the correct answer. Review the correct answer and move on to the next question. This is a safe form of review that doesn't single anyone out but includes everyone, gives you an overview of what you might need to go back over, and is engaging for all.

2. Comparison Review. Place signs in different areas of the room that list different topics or subtopics that your students are learning about. Read a statement that describes one or many of the topics. Students will stand and go to the topic that they believe is being described. If the statement reflects more than one topic, students will go to the center of the room and point to the topics they believe are being described. Review answers and lead appropriate discussions after each statement. Continue until all questions are reviewed.

Teaching Content

1. The Even/Odd Hop (classifying numbers as even or odd—elementary math). Using masking tape, create a line long enough for all students to line up on (front to back, not shoulder to shoulder). After a quick review of even and odd numbers, call out numbers and have students hop to the left of the line for odds and to the right of the line for evens. If the number 0 is called, students should stand on the line because 0 is not considered to be even or odd.

2. Editing on the Move (punctuation and mechanics—elementary language arts). Allow students to work alone or with a partner. Give each student or group a list of sentences that need to be edited. Have each person or group walk while editing one sentence at a time.

To demonstrate the editing, students should do the following:

- Have students raise their hands in the air to demonstrate a capital letter.
- Have students pause for commas and slightly bend their knees.
- Have students add a punctuation mark to the end of each sentence. The period will be demonstrated by going into a tuck position (bend down and hug your knees). The exclamation mark will be shown by jumping up and down on both feet at the same time. To demonstrate the question mark, the students will stand on one leg and make a hook-like action with the opposite arm. Also, apostrophes will be added by lifting the right arm and making a hook-like action.

After all sentences are completed, the participants will compare their edited sentences while discussing any differences they have.

The QR code below will bring you to a printable version of all activities for Chapter 9. This material may also be accessed under the "Downloads" tab at https://www.tcpress.com/move-more-learn-more-9780807784051.

CONCLUSION

Finally, there are two important ideas I will leave with you. First, if students are taught information using their bodies to help learn it, then I strongly suggest you provide them the opportunity to use it or write down what they have learned. We live in a testing culture, and your students will most likely not be tested in the way they learned the information if their bodies were involved. For some, this presents no challenge at all. They can easily change lanes in their brain from what is more of a procedural lane to one that is more semantic. Other students will have a much more difficult time and need the opportunity to practice the conversion.

Second, when using physical activities, there will be times when you must have tools at your disposal to bring students back from the activity so that they can quietly return to learning while being seated. I always preferred breathing activities while doing some short form of progressive muscle relaxation. The activities will not take longer than 60 seconds to use. These activities can be very simple such as breathing in to a 4 count, holding the breath for a 4 count, and exhaling to a 4 count. You might consider having students put their tongue on the roof of their mouth so they remain quiet. You can add simple progressive muscle relaxation by having students squeeze their hands into fists and relaxing their hands when the exhale takes place.

REFERENCES

Adams, J. (2009). *The impact of kinesthetic activities on the eighth-grade benchmark scores* (Unpublished master's thesis). Gratz College, Melrose Park, PA.

Brage, S., Ekelund, U., Haapala, E., Laaka, T., Lintu, N., Poikkeus, A., Vaisto, J., & Westgate, K. (2016). Physical activity and sedentary time in relation to academic achievement in children. *Journal of Science and Medicine in Sport, 20*(6), 583–589.

Burr, S. (2009). *The effect of kinesthetic teaching techniques on student learning* (Unpublished master's thesis). Gratz College, Melrose Park, PA.

Donnelly, J., & Lambourne, K. (2011). Classroom-based physical activity, cognition, and academic achievement. *Preventive Medicine, 52*, S3–S42.

Erwin, H., Fedewa, A., Beighle, A., & Ahn, S. (2012). A quantitative review of physical activity, health, and learning outcomes associated with classroom-based physical activity interventions. *Journal of Applied School Psychology, 28*(1), 14–36.

Gibbs, S. (2009). *Using bodily-kinesthetic activities to foster student success in a high school Spanish classroom* (Unpublished master's thesis). Gratz College, Melrose Park, PA.

Hannaford, C. (1995). *Smart moves: Why learning is not all in the head*. Great Ocean.

Harding, T. (2009). *Using gross motor activities to increase the attention span of early intervention students with developmental delays* (Unpublished master's thesis). Gratz College, Melrose Park, PA.

Hubbard, J. (2009). *Kinesthetics mathematics instruction for secondary students with traumatic brain injury* (Unpublished master's thesis). Gratz College, Melrose Park, PA.

Jensen, E. (2000). *Learning with the body in mind: The scientific basis for energizers, movement, play, games, and physical education*. Corwin.

Lengel, T,. & Kuczala, M. (2010). *The kinesthetic classroom: Teaching and learning through movement*. Corwin.

Lengel, T., & Kuczala, M. (2017). *Ready, set, go: The kinesthetic classroom 2.0*. Corwin.

U.S. Department of Health and Human Services, Centers for Disease Control and Prevention, National Center for Chronic Disease Prevention and Health Promotion, Division of Adolescent and School Health. (2010, July). *The association between school-based physical activity, including physical education, and academic performance*. https://stacks.cdc.gov/view/cdc/25616

Watson, A., Timperio, A., Brown, H., Best, K., & Hesketh, K. (2017). Effect of classroom-based physical activity interventions on academic and physical activity outcomes: A systematic review and meta-analysis. *International Journal of Behavioral Nutrition and Physical Activity, 14*, 114.

Wood, N. (2009). *The impact of movement on the student's ability to retain information* (Unpublished master's thesis). Gratz College.

Part III

WHAT TO DO (SELF-REGULATION AND SOCIAL-RELATIONAL DEVELOPMENT)

CHAPTER 10

Rhythm and Movement for Early Childhood Self-Regulation Development

Kate Williams, Australia

Self-regulation skills, our ability to control our own attention, emotions, and behavior, develop rapidly in early childhood and are critical to lifelong learning and well-being. These skills are so critical that they cannot be left to natural maturation processes alone. Indeed, many children experience challenges with self-regulation development, at times related to stressful home environments, low resource settings, disability, and the impact of world events, including the COVID-19 pandemic and natural disasters. Children with self-regulation difficulties will find transitioning to school challenging, may struggle to form relationships with teachers and peers, and will not take full advantage of classroom learning opportunities. Addressing the brain architecture underlying self-regulation development for all young children, and supporting positive social skills, requires activities that explicitly target brain processes, with rhythmic movement being an ideal medium.

In this chapter the underpinning theory and science behind the use of rhythmic movement for self-regulation and social development will be set out. Key concepts derive from the fields of neurologic music therapy, music education, and developmental psychology and include entrainment, beat synchronization, and interpersonal synchrony. When adults understand the response of the brain and body to beat and rhythm, the opportunity to use beat in everyday life as a regulator holds exciting potential. For example, this chapter will build knowledge in adults working with children about how they can use beat synchronization as a "window to the brain." Evidence from experimental studies of the Rhythm and Movement for Self-Regulation (RAMSR) program will be summarized, and several easy-to-implement rhythmic movement activities will be provided. These can be implemented by any adult working with children under 8 years old without the need for specialized music training.

THE VALUE OF RHYTHM

To be human is to be rhythmic. The first sense of rhythm, indeed, the first sound we hear, is our mother's heartbeat in utero. Fetuses, in utero, will move more rhythmically and in a patterned way to music than to speech (Kisilevsky et al., 2004). Hearing is the last sense we lose near the end of life (Blundon et al., 2020). Indeed, our very species and the things that make us unique as humans are all underlined by rhythmic patterns: social interaction and its give-and-take, music, dance, and language. If we understand more about how the brain and body respond to beat and rhythm, we can use this fantastic tool to support learning, development, and well-being.

This chapter focuses on the developmental areas of self-regulation, executive function, and social skills as critical underpinning capabilities for lifelong learning and well-being. Self-regulation refers to the ability to control our own attention, thinking, emotion, and behavior. The executive functions are related to self-regulation and include impulse control, flexible attention shifting, and working memory. Social skills, including prosocial helping behaviors, empathy, and sharing, are important underlying capacities for relationship-building.

Stronger skills in self-regulation, executive function, and social skills have been repeatedly and significantly linked with more positive learning, achievement, health, and well-being trajectories right across life. These skills develop most rapidly in early childhood through interactions with others and early learning environments, rather than simply through natural maturation. Thus, they have become an important focus of work that aims to give children the best possible chance of success, whether this be parenting programs, preschool and school, or extracurricular programs.

Importantly, a number of children can find self-regulation, executive function, and social skills challenging to develop for a number of reasons. Early economic disadvantage and experiences of trauma including abuse and neglect, as well as global stressful experiences, including the COVID-19 pandemic, can affect the underlying developing brain architecture that supports self-regulation development. Some neurodivergent children may need more support to develop these skills, and for other children there may be no apparent rhyme or reason for self-regulation development that is a little slower than others. Regardless of the underlying cause, strong support for self-regulation development by adults in all settings will only help all children.

Given that challenges with self-regulation and related skills are related to developing brain architecture, my argument is that strategies to support these skills must also in turn tap into neural processes rather than focusing solely on behavioral skills. In this chapter you will learn some of the key facts behind why rhythmic movement is an ideal medium to support developing brain architecture and in turn self-regulation, executive function, and social skills.

You will also be introduced to the Rhythm and Movement for Self-Regulation (RAMSR) program, and some useful activities you can begin to use right away.

DID YOU KNOW #1: WE ALL HAVE A SPONTANEOUS MOTOR TEMPO (SMT)

Part of being rhythmic beings is having a natural tempo that we tend to prefer or move to, known as spontaneous motor tempo (SMT). This would be the tempo that someone would tap at if you gave them a drumstick and asked them to tap a beat they felt comfortable with, without giving them any visual or auditory cues. It is the most regular, natural, and pleasant beat for that person. Across the human population, this tends to change with age and development.

In the first 6 months of life, our SMT is quite slow, at 90 beats per minute (Rocha et al., 2024). It is no coincidence that this is the same average tempo of a pregnant woman's heartbeat (slightly faster than when she isn't pregnant) and is the tempo most lullabies are sung to around the world. In the second year of life, though, our SMT tends to speed up to 112 beats per minute (Yu & Myowa, 2021). This is a similar tempo to the stressed syllables in speech, right at the time that children begin to talk! It will be no surprise to you that our SMT tends to become even faster from 2 to 5 years of age, at around 150 to 160 beats per minute (Yu & Myowa, 2021). From 5 to 8 years, children can still "run quite fast" at 120 to 150 bpm (Monier & Droit-Volet, 2019), but by adolescence, we have typically settled to on average around 120 bpm, though this can range from 60 to 150 beats per minute across adults (Desbernats et al., 2023).

Why is it important to know about spontaneous motor tempo (SMT)? When we understand the natural and comfortable speed of movement for different ages, we can empathize and understand the behaviors we see. Is it any wonder that as adults, we tend to view children as "full of beans" and "unable to sit still" when their bodies are literally running up to twice as fast as some of ours? It also helps to understand SMT when we are engaging in rhythmic and beat activities with children in which we are hoping they will synchronize or align with our tempo. If we are working close to the child's SMT, this will be much easier than if we are working far away from it.

Activity #1: What Is Your Spontaneous Motor Tempo?

What's your own spontaneous motor tempo? Grab a pen and simply tap on the desk at a pace that is comfortable to you. Are you much faster than 2 taps per second or much slower? Does this change on days when you are particularly tired or stressed?

You will likely be able to observe children's spontaneous motor tempo just by watching them play or dance in natural settings. Do some children seem particularly fast or slow compared to peers?

You can also try a tapping observation.

Find a quiet space to work one-on-one with the child. Provide them with a stick or pencil and simply ask them to tap on a desk or drum to a beat that feels comfortable to them. What sort of tempo are they beating at? Does it feel fast to you as an adult? That would be common, as children tend to simply "run faster" than adults. If this child has a particularly fast comfortable tempo when tapping alone, this gives you insight into why they might find being still or slowing down very tricky. They will find it easier to focus and also to move in time with you and others if the tempo is closer to their natural fast pace.

Note: Don't do this activity for too long, as it isn't very engaging for the child—a short snip should be enough to create an observation.

DID YOU KNOW #2: MOVING IN TIME TO THE BEAT, OR BEAT SYNCHRONIZATION, PROVIDES A SMALL WINDOW TO THE BRAIN

Beat synchronization (also called sensorimotor synchronization in the literature) refers to the ability to align our movements to an externally provided beat. Think of playing some music and asking children to clap along in time to it. While this seems like such a simple behavior and skill, it happens due to some really interesting brain responses to beat. When the brain hears a beat, it measures the distance between the sounds and only requires around three or four sounds with regular intervals to recognize a pattern and anticipate the next beat. How marvelous! Even more amazing is that once the brain has recognized a series of sounds as a regular beat, not only will the parts of the brain that process sound be excited by the beat pattern, but an area responsible for movement will also be activated. In fact, when a beat is heard, regions of the motor system are active and interacting even if you don't move a muscle (Cannon & Patel, 2021)!

This knowledge of beat synchronization and how the brain activates with the beat is important when working with children for several reasons. First, we must remember that it will be extremely difficult for children to be still when their brain perceives a beat. The motor network in their brain will literally shout, "Move, move, move, move" in time with the beat. Indeed, music therapists worldwide use this phenomenon to support the rehabilitation of coordinated movement following brain injury, such as stroke.

Rhythm supports the brain and body to better coordinate; how wonderful! In a classroom of children, if we provide an auditory beat, then for children not to move will require a key skill of impulse control, called inhibitory control in the executive function literature. So if we want to practice this control skill, as in some of the activities below (being still in the music), then this is fine. However, if we don't want to practice that inhibitory control skill in a particular activity, then when we ask children to be still when there is a beat, we will simply be draining their executive function battery (and nobody wants that). In fact, you could use music to help not drain children's batteries in times of transition and waiting.

- Children waiting in line are still and quiet—battery draining
- Children waiting in line while marching on the spot to some funky music or playing rhythm hand clapping games—more regulating and much less draining

Second, when we ask children to move in time with us during a rhythmic activity, we need to remember that this will be easier if the tempo is close to their spontaneous motor tempo (SMT). Studies have shown that around 1 year of age, infants can accelerate from their SMT to match someone else's beat, but deceleration is very hard, so a slow tempo will be challenging (see Rocha et al., 2021). From around 30 months of age, young children can decelerate, and by around 8 years of age, they may even be able to synchronize down to as slow as 85 beats per minute, even though their SMT is very fast. In adolescence, we reach our peak ability to synchronize, and we maintain this generally into adulthood. Sometimes, though, we will come across children who can't seem to synchronize as well as their peers. This is not cause for diagnosis or alarm as, like all skills, this can develop over time.

However, there is emerging evidence that poorer beat synchronization skills may be linked with potential language learning difficulties, including dyslexia (Fiveash et al., 2021; Ladányi et al., 2020), and also with attention deficit hyperactivity disorder (ADHD), where timing difficulties are a common part of the ADHD experience (Slater & Tate, 2018). That's even more reason to provide lots of fun and engaging opportunities to experience and be playful with beat and rhythmic movement for all children.

Third, when we see children not participating in our rhythmic movement activities or moving "out of time" or "not with the beat" when we work with them, it is reassuring to know that the brain is doing its work anyway. That is, even if what you see appears disengaged or completely out of sync, the brain is doing the measuring of the space between beats, and it is activating the motor network in a lovely, patterned, and regulating way. Trust the process and don't stress about nonparticipation or children being out of sync. It is essential to remember that we cannot force children to be "in time." We can only provide fun and engaging opportunities for the brain and body to experience the pattern of beat. For many children, as soon as you draw attention to them being "out of time," or put your hands on them, perhaps to move their hands for them in time, their anxiety systems will be alerted. Once this has happened, their brain will be much less likely to enjoy the patterning of beat, and their bodies will be even more out of sync.

There may be instances where a music therapist or other allied health professional uses deep pressure touch accompanied by rhythm with children they have assessed as suitable and with whom they have a rapport. The aim here is to provide and regulate sensory input rather than force or teach in-time movements.

Activity #2: Beat Matching

You can observe children's ability to synchronize with a beat simply by playing a piece of recorded music (make sure it is fairly fast to match their spontaneous motor tempo), and asking them to clap or march along. Try a few different tempos. Below are some suggestions. (But please check that these are appropriate for your children. You can also search the Internet for other options at each of these tempos).

- Taylor Swift's "Shake It Off" (quite fast, 160 beats per minute)
- Daft Punk's "Around the World" or Pitbull/Usher's "DJ Got Us Fallin' in Love Again" (both 120 beats per minute)
- Katy Perry's "Roar" or Imagine Dragons' "Demons" (slow, at 90 beats per minute, unless of course children do "double time," which is likely; then they will move at 180 beats per minute)

You could also do this in a one-on-one situation. Sit across from the child, each with a pencil or stick to tap the desk, or hands on a drum. Tap a beat that you think is close to the child's spontaneous motor tempo and then ask them to match it and play along. Start to go a little faster and then a little slower, and see if the child can come along with you to new beats. Too slow, and it will be impossible, though.

Note: It is very usual for all of us, particularly children, to come "on" and "off" the beat—perhaps be in time for a few counts, but then too fast or too slow. This is normal; just keep having fun and enjoy the movement together.

DID YOU KNOW #3: THE HUMAN BODY IS BUILT TO MATCH ITS PHYSICAL FUNCTIONS TO THE BEAT, KNOWN AS ENTRAINMENT

Entrainment refers to the inclination of the human body to match its physical functions to a heard beat (Thaut et al., 2015). While beat synchronization described above is somewhat more conscious (though the brain does the measuring and establishes patterns without us being aware of it), entrainment is typically unconscious. For example, when you are in a shop playing fast music, you will naturally move fast around the shop, and even your heart rate and breathing rate may speed up a little. When you enter a spa or massage treatment room, the music played might support your body to move more slowly, slowing your breathing and heart rate without you having to control or think too hard about it.

Music therapists often use entrainment in clinical settings to help manage anxiety, among other conditions. For example, it could be that a music therapist is called to the bedside of a highly anxious child who may be about to be prepared for surgery. The music therapist notes that the heart rate and respiration (breathing) monitors suggest that the heart is pumping fast with anxiety, and breathing is short, shallow, and quite fast. Importantly, the music therapist does not begin playing a slow and calming lullaby but instead improvises on their guitar to match the child's elevated heart and respiration rate.

Then, little by little, the music therapist slows their improvisation tempo, watches as the child's body entrains to the beat of the music, and starts to slow down in terms of heart and breath rate. This is an important process to understand, as this therapeutic technique would have been less effective if the therapist mismatched their tempo at the beginning and went straight in with a slow lullaby. The subconscious process of entrainment happens best when the beat provided is close to the current tempo of the body and changes only ever so slightly over time.

Activity #3: Using the Idea of Entrainment to Manage Your Environment

Are there times in your setting when you would like to support children to move a little faster or indeed a little slower? Perhaps it is pack-up time after a morning session, and there is a rush to get to lunch or the next activity. Try some upbeat appropriate music playing in the background and see what happens to children's movements.

Perhaps it is a wind-down or quiet time at home. Try some slower music. However, be aware of what we learned in this section. If children have transitioned from a very active or fast activity, a sudden mismatch to slow and calming music is unlikely to work. Is there a way you could match them first with a short, faster, and more energetic activity, and then introduce progressively slower music supports?

For a wind-down bundle of music designed by a highly qualified and experienced music therapist, visit https://rhythmicintegrations.com/courses/.

DID YOU KNOW #4: WHEN WE MOVE IN TIME WITH OTHERS AND EXPERIENCE INTERPERSONAL SYNCHRONY, WE BOND WITH THEM

One of my absolute favorite facts about humans is that when we move in time with others, as opposed to out of time with them, we will be more helpful and bonded with each other. Many experiments with children as young as 18 months of age have had adults sway a child in time with a researcher or out of time with a researcher (Cirelli et al., 2014). When later asked to help the researcher pick up an object, those children who moved in time with the researcher were far more likely to help than those who moved out of time with the researcher. Similarly, preschoolers who are swung on a swing set in time with each other will be much more cooperative in a later task than those who are swung out of time with each other (Rabinowitch & Meltzoff, 2017). What happens when we move in time? Certainly, our brains will experience that lovely measuring and patterning in the same way as we have discussed earlier. I think we also see each other as "kin." Someone moving in time with us is showing us, "I see you, and I am with you." Someone moving out of time with us is likely to seem suspicious and "other"—clearly even to 18-month-olds!

Research has also shown that even more frequent use of simple nursery rhymes and songs by parents with children aged 2–3 years boosts children's prosocial skills such as empathy and turn-taking 2 years later when they are 4–5 years old (Williams et al., 2015). And this effect is over and above the positive impact of shared book-reading, which is a great early learning activity. There is something very special about moving together in time that as a human society can support social bonds and likely individual social skills. How often do you provide opportunities in your setting for children and adults to move in time with each other and their peers?

Activity #4: Moving in Time With Others

Formal bush dancing, line dancing, and other simple structured dances are a great way to provide time for children and adults to move together in time. But there are also some very simple activities that can provide similar benefits without the need for detailed instruction or a lot of space.

Row, row, row your boat: A traditional nursery rhyme in which children and/or adults sit opposite each other on the floor, holding both hands and moving back and forth together to row the boat through the song.

Simple partner clapping games: Teach children a simple beat of 4—perhaps 2 pats on knees, then 2 claps. Establish this first on their own, then have them turn to a partner and complete the same move (2 knee pats, 2 claps). Then, in stage 3, have them swap out the claps for patting each other's hands (like a double high five). So, the pattern becomes 2 knee pats, 2 double high fives.

Note: There is nothing to worry about if children can't get this right and in time with each other. Just the experience of trying, and hopefully having a laugh, will boost social bonding. If one child is in time and the other isn't, you can encourage the more rhythmic child just to keep going with the pattern. You might suggest the other child just try to hit the double high five when it comes up in the pattern, as a starting point. Depending on the age and rhythmic stage of the child, coordinating a two-part pattern of knees and clap can be quite challenging.

THE RHYTHM AND MOVEMENT FOR SELF-REGULATION (RAMSR) PROGRAM

RAMSR (Rhythm and Movement for Self-Regulation) is a program for young children that supports attentional and emotional regulation skills, as well as mental flexibility, inhibition, and working memory (the executive functions), and social skills.

The program was first designed and piloted in 2016, led by myself and a wonderful team of music therapy and early childhood music education colleagues at the Queensland University of Technology. The program is a carefully designed set of rhythmic movement activities that can be done in a group or with individual children. Activities aim to stimulate some of the same brain benefits that participating in music therapy or learning a music instrument might provide.

We know that children who formally train in music gain some great brain benefits, but often music training is not available or is financially out of reach for many families. RAMSR seeks to bring the advantages of formal music training and music therapy to the masses. RAMSR is based on the kinds of scientific areas discussed in this chapter (Williams, 2018).

The vision for RAMSR is for all adults living or working with young children to have the confidence, skills, and resources to use evidence-based rhythm and movement activities for self-regulation and social support for children.

So that this can happen, we designed a low-cost, low-resource, easy-to-use-and-implement program that all early childhood practitioners can use, whether or not they have any prior music skills. Training is available online at https://rhythmicintegrations.com/rhythm-and-movement-for-self-regulation/.

There is a free introductory course followed by options to access the program for children aged 3–8 years (RAMSR-O), and the program for children aged 18 months to 3 years (RAMSR-T for toddlers). Accessing the courses will provide you with session plans, specifically produced audio tracks (easily accessed through our app), a 120-page teacher resource, demonstration videos, and all knowledge and resources you need to deliver a full-year program to individual or groups of children.

Several experimental studies of RAMSR in Australia and Hong Kong have now shown that children who engage in RAMSR, compared to those who don't, show steeper growth in self-regulation, executive function, and social skills, and reduced behavioral problems (Bentley et al., 2023; Williams et al., 2023; Williams & Berthelsen, 2019).

We have now trained thousands of adults across the world who work with children in groups or one-on-one, or who live with children, to use these activities to support development.

RAMSR activities look deceptively simple, and they are always fun, even when challenging. The next four activities are just some examples of the 48 base-level activities you can access through the RAMSR program (with many more extensions and alternative activities also provided).

Activity #5: "Heads, Shoulders, Knees, Toes"

Sing this classic children's song with actions as usual and ask the children to sing along with you.

Then say, "I have a trick for you; let's leave out the word 'shoulders.' Sing the song again with actions, but not singing the word *shoulders*. Add other items to leave out.

"Then say 'I have another trick for you. What if we sang the song forwards like usual, but did the actions backwards. That would mean we would start with our hands on our toes instead of our head! Let's go."

Sing the song forward, but the actions will be in the order of toes, knees, shoulders, head.

This seemingly simple activity targets a whole range of skills, including:

- Beat synchronization
- Coordinated movement
- Working memory (holding instructions in mind)
- Inhibition (missing out some words)
- Dual-task (doing opposite actions to words)
- Attentional regulation, especially auditory attention
- Interpersonal synchrony

Video: https://youtu.be/kc8AWmt8QDY

Activity #6: Copy Me

Pick a lively piece of music, ideally without lyrics, at around an easy march tempo (not too fast, not too slow). As the leader, demonstrate a move that children can copy. Start with single actions like tap knees, stomp feet, tap nose, clap hands. Do each for at least 16 beats before moving to the next one (or 8 beats each if your children have the hang of it).

For something a little trickier, bring in cross-body actions like tapping right arm to left knee. For something even trickier, create some double-action movements like knee, knee, clap, clap. This activity warms up children's auditory and motor systems. The beat is set by the music, and the teacher models the body percussion (coordinated movement). There is no need for any verbal directions. Leaping straight into this is a great way to begin. Often, we find that adults working with groups of children use too much talk to gain group attention, or they might drain children's batteries by waiting until all are sitting and quiet to begin an activity. Instead, use the music as your co-teacher and just press Play and begin leading the actions. The music and actions from the leader will cue children to sit down, join the group, and attempt the movements together (interpersonal synchrony). This activity can act as a warm-up/transition activity preparing children for the rest of the session and can go on for as long as needed (i.e., once all children have joined the session area).

This simple activity is targeting many skills:

- Beat synchronization
- Coordinated movement
- Interpersonal synchrony
- Attentional regulation

Video: https://youtu.be/63lc2lj3TnU

Activity #7: This Is the Way We . . . With a Trick

Sing the traditional song that begins, "This is the way we clap our hands, clap our hands, clap our hands . . ." If you aren't familiar with this tune, see the URL below. Each time, sing a different action and model the action. This could be clapping hands, patting knees, stomping feet, and so forth (keep it simple).

Then explain to the children that you want them to do what they see but not what they hear. Now it is time for you to mismatch your singing with your actions (and this is tricky). So you might sing, "This is the way we clap our hands," but while you sing that, you are tapping your knees. You might then sing "This is the way we pat our head," but while you sing that, you are stomping your feet. Try getting your friends to do this at a party for a laugh and some practice!

Children will get a different cue from your actions, compared to your voice. You have asked them to do what they see.

But then the tricker part comes. Next, ask them to do what they hear. You keep doing mismatched singing and actions, and children have to switch to wait to hear what your vocal instruction is and do that. Children will naturally more readily do what they see, and it will be interesting to see who can wait to hear what the verbal direction is and do that instead. For example, if you are singing "This is the way we clap our hands" but you are tapping your head, the children need to clap their hands. We see many adults get mixed up with leading this activity and participating in it, but don't worry—just laugh and have some fun.

This activity is targeting the following:

- Beat synchronization
- Coordinated movement
- Inhibition
- Attentional regulation

Video: https://youtu.be/zoJjUHBNufY?si=JHyNqVyesDQPT4Kr

Activity #8: Tricky Dancing to Engage the Executive Functions

For this one, pick an appropriate piece of music with a strong beat that is good to dance to. Play the music and have children free-dance to the music, then stop the music at random times and have them freeze. You won't have to instruct them on this; instead, when you stop the music, just hold one hand to signal a stop. Make sure you dance along with the children as well! This seems like a simple statue game right now.

Next, though, tell the children you are going to play the tricky game and do the opposite. This means being still statues when the music is on (as you know, this will be very tricky and take lots of inhibitory control), and then move when the music is silent (and this will look like a strange silent disco!).

Once children have the hang of that, you can add other extensions, like perhaps instead of free dancing you provide the children with a series of moves they need to remember. The number of moves should depend on their age and stage. This is very basic choreography. For example, you might have four children pick the moves and show that the group will do 8 beats of each. It might be 8 stomps, 8 star jumps, 8 hops, and 8 claps. Children need to move through this pattern when the music is on, but when the music stops, they freeze—and then try to start again at count 1 of the move that they finished on—tricky and for older children!

Then you could reverse this as we did before and have the children freeze in the music and then work through the choreography in the silence (when you stop the music). You could then even ask children to remember the same sequence but perform it in reverse (8 claps, 8 hops, 8 star jumps, 8 stomps).

The possibilities are endless when you get creative and consider the age and stage of your children and what you can do here.

This activity is working on:

- Beat synchronization
- Aerobic exercise
- Coordinated movement
- Working memory
- Inhibition

- Shifting
- Attentional regulation
- Interpersonal synchrony

The QR code below will bring you to a printable version of all activities for Chapter 10. This material may also be accessed under the "Downloads" tab at https://www.tcpress.com/move-more-learn-more-9780807784051.

CONCLUSION

You may already be doing some similar rhythmic movement games like those described above in your practice, and I hope that now you have gained some knowledge and confidence in the power of these activities to support brain development, self-regulation, and social skills. We find in RAMSR that the theory and science that we provide, along with the activities, the specific audio tracks, and the mapping of key target skills, support adults to use RAMSR, and also help them develop and extend activities using their own experience and creativity.

RAMSR courses are most conveniently accessed online, which means you can participate on your own time and flexibly around your schedule. You can start at any time and have one year to complete your materials. There are no rigid schedules. The course is entirely online and self-paced, with the option of participating in four optional live online Q&A webinars throughout the year.

REFERENCES

Bentley, L., Eager, R., Savage, S., Nielson, C., White, S., & Williams, K. (2023). A translational application of music for preschool cognitive development: RCT evidence for improved executive function, self-regulation, and school readiness. *Developmental Science*, *26*(5), 1–16.

Blundon, E., Gallagher, R., & Ward, L. (2020). Electrophysiological evidence of preserved hearing at the end of life. *Scientific Reports*, *10*(1), 10336.

Cannon, J., & Patel, A. (2021). How beat perception co-opts motor neurophysiology. *Trends in Cognitive Sciences*, *25*(2), 137–150.

Cirelli, L., Einarson, K., & Trainor, L. (2014). Interpersonal synchrony increases prosocial behavior in infants. *Developmental Science*, *17*(6), 1003–1011.

Desbernats, A., Martin, E., & Tallet, J. (2023). Which factors modulate spontaneous motor tempo? A systematic review of the literature [Systematic Review]. *Frontiers in Psychology*, *14*, 1161052.

Fiveash, A., Bedoin, N., Gordon, R., & Tillmann, B. (2021). Processing rhythm in speech and music: Shared mechanisms and implications for developmental speech and language disorders. *Neuropsychology, 35*(8), 771–791.

Kisilevsky, S., Hains, S., Jacquet, A., Granier-Deferre, C., & Lecanuet, J. (2004). Maturation of fetal responses to music. *Developmental Science, 7*(5), 550–559.

Ladányi, E., Persici, V., Fiveash, A., Tillmann, B., & Gordon, R. (2020). Is atypical rhythm a risk factor for developmental speech and language disorders? Wiley interdisciplinary reviews. *Cognitive Science, 11*(5), e1528–n/a.

Monier, F., & Droit-Volet, S. (2019). Development of sensorimotor synchronization abilities: Motor and cognitive components. *Child Neuropsychology, 25*(8), 1043–1062.

Rabinowitch, T., & Meltzoff, A. (2017). Synchronized movement experience enhances peer cooperation in preschool children. *Journal of Experimental Child Psychology, 160*, 21–32.

Rocha, S., Attaheri, A., Ní Choisdealbha, Á., Brusini, P., Mead, N., Olawole-Scott, H., Boutris, P., Gibbon, S., Williams, I., Grey, C., Alfaro e Oliveira, M., Brough, C., Flanagan, S., Ahmed, H., Macrae, E., & Goswami, U. (2024). Precursors to infant sensorimotor synchronization to speech and non-speech rhythms: A longitudinal study. *Developmental Science, 27*(4), e13483.

Rocha, S., Southgate, V., & Mareschal, D. (2021). Infant spontaneous motor tempo. *Developmental Science, 24*(2), e13032.

Slater, J., & Tate, M. (2018). Timing deficits in ADHD: Insights from the neuroscience of musical rhythm. *Frontiers in Computational Neuroscience, 12*, 51.

Thaut, M., McIntosh, G., & Hoemberg, V. (2015). Neurobiological foundations of neurologic music therapy: Rhythmic entrainment and the motor system. *Frontiers in Psychology, 5*, 1185.

Williams, K. (2018). Moving to the beat: Using music, rhythm, and movement to enhance self-regulation in early childhood classrooms. *International Journal of Early Childhood, 50*(1), 85–100.

Williams, K., Barrett, M., Welch, G., Abad, V., & Broughton, M. (2015). Associations between early shared music activities in the home and later child outcomes: Findings from the longitudinal study of Australian children. *Early Childhood Research Quarterly, 31*, 113–124.

Williams, K., Bentley, L., Savage, S., Eager, R., & Nielson, C. (2023). Rhythm and movement delivered by teachers supports self-regulation skills of preschool-aged children in disadvantaged communities: A clustered RCT. *Early Childhood Research Quarterly, 65*, 115–128.

Williams, K., & Berthelsen, D. (2019). Implementation of a rhythm and movement intervention to support self-regulation skills of preschool-aged children in disadvantaged communities. *Psychology of Music, 47*(6), 800–820.

Yu, L., & Myowa, M. (2021). The early development of tempo adjustment and synchronization during joint drumming: A study of 18-to 42-month-old children. *Infancy, 26*(4), 635–646.

CHAPTER 11

"MovementWorks" for Neurotypical and Neurodivergent Learners

Ali Golding, UK

Current research indicates that over 30% of children across England are starting school unready to learn (University of Leeds, 2024), with a significant proportion presenting with additional support needs and/or symptoms typically associated with learning difficulties; for example, 46% are unable to sit still (Savanta, 2024). Schools are seeing high numbers of children unable to meet formal learning expectations and approaches and struggling to cope at school, with twice as many having underdeveloped language and poor communication skills (Hobbs & Bernard, 2021). Peer interaction and behavior, self-regulation, and anxiety are all areas of concern (Education Endowment Foundation, 2022). The issue has risen exponentially since the lockdowns, especially for children from low economic backgrounds who have greater social and educational needs than pre-pandemic (Taylor, 2021).

The Sheffield University 2024 report "An Evidence-Based Approach to Supporting Children in the Preschool Years" highlights the alarming rise in developmental delays since COVID-19 (Powell et al., 2024), correlating with a downward trend in motor skill proficiency (Brian et al., 2019). School resources are being redirected to offer extra targeted support to ever-increasing numbers of children, but the landscape of diminishing school finances means this response is ineffectual and unsustainable. Small-group academic skill "catch-up" interventions or the one-to-one support that is put in place for a few children with the highest level of needs is not addressing the broader exigency or getting to the root of the underlying issue that exists; neither are these approaches truly inclusive. As a result, these children often miss out on social interaction and active free play time opportunities and become more marginalized from the rest of their cohort.

Concurrently, there is an acknowledged physical inactivity crisis. Findings indicate that just 14% of preschool children meet the daily recommended activity levels (University of Stirling, 2024), with the World Health Organization and UK guidance promoting whole-school approaches to tackle the problem while emphasizing the need to provide more inclusive opportunities. Physically active learning approaches have been considered as a way to tackle the sedentary nature of the school curriculum (Eddy et al., 2024). As well as improving levels of activity, they have been found to have a positive impact on educational outcomes (Norris et al., 2020). However, their use is still limited as teachers are lacking the knowledge and/or skills to implement these approaches (Eddy et al., 2024).

The big picture suggests that low-cost, effective, and physically active learning embedded into the curriculum is the way forward but there needs to be an awakening and a joining of the dots between what are generally perceived to be two unrelated crises when they are in fact symptoms of the same environmental influences. A combination of technology-driven "modern enhancers," more sedentary lifestyles, cramped living conditions, and lack of opportunity are creating deficits in our children's development. One source explains, "Evidence has mounted from imaging studies, developmental disorders, and typically developing children to suggest that cognitive and motor development are more closely related than previously assumed and have similarly protracted developmental trajectories" (Davis et al., 2011).

This chapter contributes to *Move More, Learn More* by signposting pioneering dance-movement approaches and evidence-based programs that address the needs of all children in the classroom, for both typically developing and neurodiverse learners. because borrowing from the perspectives of Baroness Sheila Hollins, when we get it right for children with disabilities and learning difficulties we get it right for all children.

As barriers to learning are minimized, improvements in class integration have a positive effect for all children and the class teachers.

WHY "MOVEMENTWORKS"

The common misconception is that movement resides in and for the body when, in fact, it is really about the brain. If this sounds like a contentious idea, it is worth considering why we have brains at all. As Daniel Wolpert (2011) explains, our brains evolved to move.

It is increasingly acknowledged in the academic literature that individuals with learning differences experience difficulties with movement that negatively impact their development (Bhat, 2020; Ohara et al., 2019).

Furthermore, when the current context as described above is viewed through this lens, through informed observation, these difficulties become apparent sooner than the emergence of communication, social interaction, and/or behavior challenges (Hardy & LaGasse, 2013). Movement difficulties are early indicators of developmental delay as they mirror the neurological organization of the brain. Yet there still has not been a broad formal recognition of these difficulties (Golding et al., 2024; Wright et al., 2019).

With deeper understanding of the body-brain relationship, it becomes easier to recognize and better support those presenting with sensorimotor difficulties and to appreciate how providing optimal movement experiences can improve brain development and function.

In fact, recently published research reframes autism as a condition primarily concerning connectivity of sensory, perception, and motor control affecting cognition (Leisman et al., 2023).

This relates to movement and physical experience being the very foundation of thinking (Llinas, 2002; Tversky, 2019). Therefore, all young children are predominantly kinesthetic learners. They are biologically programmed toward full-bodied experiences for healthy growth of the nervous (body-brain) system. What's important to most strongly communicate is that a lack of optimal physical experience doesn't just affect children's weight and general health; it actually impacts and limits their brain development (Bryck & Fisher, 2012) and therefore their learning potential.

THE BRAIN IS A PROCESSING WONDER

The brain is an information processing wonder. We process and store information in either long-term or short-term areas of the brain. When we need that information again, we retrieve it via a pathway (white brain matter) in the mapping area (gray matter) of the brain. Brain mapping is an interesting process. In simple terms, it's like moving into a new home when at first you don't know where to find the grocery store, the dry cleaner, the gas station, or any other neighborhood establishments you need daily. But within a short period of time, you've found these places, and you no longer have to think about the specific directions to get there. You get in your car and drive right to the spot, almost as though you're on automatic pilot. Daily we map hundreds of pieces of information by placing them in a file in our brain and without even having to think about it. When we need the information we retrieve the file by going straight to it, via cognitive maps or highway pathways.

Autistic individuals have difficulty accessing and retrieving information in both long- and short-term memory banks. Either the pathway does not exist or the transmitters are impaired. This makes learning information more challenging. The analogy is that the neurodivergent brain functions like a library, where the information is stored in a differently organized and/or non-categorized way, causing degrees of confusion. The good news is that through developments in neuroscience, we now know about the phenomenon of neuroplasticity; the brain is not fixed but has the ability to change and will adapt according to our experiences (Arrowsmith-Young, 2012). We can jumpstart impaired informational pathways and create new pathways through a process called cognitive redirection.

In other words, cognition is not passive but "enactive"—that is to say, it is an embodied activity that necessitates an involvement with the internal world and sensorimotor coupling (Engel et al., 2013).

For example, the rocking motion that children are often restricted from doing in the classroom environment is serving them a purpose. As Dr. Temple Grandin says in the documentary *Generation A: Portraits of Autism in the Arts*, "The repetitive rocking motion that requires a person to continually find and refine their balance stimulates areas of the brain where learning receptors are located" (Shils, 2015).

As a dance practitioner and movement scientist, I have been instrumental in advocating for the therapeutic use of dance movement in the educational environment, as it provides a powerful tool for expression and learning (Golding et al., 2024) and is useful to the educator as simultaneously an early indicator and an appropriate, fully inclusive, and low-cost whole-class group intervention.

In 2011, I set about to address the acknowledged "paucity of interventions that exist with a theoretical framework" (Kirk & Rhodes, 2011). The direct response was the creation of a dance-movement-based program, which was to become Developmental Dance Movement® (DDM). The pilot project, subject to a peer-reviewed publication (Golding et al., 2016), found that visual-motor integration and developmental maturity measured across two Reception (kindergarten) classes increased by 7% across one term and accelerated the learning trajectories for children with additional needs (TEDXTalks [Golding], 2017).

This led to the establishment of the UK charity MovementWorks®, a groundbreaking not-for-profit organization and pioneer of evidence-based inclusive dance movement programs specifically to support development and learning through improving cognitive function. Developmental Dance Movement® (DDM) and Autism Movement Therapy® (AMT) (Lara, 2015) are examples of our flagship models applied in this context.

Dance movement provides multiple channels for learning and skill acquisition as well as self-expression and group interaction that may shift expectations through active and enjoyable engagement. Programs that integrate sensory and movement experiences may thus provide a basis for learning as well as positive participatory experiences, particularly for children who find traditional teaching methods difficult to access.

The reason teachers are currently struggling to apply formal elements of the curriculum is that we cannot rule a child's need to orient their senses from a top-down approach—we can only provide for it. Teachers are experiencing increasing levels of needs and perceive the nature of the problem to be worsening because they are being asked to adopt learning approaches that are simply not appropriate for the stage of development of the children (Savanta, 2024). Simultaneously, it is becoming more and more difficult to decipher which children have a real underlying neurological condition from those with developmental delay due to "environmental insults." However, a child who receives appropriate and adequate stimulation will in time be able to engage, remain calm, decipher, and absorb information from the world.

While language-based tasks can be a barrier to understanding and expressing thoughts, music, movement, and dance are, by nature, multimodal. They are learned by seeing, hearing, feeling, and doing simultaneously and are accessible in nonverbal ways; music and movement have the potential to be effective via multisensory systems for typical and neurodiverse children (Amonkar et al., 2021; Golding et al., 2016; Stamou et al., 2019; Su et al., 2022).

Refining imitation skills, sense of self, and environmental awareness through building experiences across the combination of modalities used in dance can contribute to recommended sensory enrichment programs for autistic children (Woo & Leon, 2013). Since we generally dance with others, dance-based activities and games can simultaneously support psychosocial and cognitive development (Ketcheson et al., 2016; Rintala et al., 1998). The rhythmic and musical elements that anchor dance practice are also significant contributing factors in its efficacy in supporting key areas of development.

Entrainment theory underpins the clinical application of the positive effects that rhythmic synchronization has on sensory perception, social, emotional and speech development, and aspects of cognition (Thaut et al., 2015). Temple Grandin acknowledges that "rhythmic and balancing activities seem to have a stabilizing effect on the brain" (Shils, 2015). Speech development may be supported additionally through the cognitive relationship between speech and gesture, thus enhancing understanding and pragmatic language acquisition. Since the neural pathways of speech articulation and gesture work intentionally, in a tightly coupled system use of gesture can enhance brain integration, language, and memory (Clough & Duff, 2020).

For those with disrupted/impaired speech communication pathways, it is essential to note that since music and singing occupy different circuitry in the brain compared to spoken language, they are activated in different regions (Hamilton, 2022). Therefore, using music and song intrinsically integrated with dance movement may be beneficial for supporting non/preverbal and neurodivergent individuals. Thus, intentionally devised dance movement programs, such as those offered by MovementWorks®, can positively impact a broad range of learning and behavior outcomes for children, supporting the context of this chapter.

Originally devised independently, the programs DDM (Golding) and AMT (Lara) are taught separately and together as an all-through-PreK–12 approach in educational and community settings to improve learning, physical skills, emotional maturity, and self-esteem and to support positive social engagement. Methods involve the use of dance movement therapeutically and as an intentional learning tool, including direct instruction of choreographic content provided within meaningful learning contexts and guidance of creative imaginative tasks that support broader occupational outcomes. The underlying theories and methods of DDM and AMT are so complementary that they are delivered by MovementWorks® in the UK as an all-through-school approach to support the traditional therapies offered for autistic children. In addition, MovementWorks® is the global lead for AMT training.

The following subsections will introduce the fundamentals of both programs. The end of the chapter I will provide some stand-alone take-away activities from the approaches that support specific objectives.

WHAT IS DEVELOPMENTAL DANCE MOVEMENT®? (ALI GOLDING)

Developmental Dance Movement® is an innovative, unique, whole-body multisensory early intervention program designed for young children (from around 2.5 years to age 8) facilitate optimal physical and cognitive development in a fun, imaginative, and engaging way made relevant to the curriculum.

The results of a structured program of DDM as an early intervention indicate accelerated and cross-curricular learning for all children and suggest that children with special educational needs (SENs) and particularly those on the autistic spectrum with related differences benefit significantly (Golding et al., 2016). The full DDM program is designed to run across an academic year. Sessions are scaffolded to gradually increase in difficulty/challenge, with positive results being determinable after one term of weekly sessions (Golding et al., 2016). Activities can also be differentiated to support the needs of specific groups/individuals, creating a fertile opportunity to balance fun with a growth environment. This makes for a highly enjoyable experience, which is the key to engagement.

What Happens in a DDM Session?

Sessions normally last between 35 and 45 minutes. They have a structure that the children quickly become familiar and comfortable with. The structure allows them to feel safe and anticipate activities, and it gives them the opportunity to repeat and master tasks before moving on to the next level/challenge.

Underpinned by educational theory, scientifically validated and carefully crafted, they are grounded in academic research and informed by Montessori pedagogy and observational practice, with sessions taking the form of various dance movement–based games and activities. They are not focused on learning particular dance styles or steps and are therefore appealing to all genders. The work is process- rather than performance-led, which nurtures a safe, encouraging, and supportive learning environment; sessions are physiologically sound and are designed to promote inclusivity.

Physical experiences are carefully crafted to maximize the positive impact on brain plasticity, development, and function. Contributing factors include consideration of the following: increasing levels of neurotransmitters, which support brain building; complex movement patterns that promote whole-brain connectivity; and those that appropriately stimulate reduction of habitual limiting movement patterns and bring awareness to the visual, vestibular, proprioceptive, and interoceptive senses likely to reduce deficits and barriers to learning.

Activities are designed to maximize global understanding through the act of moving and anchoring learning physically and intellectually (embodied learning). DDM embraces the scientific notion of multilevel processing and provides a multifaceted pathway for learning, facilitating opportunities for growth for all children. This multilevel processing has benefits for both conceptual learning and the development of language and communication skills. Speech and language development is augmented during sessions with additional visual communication systems such as Makaton (Makaton, n.d.).

DDM is a genuine model of inclusion that considers the developmental needs of neurodivergent individuals with physical and intellectual disabilities, while supporting them to learn alongside their typical peers.

Appropriate stimulation lays a strong foundation for learning. Children are provided with optimal experiences and encouraged to practice fundamental physical skills that suitably engage the senses: visual, aural, tactile, olfactory, vestibular, proprioceptive, and interoceptive. These experiences foster awareness and specific coordination and control, which directly contribute to the developmental maturity needed for school readiness and enable children to excel in all areas of learning. All children need a sensory-rich diet, and as highlighted in the contextual background, an increasing number of children are showing developmental delays due to a lack of optimal movement opportunities. The DDM program can be paired with specially developed integrated progress checks, which support early observational practice and enhance the knowledge of teachers and parents/caregivers. Informed observations can identify underlying needs that may not be recognized until much later stages of development, allowing children who might eventually receive a diagnosis of autism or related differences to benefit from appropriate intervention at the earliest possible point.

Fun and Informative

The program takes into careful consideration both the recreational and educational potential dance movement has to offer. Sessions offer cross-curricular learning opportunities closely linked with specific areas of learning, particularly literacy and math, and so contribute to the forming of a baseline for teaching curriculum. Concepts taught experientially have a greater impact on understanding and retention. Enjoyable whole-body recreational group activity fosters the physical, social, emotional, and cognitive potential of each child and provides multisensory learning opportunities that are complementary to differing learning dispositions and needs.

WHOLE-BODY RECREATIONAL GROUP ACTIVITIES

Activity #1: Warm-Up Sequence—Overview

Clapping side-to-side to a favorite song with a freeze element.

Benefits

This warm-up activity stimulates/engages the whole brain for focus, attention, and learning. It should be done to a moderate steady beat using a favorite rhyme or song.
It can be done opposite a partner for imitation/mirroring (supporting mirror neuron brain activity).
Freeze the clapping activity in rhythmic phrases; for example, 8×8, 4×8, 2×8, 1×8.
Introduce a novel movement after the freeze that stimulates the vestibular system; for example, a turn, swing, or a balance (on one foot, or on one hand and one foot, or even the hips).

Tip

The rhymes, songs, rhythmic phrases, and the novel movements can be changed regularly to retain interest and engagement.

Activity #2: Locomotor Skipping and Galloping Sequence

"It takes both sides of the brain to dance."
—Joanne Lara

Benefits

Skipping and galloping are fundamental rhythmic movements. Like walking and running, they do not need to be taught/broken down into steps. They require whole-brain engagement and are great fun and mood enhancing. This notion is literally embedded in our common language; we "jump for joy" and "skip the light fantastic."

Tips/Additional Activities

This can take place in a hall, classroom, or studio space.
Choose appropriate music and tempo for skipping/galloping in a simple 2/4 or compound 6/8 meter. Drawing from Irish jig folk music and classical polka works well. Students can start the work in pairs, enhancing their imitation/mirroring skills.
These skipping and/or galloping activities may be done in pairs across the room or around in a circle. Students may hold hands traveling side by side or traveling opposite each other with a partner.
All students keep the temp by clapping/patting on their legs/other body parts.
This can progress in challenge as a group activity for environmental/spatial awareness, anticipating rhythm, social interaction, and skills such as turn-taking.

Variations

Skipping forwards/backwards
Galloping sideways/forwards
Incorporating combinations of phrases/counts in 8s, 4s, or 2s.

Further Variations

Adding 1/2 turns, different facings, full turns
Traveling diagonally from corner to corner
Changing partners
The combinations are infinite.
More able/older students can be given creative tasks in small groups.

Activity #3: Walking the Line (Montessori)

Overview

Why do children enjoy walking on walls?
There is an interrelationship between physical development and emotional maturity. The period referred to as the Terrible Twos marks the transition from infanthood to young child. A toddler finds it challenging to control their emotions, and at the same time they are physically unstable. When physical stability improves, there is often also a shift in emotional maturity.

Benefit

Movement activities that harness this correlation, supporting development of physical balance and control, are of great benefit for more general control and balance of self/behavior, emotional stability, and concentration.
Traditionally, this gentle and focused physical activity is employed in a Montessori classroom between work cycles to support the above.

Instructions

Draw a line on the floor with masking/painter's tape.
Choose slow music to anchor the pace and your approach as desired. Adult model walks heel to toe along the line with children following. Children should be guided to maintain an arm's distance (personal kinesphere).

Additional Variations

Rhythmic walking, zigzag pathways, reverse walking, and balancing challenges

Activity #4: Co-regulation Activities—Partner Breathing

Overview

Calming, mindful, and grounding activities are recommended at the end of any stimulating dance movement activity session.

Benefits

They are also highly useful as stand-alone activities and very helpful strategies in an autism-specific learning environment and/or where individuals struggle with sensory overload. The ability to self-regulate comes from building an awareness and gaining skills from co-regulating opportunities. In other words, skills of immobility and energy management have to be modeled, learned, and practiced.

Instructions

Partners can be a scarf; a small, soft toy; an adult model; or another child.
Calming, non-rhythmic music best supports this activity; however, some rhythmic grounding can also be appropriate.
Using chiffon juggling scarves is a good place to start from, as they are both a good visual and qualitative support for the activity.

Approaching this task with curious exploration, children can start with gentle, unstructured improvised fluid movement, in their own body and through the space.

The concepts of inhale and exhale can be introduced with rising and falling and/or expanding and contracting movements in various ways through visual and/or verbal cues, working toward bringing an awareness to the breath itself.

Scarf breathing involves breathing in through the nose and out through the mouth, lifting the scarf in front of the face so that it moves away gently on the exhale. This can transition to lying on the floor to practice chest and belly breathing with the scarf or a small, soft toy.

Start with 3 breaths and gradually extend the rounds. With practice you may be surprised how long children will be willing to collectively engage with down regulating.

Benefits

Many children enjoy and benefit from some gentle pressure as an additional grounding element of closing the practice. Head, shoulder, arm/finger, and legs/ankles/feet squeezes can be helpful.

Variation

Partner breathing involves sitting back to back with legs crossed or outstretched; children take turns leading and following their partners' breath rhythm. Adding the element of gentle pressure can be incorporated by sharing body weight in a slow sway and/or see-saw action.

The QR code below will bring you to a printable version of all activities for Chapter 11. This material may also be accessed under the "Downloads" tab at https://www.tcpress.com/move-more-learn-more-9780807784051.

WHAT IS AUTISM MOVEMENT THERAPY®? (JOANNE LARA)

Autism Movement Therapy® (AMT) is an *empowering* strategy that improves connectivity in and between the left and right hemispheres of the brain by combining patterning, visual movement calculation, audile receptive processing, rhythm, and sequencing into a "whole brain" cognitive thinking approach that can significantly impact brain function and positively influence behavioral, emotional, social, speech and language, and academic skills for autistic/neurodivergent individuals.

The primary goal of AMT is that after repeated practice the individual will be better able to complete on-task activities, will interact with peers more frequently, and will be using both sides of the brain for processing. Increased overall self-determination as well as self and environmental awareness, along with improved self-esteem and greater independence, is the ultimate end goal.

What Is the Theory Behind AMT?

In autistic individuals, the left and right hemispheres of the brain are often not functioning cohesively. The left (analytic) or logical hemisphere of the brain is verbal, responds to word meaning, is sequential, processes information linearly, responds to logic and plans ahead, recalls people's names, is ordered, and prefers formal study. The right (global) or artistic hemisphere is visual, responds to tone of voice, is random, processes information in varied order, responds to emotion, nonverbal cues, is impulsive, recalls people's faces, and prefers sound or music in the background and frequent mobility while studying. Integration occurs across the corpus callosum, which serves as the conduit or bridge between the left and right hemispheres (Goldstein et al., 2023).

AMT is designed to cognitively redirect or remap the brain. Repetition of movement patterns and sequences establishes legitimate pathways or highways for the information to travel along. This helps with information processing and storing and retrieving information in a more efficient and effective manner. How can this be possible? Think of it this way: You buy a new home with a guest house in the backyard. No one has ever lived in the guest house, and the backyard grass is green and lovely and covers the entire yard. Someone moves into the guest house, and they use your laundry room, located at the back of your house. After a while, inevitably a pathway forms from the guest house to the laundry room. This is how we make new pathways in the brain, by having the information travel back and forth, over and over again, along the same white brain matter transmitters until the brain establishes that the traveled route is the preferred pathway to the stored information.

Parents and professionals will find the following "mis-association" example familiar. An autistic child goes to the park with his father. He sees a dog and as he leans down to pet it, his father looks up at the sky and says, "What a lovely blue sky." A month later the boy sees a dog at a friend's home. He immediately rushes over and as he lovingly pets the dog he says, "blue sky"—the words he cognitively mapped and stored in his memory bank during his trip to the park with his father. Because he is now re-experiencing the same activity, one that he enjoyed, his brain retrieves the words (speech) he heard from his father (receptive audio information) that were stored along with the picture of the dog (language) and the action of petting the dog (gross motor). When the child says, "blue sky," adults may then misinterpret the child as thinking the name of the dog is "Blue Sky." In actuality, the image of the dog was the visual trigger for the retrieval of the stored information in the boy's brain.

The difference in the processing, as in the above example, is a disconnect in areas of the brain affecting the interpretation of the information. We process information through audio, visual, and sensorimotor cues, which in turn become triggers. AMT harnesses these different forms of information processing and triggers in supporting the remapping of the brain. In doing AMT, students are simultaneously listening to instructions/responding to the music, using visual processing to see the instructors and their own physical image, and employing gross motor skills to be able to reproduce/imitate/mirror what they see.

What Does an AMT Session Look Like?

Doing AMT is fun, involving music and dance that appeals to all ages. The full program is available through live sessions delivered by a professional-level certified AMT practitioner. A library of prerecorded "Dance on Demand" sessions has been developed by MovementWorks, the global lead for Autism Movement Therapy® training. A method book is available as a reference book (Lara, 2015).

An AMT session is structured to include warm-up; stationary movement; locomotor movement; improvisation and creative tasks; cool-down; and relaxation. Activities are designed to scaffold, and through repetition and predictability, the student is able to move on to the next level when they have mastered the foundation movement patterns and sequences tempo and rhythms. In other words, they move on when they have "mapped" the patterns and sequences (information), and when their body will reliably respond to that information (triggers).

AMT can be applied for individuals with emerging gross and fine motor and cognitive skills, and basic imitation—Listen, See, and Do skills. Students do not have to have verbal skills or be able to follow a verbal instruction (expressive or receptive language) to access the work. However, more complex patterning and sequencing—with the addition of creative improvisation exercises that require imaginative novel contributions and working with others—support more able students to develop higher-level thinking and social skills and their overall personal and academic confidence.

How long that takes depends on each student, how easily the brain responds to the remapping, and how quickly transmitters are reorganized. The ultimate goal is that the student be able to execute tasks independently, without an adult model/prompt.

Cognitive redirection or remapping requires dedication and perseverance, along with the ideal balance of predictability, repetition, and novel challenge.

These are all elements intrinsic to the method. We all want our students to perform well and work on-task; mastering these basic skills can have an enormous impact in all other areas of learning. Autism Movement Therapy® stimulates the brain and wakes up areas that are dormant. But it is a journey, and no two individuals respond in exactly the same manner. AMT can be introduced to children as young as age 6 and is effective with teenagers and young adults, too.

AUTISM MOVEMENT THERAPY® ACTIVITIES

Activity #1: Mouse

Overview

Many autistic individuals struggle with body-spatial awareness. It may be more difficult to discern where the body ends and the environment begins. As Dr. Stephen Shore says in *Generation A: Portraits of Autism in the Arts*, "We take for granted we know where the back of a chair is, but an autistic person may not be able to tell. Movement helps sort that out!" (Shils, 2015).

Benefits

The following exercise focuses on the somatosensory area of the brain, which in neuroanatomical terms resides next to the primary motor cortex, meaning that when we consciously stimulate and bring these areas to awareness, we can expect better function.

Instructions

In the Mouse Activity, the student uses their fingertips to draw awareness to their body with light touch proprioceptive stimulation, by playfully wiggling their fingertips. Imagine how a mouse would groom themselves.

Starting at the very top of the body from the head, and drawing awareess to their hair, eyes, ears, nose, cheeks, and chin, the student then shifts to gentle tapping motions with the flat of their fingers to touch their chest (chest-chest—shoulder-shoulder—elbow-elbow—knee-knee—foot-foot), touching the body parts in opposition (crosslateral/contralateral movement). This exercise works best with increasing tempo (cognitive loading).

Further variations add more cognitive loading to the activities by keeping the beat with the feet (tempo) while responding to in-the-moment instructions for changes of direction.

Activity #2: Partner Clapping—Cross-Hemispheric Clapping

Benefits

This exercise is useful for students with limited language skills and/or social anxiety.
Partners sit *"criss-cross applesauce"* or stand opposite each other.
Both clap in front of the body, then reach across the midline of their body with their right hand and pat their partner's right hand, switching sides in tempo. This activity is best done to a steady drumbeat.
Once students master this activity, language can be added for cognitive loading: counting/letters of the alphabet. All numbers/letters are said by the first student; then the second student repeats the sequence.
Level up with an alternate partner and/or different sequence challenges.

Activity #3: Movements With Sounds

Overview

This exercise is highly suitable for pre-verbal students. Expressive language (sound articulation) *is movement*. Neuroanatomically, Broca's area, which resides in the left hemisphere and is associated with language production, lies specifically in the third frontal convolution, just anterior to the face area of the motor cortex.

Benefits

As highlighted earlier in this discussion, speech is neurologically connected with gesture, so when we consciously stimulate them simultaneously, we can get spoken language kicking in.

Instructions

Students sit on the floor in a circle. Each student leads (demonstrates) a movement with a sound (sounds, not words), and the whole group reproduces the student's movement and sound before moving on to the next student in the circle.
The student who has just led touches the student on their right on the knee or shoulder to let them know who is next to go.
Higher-level variations add more to the sequence and a memory element to the task.

Activity #4: Breathing Ball—Hoberman Sphere

Overview

Autistic individuals may struggle with any kind of transition. It is important to establish a closing ritual, and a three-breath reset is a useful tool to employ in an educational setting for use as group closing, for individual students in moments of anxiety/conflict, and as a technique for teaching self-regulation.

Benefits

With or without supporting music to anchor mood, this simple restorative breathing exercise uses a "breathing ball," or Hoberman sphere, as a visual focus and as a physical proprioceptive/interoceptive enhancing prop.

Instructions

Sit with legs straddled with a partner or in a group. The ball is rolled back and forth between participants for a few minutes, combining cooling down and gentle stretching with a proprioceptive and social interaction task. Then each student takes a turn (up to 3 breath rounds) to inhale and exhale with the ball opening and closing.

The QR code below will bring you to a printable PDF version of the Autism Movement Therapy® Activities. This material may also be accessed under the "Downloads" tab at https://www.tcpress.com/move-more-learn-more-9780807784051.

CONCLUSION

We want our children to be the best version of themselves they can be. Developmental Dance Movement® and Autism Movement Therapy® are artistic and scientific applications of an interdisciplinary approach among dance in education, occupational therapy, speech and language therapy, and dance movement therapy, working to enhance brain function and school performance, support other therapeutic and educational goals, and address complex learning and behavior challenges. These dance movement approaches impact upon areas that cross over to the behavioral and communication sciences, reflecting the complex interactions between physical experience, learning, behavior, and social interaction. In our most recently published paper (Golding et al., 2024), positive outcomes were identified by teachers, parents, and therapists of children participating in the MovementWorks® program. The next stage of the research is to develop a specific validated measurement tool aligned to the International Classification of Function (ICF).

REFERENCES

Amonkar, N., Su, W., Bhat, A., & Srinivasan, S. (2021). Effects of creative movement therapies on social communication, behavioral-affective, sensorimotor, cognitive, and functional participation skills of individuals with autism spectrum disorder: A systematic review. *Frontiers in Psychiatry*, *12*, 722874.

Arrowsmith-Young, B. (2012). *The woman who changed her brain*. Square Peg.

Bhat, A. (2020). Is motor impairment in autism spectrum disorder distinct from developmental coordination disorder? A report from the SPARK study. *Physical Therapy*, *100*(4), 633–644.

Brian, A., Pennell, A., Taunton, S., Starrett, A., Howard-Shaughnessy, C., Goodway, J., Wadsworth, D., Rudisill, M., & Stodden, D. (2019). Motor competence levels and developmental delay in early childhood: A multicenter cross-sectional study conducted in the USA. *Sports Medicine*, *49*(10), 1609–1618.

Bryck, R., & Fisher, P. (2012). Training the brain: Practical applications of neural plasticity from the intersection of cognitive neuroscience, developmental psychology, and prevention science. *American Psychologist*, *67*(2), 87–100.

Clough, S., & Duff, M. (2020). The role of gesture in communication and cognition: Implications for understanding and treating neurogenic communication disorders. *Frontiers in Human Neuroscience*, *14*(323).

Davis, E., Pitchford, N., & Limback, E. (2011). The interrelation between cognitive and motor development in typically developing children aged 4–11 years is underpinned by visual processing and fine manual control. *British Journal of Psychology*, *102*(3), 569–584.

Eddy, L., Bryant, E., Daly-Smith, A., & Wood, M. (2024). *A country that works for all children and young people: An evidence-based plan for supporting physical activity and healthy nutrition with and through education settings.* Children of the North.

Education Endowment Foundation. (2022). *Socio-economic attainment gap remains stubbornly wide after pandemic.* EEF. https://educationendowmentfoundation.org.uk/news/socio-economic-attainment-gap-remains-stubbornly-wide-after-pandemic-with-reading-skills-particularly-affected

Engel, A., Maye, A., Kurthen, M., & König, P. (2013). Where's the action? The pragmatic turn in cognitive science. *Trends in Cognitive Sciences*, *17*(5), 202–209.

Golding, A., Ambrose, Z., Lara, J., Malamateniou, C., & Green, D. (2024). Expectations and experiences of a dance programme for autistic children: A qualitative study of parents, teachers and therapists. *Journal of Research in Special Educational Needs*, *24*(3) 653–666.

Golding, A., Boes, C., & Nordin-Bates, S. (2016). Investigating learning through developmental dance movement as a kinaesthetic tool in the Early Years Foundation Stage. *Research in Dance Education, 17*(3), 235–267.

Goldstein, A., Covington, B., Mahabadi, N., & Mesfin, F. (2023). *Neuroanatomy, corpus callosum.* StatPearls Publishing.

Gutek, G. L. (Ed.). (2004). *The Montessori method: The origins of an educational innovation: Including an abridged and annotated edition of Maria Montessori's The Montessori method.* Rowman & Littlefield Publishers.

Hamilton, L. (2022). Human song: Separate neural pathways for melody and speech. *Current Biology, 32*(7), R311–R313.

Hardy, M., & LaGasse, A. (2013). Rhythm, movement, and autism: Using rhythmic rehabilitation research as a model for autism. *Frontiers in Integrative Neuroscience, 7*(19).

Hobbs, A., & Bernard, R. (2021). The impact of COVID-19 on early childhood education and care. *Education Journal Review, 27*(3), 17.

Jabr, F. (2021). *John A. Long—publications list.* Publicationslist.org, *14*(6).

Ketcheson, L., Hauck, J., & Ulrich, D. (2016). The effects of an early motor skill intervention on motor skills, levels of physical activity, and socialization in young children with autism spectrum disorder: A pilot study. *Autism, 21*(4), 481–492.

Kirk, M., & Rhodes, R. (2011). Motor skill interventions to improve fundamental movement skills of preschoolers with developmental delay. *Adapted Physical Activity Quarterly, 28*(3), 210–232.

Lara, J., with Bowers, K. (2015). *Autism Movement Therapy® method: Waking up the brain!* Jessica Kingsley Publishers.

Leisman, G., Melillo, R., & Melillo, T. (2023). Prefrontal functional connectivities in autism spectrum disorders: A connectopathic disorder affecting movement, interoception, and cognition. *Brain Research Bulletin, 198,* 65–76.

Llinas, R. (2002). *I of the vortex: From neurons to self.* MIT Press.

Makaton. (n.d.). *About Makaton.* Makaton.org.

Norris, E., van Steen, T., Direito, A., & Stamatakis, E. (2020). Physically active lessons in schools and their impact on physical activity, educational, health and cognition outcomes: A systematic review and meta-analysis. *British Journal of Sports Medicine, 54*(14), 826–838.

Ohara, R., Kanejima, Y., Kitamura, M., & Izawa, K. (2019). Association between social skills and motor skills in individuals with autism spectrum disorder: A systematic review. *European Journal of Investigation in Health, Psychology and Education, 10*(1), 276–296.

Powell, L., Spencer, S., Clegg, J., & Wood, M. (2024). *A country that works for all children and young people: An evidence-based approach to supporting children in the preschool years.* Child of the North.

Rintala, P., Pienimäki, K., Ahonen, T., Cantell, M., & Kooistra, L. (1998). The effects of a psychomotor training programme on motor skill development in children with developmental language disorders. *Human Movement Science, 17*(4–5), 721–737.

Savanta. (2024). *School Readiness Survey.* https://kindredsquared.org.uk/wp-content/uploads/2024/02/Kindred-Squared-School-Readiness-Report-February-2024.pdf

Shils, B. (Director). (2015). *Generation A: Portraits of autism in the arts* [Film]. Goldstreet Pictures & Autism Movement Therapy.

Stamou, A., Roussy, A., Ockelford, A., & Terzi, L. (2019). The effectiveness of a music and dance program on the task engagement and inclusion of young pupils on the autism spectrum. *Music & Science, 2*.

Su, W., Amonkar, N., Cleffi, C., Srinivasan, S., & Bhat, A. (2022). Neural effects of physical activity and movement interventions in individuals with developmental disabilities–A systematic review. *Frontiers in Psychiatry, 13*, 794652.

Taylor, R. (2021). *Covid-19: Impact on child poverty and on young people's education, health and wellbeing*. House of Lords Library. https://lordslibrary.parliament.uk/covid-19-impact-on-child-poverty-and-on-young-peoples-education-health-and-wellbeing

TEDXTalks (2017). *Why Movement Works for Learning/Ali Golding.* YouTube.

Thaut, M., McIntosh, G., & Hoemberg, V. (2015). Neurobiological foundations of neurologic music therapy: Rhythmic entrainment and the motor system. *Frontiers in Psychology, 5*(1185).

Tversky, B. (2019). *Mind in motion: How action shapes thought*. Basic Books.

University of Leeds. (2024). *New school starters not ready for learning*. Author.

University of Stirling. (2024). *Only 1 in 10 children meet global health guidelines, researchers discover*. Medicalxpress.com; Medical Xpress.

Wolpert, D. (2011, July). *The real reason for brains*. In TED Conferences.

Woo, C., & Leon, M. (2013). Environmental enrichment as an effective treatment for autism: A randomized controlled trial. *Behavioral Neuroscience, 127*(4), 487–497.

Wright, K., Furzer, B., Licari, M., Thornton, A., Dimmock, J., Naylor, L., Reid, S., Kwan, S., & Jackson, B. (2019). Physiological characteristics, self-perceptions, and parental support of physical activity in children with, or at risk of, developmental coordination disorder. *Research in Developmental Disabilities, 84*, 66–74. Science Direct.

CHAPTER 12

Promoting Social Connections Through Group Activities

Andy Milne, United States

During early childhood, children learn to navigate the complexities of relationships, from understanding others' perspectives to managing their own emotions (Thompson, 2015). Positive social interactions in early childhood foster emotional well-being and lay the foundation for essential life skills like cooperation, empathy, and effective communication (Hosokawa et al., 2024). Considering that many adults themselves find these skills challenging, it is necessary to intentionally provide children with regular opportunities to practice and develop them through age-appropriate activities. Suppose the high hopes mentioned earlier include a lifetime of meaningful relationships, resilience, collaboration, conflict management, and successful engagement in group settings. In that case, you can nurture social connections by harnessing the benefits of structured and unstructured physical play and physical education activities.

The purpose of this chapter is to explore how adults can promote meaningful social connections among children aged 3–9 through intentional design and facilitation of age-appropriate physical activities. Practical strategies and inclusive approaches are provided for educators, caregivers, and community leaders to feel empowered to harness the benefits of a variety of movement-based experiences. This chapter aims to inspire thoughtful, developmentally appropriate practices prioritizing connection, inclusion, and joy in early childhood physical activity settings.

SOCIAL-RELATIONAL CONNECTIONS

I have fond memories from early childhood, thriving in environments that allowed me to move and explore beyond the confines of a desk. Only now do I recognize the purpose behind those fun activities and the opportunities they provided to connect with my peers in a shared space.

Simple games of tag, team-building challenges, and cooperative activities like parachute play encouraged my classmates and me to work together, communicate, and problem-solve in real time. We made friends, strengthened bonds (or resolved disputes), and improved our motor skills, coordination, and overall fitness. We practiced taking turns, sharing implements, helping one another, and fostering a sense of belonging and community. These skills and experiences continue to shape me as an adult, reminding me that growth in these areas is a lifelong journey.

If life is indeed a journey, then these early years see children develop at quite a speed, and as such, we need to modify our spaces, games, and activities to suit the developmental milestones in both social and physical domains. Creating inclusive and engaging group activities requires thoughtful planning to accommodate children with diverse skill levels, abilities, and interests.

At age 3, children begin to understand the concept of sharing and are learning to communicate their needs and emotions (Malik, 2022). By age 5, many children can participate in cooperative play, showing the ability to take turns and follow simple group rules (Malik, 2022). By age 8, they are more adept at forming friendships, resolving minor conflicts independently, and demonstrating empathy toward others (Malik, 2022). These years are pivotal for teaching children how to navigate group dynamics, as they are naturally curious and eager to explore their environment through play.

THE MOVEMENT LENS

Planning and leveraging age-appropriate activities becomes clearer and more manageable once we see our time with young children through a movement lens. This lens is whole-child, student-centered, and physical. This can be achieved with the following:

- Offering variations or modifications within activities can help ensure meaningful participation by all children. For instance, in a game of tag, providing alternate movement options, such as walking instead of running or allowing a "safe zone" for children who need breaks, can help foster inclusivity.
- Connecting with others while engaging within individual comfort levels can be attained by mixing personal and cooperative challenges.
- A sense of belonging and teamwork develops when we encourage peer support and give children opportunities to work together to problem-solve or assist one another. Ask a child what supporting someone looks, sounds, and feels like, and they'll impress you with their responses.

- We can promote inclusion by using clear, simple instructions and offering choices within activities, allowing children to select roles or tasks that align with their strengths and preferences.

By intentionally designing activities that embrace a range of abilities and interests, adults create an environment where every child feels valued, supported, and engaged in meaningful social interactions. This approach benefits young children in the moment and lays the foundation for them to become compassionate, collaborative, and confident individuals who contribute positively to society. Furthermore, by fostering a love for movement through inclusive and enjoyable experiences, we increase the likelihood that they will carry an active lifestyle into adulthood, embracing physical activity as a lifelong pursuit. Everybody benefits from movement.

Advocating for movement is crucial. This means recognizing the profound impact of physical activity on young children's development, including embracing physical health, cognitive abilities, emotional well-being, and social skills, to ensure that its importance is widely understood. As educators, parents, and caregivers, we are responsible for sharing our knowledge and success stories with others, whether through conversations with colleagues within our building, discussions with families within our community, or influencing local and statewide policies that prioritize movement-based learning. By championing the value of structured and unstructured physical play, we can inspire others to embrace and implement meaningful movement experiences for children. The more we advocate, the more we can collectively ensure that every child can thrive socially, emotionally, and physically.

The QR code below will bring you to a printable version of all the activities for Chapter 12. This material may also be accessed under the "Downloads" tab at https://www.tcpress.com/move-more-learn-more-9780807784051.

Creating Groups/Teams Activity

Creating groups for activities or teams can be challenging at times. Friendship groups are reluctant to separate, or athletic students often want to stick together if they sense that competition is coming.

The following engaging activity helps children form groups and fosters social connections by encouraging them to discover commonalities with their peers. It's a simple yet powerful way to nudge children out of their comfort zones in a supportive and low-pressure manner. The activity can be easily modified based on the children's developmental stage and the teacher's needs.

In an open space, the teacher calls out a category or theme, and students must quickly form groups based on their responses. For younger children, the categories should be more concrete, such as "Do you prefer cats or dogs?" or "What's your favorite ice cream flavor—chocolate, vanilla, or strawberry?" For older children, the prompts can be more open-ended, such as "What's your favorite season?" or "Choose a group based on your favorite color," allowing for more individuality and naturally varying group sizes.

To deepen the experience, conclude the activity with a connection-building prompt. Once in their final groups, ask children to high-five or fist-bump their group members and work together to identify three things they have in common. This act reinforces a sense of belonging and highlights shared interests, laying the foundation for stronger peer relationships and a more inclusive community.

Tag Games

Tag games remain a staple of childhood play, but thankfully, modern variations have moved away from elimination, survival of the most agile, and rough two-handed tagging. Best practices mean that today's tag games prioritize safety, inclusivity, and engagement for all participants. These games provide opportunities for children to develop physical skills such as agility, coordination, and spatial awareness while reinforcing social-emotional skills like teamwork, empathy, and problem-solving.

To ensure a fun and safe experience, the adult should begin by modeling an appropriate two-finger tag, demonstrating a light and controlled touch instead of a forceful tag. This step helps prevent unnecessary collisions or rough play while reinforcing respect for personal space—an essential skill in movement and social interactions. Framing the game around this safe tagging method allows children to feel more comfortable and confident in participating.

Many modern tag games incorporate different roles to keep all children engaged and promote teamwork. For example, rather than having tagged players remain frozen indefinitely, introduce a designated "rescuer" role. This student might unfreeze a tagged player by offering a high-five, linking elbows, or performing a quick movement task like a squat or a jump together. Playing the role of a rescuer develops leadership, responsibility, and cooperative problem-solving, as students must be aware of their surroundings and support their peers.

Modifications to tag include lower-paced movement, such as skipping or walking instead of running. Consider playing shadow tag, where children step on each other's shadows instead of physically tagging their peers, or amoeba tag, where those who are tagged join hands to form a line (amoeba) of taggers.

By modifying traditional tag games to include safe tagging techniques and varied roles, educators create a dynamic environment where every child—regardless of speed, confidence, or ability—can actively participate, enjoy movement, and strengthen physical and social skills.

Activity #1: Amoeba Tag

Decide on a safe playing surface and area. The boundary will be the confines of the game. With the remaining players spread around the playing area, select two players who are "it"; they are the amoeba. These two players join hands and travel together searching for players to tag. Tagged players join the amoeba and the tagging continues until the amoeba numbers four players, whereupon the amoeba splits down the middle into two. Play continues as amoebas grow and divide until the last person is tagged. Facilitators can look for and acknowledge cooperation, communication, encouragement, empathy, and leadership from the players.

WALKING ACTIVITIES

Walking activities provide a natural and accessible way to foster positive social interactions, support emotional well-being, and build essential life skills in early childhood. Unlike competitive or high-energy games, walking activities create a safe and relaxed environment where children can engage in conversation, observe their surroundings, and connect with their peers meaningfully.

When children walk together—whether on a nature walk, a themed scavenger hunt, or a simple partner walk—they practice cooperation by matching each other's pace, navigating shared spaces, and taking turns leading or following. Walk in time to music or instruct children to move like their favorite animal, and you can see how we can take this simple activity in so many directions. These activities encourage empathy as children become more aware of their peers' needs, whether slowing down for a friend, waiting at a designated spot, or offering a helping hand. Walking side by side also fosters effective communication, giving children opportunities to share observations, ask questions, and engage in storytelling, all of which contribute to their social-emotional development.

Beyond social benefits, walking activities support emotional regulation by providing a calming and rhythmic movement that can reduce stress and enhance focus. When used intentionally, these activities can be powerful tools for setting a positive tone, reinforcing a sense of community, and ensuring that all children—regardless of skill level or ability—feel included and connected.

Considering that almost 60% of adults walked for leisure in the past 7 days, we see how valuable walking is as a lifelong movement practice (Adjaye-Gbewonyo & Briones, 2024). When we are intentional about *how* students walk, *where* they walk, *how often* they walk, and *who* they walk with, we transform a simple activity into something significant and lay the groundwork for a lifetime of movement.

Activity #2: Lovely/Unlovely Walk

Take a walk with your children, challenging them to identify as many lovely or pleasing things as possible. The "lovely list" might include sights and sounds, the natural or built environment, smells, or sensations. Now ask the children to add to an "unlovely list," identifying things around them that don't give them pleasure. The culminating task is to find something positive in the things on the "unlovely list." Litter reminds us that we can all do our part in caring for the environment; noisy trucks might be delivering food to stores for us to eat, and unpleasant-looking trees provide shelter when it rains.

Facilitators can ask guiding questions to the young walkers, encouraging them to connect with one another and the environment. This question-guided walk, along with many others, can be found in *A Walking Curriculum: Evoking Wonder and Developing a Sense of Place (K–12)* (Judson, 2018).

Relay Games

Relay games are a favorite among young children because they are fast-paced, exciting, and energetic. They certainly sound as exciting as they look, but beyond the fun, they also offer valuable opportunities to develop essential life skills such as cooperation, patience, and communication. At their core, relay games teach children how to take turns—a fundamental social skill that requires both self-regulation and an awareness of others. While waiting their turn, children practice managing anticipation, supporting teammates, and understanding that success is a shared effort rather than an individual pursuit. The nature of relay games provides adults with the perfect setting to observe the children in their care. Do they cheer on their peers, show patience, or express frustration? During transitions, do they communicate effectively with teammates, offer encouragement, or struggle with the pressure of performing? By paying attention to body language, facial expressions, and verbal interactions, adults can identify children who need support in developing patience, resilience, or confidence and step in with meaningful interventions.

It is important to be intentional about structure and tone to ensure that relay games foster positive social interactions rather than overly competitive dynamics. Teachers and caregivers can emphasize teamwork over winning by designing relays that focus on collective achievement rather than speed alone. Cooperative relays encourage children to work together toward a common goal rather than racing against one another.

For example, instead of a traditional race, children could take turns gathering puzzle pieces or building blocks and work as a team to assemble the final structure. Another variation might involve collecting and sorting different-colored objects, where each player's contribution brings the group closer to completing a shared task. Relays involving transferring water to fill a container, moving objects without using hands, or passing a ball creatively promote problem-solving, teamwork, and inclusive participation.

By framing relay games as opportunities for collaboration rather than competition, we allow children to develop a sense of belonging, mutual support, and shared success. This reinforces the idea that movement is not just about winning but about working together, celebrating effort, and appreciating the process.

Activity #3: Hula Hoop Tower Relay

For each team, lay out six hula hoops in a straight line with space between each one. Use cones to mark a clear starting line where teams will line up.

To start the game, teams line up behind the starting line/cone. Give one beanbag to each team. The first player runs from the team to the nearest hula hoop and stands inside it. A teammate at the starting line throws them a beanbag. If it is caught, the player returns to their team with the beanbag and hoop. If it is dropped, the player leaves the hoop and returns with the beanbag. The next teammate runs to that hoop and tries again. The relay continues, with each player running to the next available hoop (each one getting progressively farther away), catching the beanbag and returning with the hoop. Once all six hoops have been collected, the team works cooperatively to build a Hula Hoop Tower using the hoops. This cooperative relay allows facilitators to discuss frustration and perseverance, as well as encouragement and leadership, with the participants.

PARACHUTE PLAY

Watch children's expressions at the mere mention of parachute games. It could be the bright colors, the tactile nature of the parachute itself, or the thought of small bodies controlling such a large item, but there is something unique to parachute games. They are a powerful tool for fostering positive social interactions, emotional well-being, and essential life skills in early childhood. Unlike competitive activities, parachute play naturally encourages cooperation, with every child working together to make the parachute move in unison. Whether shaking it to create waves, lifting it high to form a tent, or working as a team to keep a ball bouncing on top, children quickly learn that success depends on collaboration rather than individual achievement. This shared experience strengthens teamwork and nurtures a sense of belonging and collective accomplishment.

Modifying our spaces, games, and activities to suit developmental milestones in both social and physical domains can be challenging, and that is where parachute games come into their element. I have had great success in using parachutes with diverse groups of students, and this is one activity where every child, regardless of ability, can find a meaningful role. Whether a child takes on a leadership role by calling out commands, enjoys the sensory experience of the fabric moving through their hands, or delights in the cooperative nature of the play, parachute games ensure that no one is left out.

Parachute play also provides opportunities for children to develop empathy and effective communication. As they work together to control the parachute, they must listen, take turns leading, and adjust their movements based on the group's rhythm and pace. Games that require eye contact and verbal coordination, such as calling out a peer's name before swapping places under the parachute, help children practice social awareness and build connections with others. Additionally, parachute activities can be calming and emotionally supportive, especially when using slow, rhythmic movements that create a soothing, sensory-friendly experience.

By incorporating parachute play into early childhood settings, adults can create a playful yet structured environment that nurtures essential social-emotional skills. Encouraging children to reflect upon and appreciate their role in the group reinforces the importance of teamwork, respect, and shared joy in movement.

Activity #4: Parachute Igloo Activity

Set up a safe, open space where the parachute can be spread out fully. Have all participants stand around the edge of the parachute, evenly spaced, holding the handles with both hands.

This activity aims for all participants to work together to create an igloo shape by lifting the parachute high and quickly sitting down inside, trapping air. You can stay here until the parachute floats to the ground. For this to work well, everyone must communicate, time their movements together, and listen to the group leader.

This activity is ideal for designating a young leader to give the commands:

"Up!" Everyone lifts the parachute high above their heads. "Under!" Everyone takes a small step in and pulls the parachute behind them, ready to sit on the edge.

Facilitators can find many age-appropriate parachute games at OPEN Physical Education Curriculum (www.openphysed.org).

RECESS

In England, recess is known as "playtime," highlighting its purpose. However, not all recess experiences are the same, making it essential to distinguish between unstructured and structured play. Understanding this difference helps us see how each supports a child's development and reinforces adults' important role in creating a positive and successful playground experience.

Unstructured play allows children to explore, create, and engage in their own chosen activities. This type of play fosters creativity, independence, and problem-solving, giving children the space to navigate social interactions, negotiate roles, and practice self-regulation. However, unstructured play does not mean unsupervised or unsupported play. Without guidance, conflicts may arise, exclusion may occur, and some children may struggle to engage. Therefore, it is recommended that adults support positive behaviors by teaching and reinforcing rules, protocols, and expectations for recess and the consequences of not following them. Teaching children how to prevent or handle conflicts can promote positive behavior, leading to a more inclusive and enjoyable play experience where all children feel valued, respected, and empowered to engage

In 2017 the Centers for Disease Control and Prevention and SHAPE America (Society of Health and Physical Educators) released a report titled *Strategies for Recess in Schools*, which defined recess, highlighted its benefits, and provided guidance for the implementation of recess. The highlighted guidance includes separating recess and physical education, providing adequate (and safe) spaces and equipment, not excluding students for behavioral or academic reasons, not using physical activity as punishment during recess, providing recess before lunch, and providing supervisory individuals with professional development.

Structured play, conversely, provides more defined activities with clear expectations, whether through organized games, teacher-facilitated activities, or guided play scenarios. This type of play is particularly beneficial for teaching cooperation, turn-taking, and conflict resolution, as children receive direct support in developing positive social behaviors.

For recess to be effective in fostering social and emotional well-being, adults must actively teach children *how* to play. This includes modeling appropriate interactions, demonstrating how to include others, and equipping children with simple strategies to resolve conflicts independently. Teaching students how to initiate a game, handle losing with grace, or invite a peer to join can make the difference between a recess filled with connection and one marked by frustration or isolation.

While recess might feel like a break, it is far from that. Adults still have an active role in providing adequate supervision and guidance, ensuring appropriate behavior, and reducing injury. Students, too, might be taking a "brain break" from the classroom, but the learning continues. Recess is an excellent learning opportunity for young children; they can even be involved in your planning. Ask children what games they like and what equipment they need, and you start to develop their young advocacy voices. Providing children with a safe and engaging recess experience will create an army of young voices that will speak up in support of recess should it ever be devalued by decision-makers in your community.

One of my advocacy passions is raising awareness of the benefits of providing recess. Recess is not a privilege to be earned—it is a fundamental right that supports the healthy development of young children (Mader, 2022). Too often, recess is withheld because of misbehavior or unfinished work when unstructured playtime is one of the most effective tools for addressing the very challenges that lead to these issues (Lee et al., 2020). Recess provides children with the movement, social interaction, and brain breaks they need to regulate their emotions, improve focus, and develop essential problem-solving skills. When we deny children recess, we are not just taking away play—we are taking away opportunities for them to build resilience, manage their energy, and learn cooperation through natural interactions.

As advocates for children's well-being, we must push for policies that protect recess as a non-negotiable part of the school day. Through conversations with school leaders and parent groups, or through policy initiatives, we need to shift the mindset from seeing recess as an earned reward to recognizing it as an essential component of a child's physical, social, and emotional development. Investigate whether your state is one of those who have enacted laws to ensure that recess is a protected and integral part of the school day for young children. In 2018, 20 states had a law recommending or requiring recess (Clevenger et al., 2022). And, as of 2023, California, Louisiana, Washington, Georgia, Illinois, Arkansas, New Jersey, Arizona, Florida, Rhode Island, Connecticut, Missouri, and Virginia all had laws on the books requiring recess (https://kidsneedrecess.com/states/). Several other states had recess laws pending, and yet others have physical activity laws but no recess laws. Twenty-three states have no recess or physical activity laws.

Recess naturally reinforces cooperation, empathy, and communication, laying a foundation for positive interactions that extend far beyond the playground. For those reasons, recess must be viewed as a right, not a reward.

TEAM-BASED AND SPORT-INSPIRED ACTIVITIES

Sports provide many of us with teams to follow and athletes to emulate. Just as adults come together to "root, root, root for the home team," young children also cheer for their favorite players, imitate their moves, and bring that enthusiasm into their play. Team games and sport-inspired activities can incorporate elements of traditional sports while being thoughtfully modified to emphasize fun, effort, and teamwork over winning. Games like balloon volleyball or kickball with smaller fields and soft balls introduce young children to the structure and teamwork of more complex sports like softball and baseball, while keeping the focus on fun and skill development. Although competition will inevitably find its place in children's lives as they grow, we can harness the unique benefits of team play to foster a growth mindset, emotional well-being, and social connection in a supportive, dynamic environment.

By mixing skill levels and personalities, adults can create an atmosphere where inclusive play flourishes, limiting the tendency for a few dominant players to overshadow others. Modeling supportive language and openly acknowledging acts of cooperation help children feel valued, reinforcing the idea that good teammates contribute beyond just skill. This might sound like "I'm proud of you for cooperating with each other," "I like how you all support each other," or "Thank you for sharing and cooperating. It makes it easier for others to do the same for you." We want children to be someone others want to play with, uplifting and including those around them. When adults step in to guide children through disagreements and rule disputes, they equip them with the tools to manage conflict independently as they grow.

Sport-inspired activities also provide a natural setting for emotional regulation (Martín-Rodríguez et al., 2024). Success and setbacks are both part of the experience, giving children a safe space to navigate frustration, disappointment, and excitement in real time. Learning to manage emotions in the context of play—whether celebrating a shared victory or bouncing back from a mistake—builds resilience. When children see positive reactions modeled by peers and supportive adults, they develop healthier ways to cope with challenges on and off the field.

Beyond childhood, the benefits of these early team-based experiences extend into essential life skills. Playing in teams teaches children to work with others while recognizing and responding to their own emotions. Children also strengthen their ability to understand different perspectives and communicate and collaborate effectively. Encouraging both verbal and nonverbal communication during play builds confidence in expressing thoughts, listening to peers, and offering encouragement. These valuable skills will serve them well in later life.

Structured team-based and sport-inspired play offers more than physical skill development—it plays a significant role in developing children into empathetic, communicative, and cooperative individuals. When adults prioritize inclusive, well-facilitated play experiences, they lay the groundwork for children to be successful not just in games, but in life.

CONCLUSION

A child's relationship with movement starts during their foundational years, connecting and collaborating with others through shared experiences. Understanding and harnessing the power of purposeful physical activity and inclusive experiences enables us to equip children with the social and emotional tools needed to thrive. As a "movement advocate," you understand that what we are doing is more than keeping children active; there is meaning behind our methods and depth to our actions. We can foster a generation of confident, compassionate individuals who understand and value teamwork, empathy, and joy. When we prioritize and advocate for positive movement experiences for children, we help them develop skills that will serve them far beyond the playground and into adulthood.

REFERENCES

Adjaye-Gbewonyo, D., & Briones, E. (2024). *Walking for leisure and transportation among adults: United States*. National Center for Health Statistics Data Brief. https://www.cdc.gov/nchs/products/databriefs/db504.htm

Centers for Disease Control and Prevention and SHAPE America—Society of Health and Physical Educators (2017). *Strategies for recess in schools*. https://www.shapeamerica.org/MemberPortal/standards/guidelines/strategies_for_recess_in_schools.aspx

Clevenger, K., Perna, F., Moser, R., & Berrigan D. (2022). Associations between state laws governing recess policy with children's physical activity and health. *Journal of School Health*, 92(10), 976–986.

Hosokawa, R., Matsumoto, Y., Nishida, C., Funato, K., & Mitani, A. (2024). Enhancing social-emotional skills in early childhood: Intervention study on the effectiveness of social and emotional learning. *BMC Psychology*, 12(1), 761.

Judson, G. (2018). *A walking curriculum: Evoking wonder and developing a sense of place (K–12)*. KDP/Canadian ISBN Service.

Lee, R., Lane, S., Brown, G., Leung, C., Kwok, S., & Chan, S. (2020). Systematic review of the impact of unstructured play interventions to improve young children's physical, social, and emotional wellbeing. *Nursing & Health Sciences*, 22(2), 184–196.

Mader, J. (May 12, 2022). Kids' access to research varies greatly. *The Hechinger Report*. https://hechingerreport.org/kids-access-to-recess-varies-greatly/

Malik, F., & Marwaha, R. (2022). Developmental stages of social emotional development in children. StatPearls Publishing. https://www.ncbi.nlm.nih.gov/books/NBK534819/

Martín-Rodríguez, A., Gostian-Ropotin, L., Beltrán-Velasco, A., Belando-Pedreño, N., Simón, J., López-Mora, C., Navarro-Jiménez, E., Tornero-Aguilera, J., & Clemente-Suárez, V. (2024). Sporting mind: The interplay of physical activity and psychological health. *Sports (Basel)*, 12(1), 37.

Thompson, R. (2015). Infancy and childhood: Emotional development. In J. D. Wright (Ed.), *International Encyclopedia of the Social & Behavioral Sciences, Volume 26*. Elsevier.

CHAPTER 13

Creating Meaningful Movement Experiences Before, During, and After School

Andy Vasily, Belgium

Keeping children active throughout the school day is crucial for their physical, mental, emotional, and social well-being (Llewellyn et al., 2022). While encouraging movement is essential, we can be more precise, intentional, and purposeful in designing activities before, during, and after school to engage every child more deeply in physical activity.

This chapter explores a specific framework that centers students in their own physical activity and movement learning. This framework allows all students to find their entry points into physical activity by exploring what is possible. Whether through before-school clubs, physical education lessons, recess, or after-school programs, movement activities can be designed with much more intentionality to meet each student's skill level while also considering their relationship with physical activity, sport, and movement. The key takeaways or goals for the reader intended in this chapter include the following:

- Emphasizing the profound impact of student-driven exploration and self-assessment
- Creating meaningful movement experiences
- Understanding why exploration in movement matters
- Pedagogical strategies to deepen learning and engagement
- An example of one student's success with this type of engagement
- Developing self-assessment capabilities with our young learners
- How to approach the end of units or clubs

The aim of applying such a framework is to provide the psychological safety and trust needed for each young person to participate in physical activity in ways that are truly relevant and meaningful to them. In this chapter, you'll find practical examples of how to implement these strategies and use entrance/exit ticket assessments to help students reflect on their learning and continually improve their skills. The goal is to help pre-K through 3rd-grade students find more meaning and joy in their movement experiences before, during, and after school.

In her book *The Differentiated Classroom: Responding to the Needs of All Learners*, Tomlinson (2014) writes:

> In differentiated classrooms, assessment is diagnostic and ongoing. It provides teachers with day-to-day data on students' readiness for particular ideas and skills, their interests, and their approaches to learning. These teachers don't see assessment as something that comes at the end of a unit to find out what students learned (or didn't learn); rather, assessment is today's means of understanding how to modify tomorrow's instruction. (p. 17)

Therefore, the approach in this chapter is to involve students in the ongoing assessment and exploration process so that it becomes learner driven.

A PERSONAL JOURNEY: FINDING PURPOSE THROUGH MOVEMENT

Growing up in a dysfunctional family marked by mental health challenges and addiction, physical activity and sport became my escape from a turbulent and often violent environment. They gave me meaning and purpose and led to incredible opportunities along my journey. I have experienced the profound loss of two brothers—one to suicide and the other to drug addiction. Yet, through these hardships, physical activity and sports gave me a different lens through which to look at my life. These pursuits helped me forge essential social connections, encouraged me to strive for my best self, and allowed me to find meaning in significant ways.

This personal journey led me to a career in education, where I've had the privilege of connecting with young people around the globe. Over the past 25 years, I have worked in educational organizations across Japan, Azerbaijan, Cambodia, China, Saudi Arabia, and Belgium. What I've seen is that regardless of country or culture, young people share a natural love for movement in all its forms. Yet many barriers can hinder their intrinsic motivation to engage in physical activity and sports in ways that resonate with them.

THE MISSION: CREATING MEANINGFUL MOVEMENT EXPERIENCES

My mission has become clear: to help build programs that consistently create the conditions for students to find genuine meaning and purpose in movement—whether through team sports or individual pursuits. Schools play a critical role in this engagement, whether it is before, during, or after school—through clubs or physical education classes. We have the unique opportunity to introduce students to a wide variety of activities that highlight many forms of physical engagement and expression.

EXPLORATION BEFORE EXPLANATION

A transformative conversation with Professor Guy Clayton on my podcast in 2019 crystallized a core principle of my approach: "Exploration Before Explanation." As Carl Sagan once said, "Somewhere, something incredible is waiting to be explored." This principle fundamentally shapes how we should approach physical education and sports programming.

WHY EXPLORATION MATTERS

Too often, schools and teachers place enormous pressure on students to immediately demonstrate knowledge without providing genuine opportunities for exploration. Our role as educators is to reveal what may be possible for students based on their unique needs and experiences. When students are encouraged to explore freely, they

- Engage more deeply with physical activities
- Develop critical thinking skills
- Take ownership of their learning journey
- Build confidence through self-directed discovery
- Feel psychologically safe to try new things.

Table 13.1 provides a brief overview of what this type of exploration could look like in both before- and after-school programs, as well as during physical education classes. It is broken up into Program, Structure, and Key Elements.

PEDAGOGICAL STRATEGIES TO DEEPEN LEARNING AND ENGAGEMENT

Our shared goal as physical educators remains constant across cultures: to deeply engage young learners in physical activity and sports and to provide safe and accessible entry points for their growth and skill development (Greenberg et al., 2024). Through the framework of exploration before explanation, we can create environments where students discover their own path to physical literacy and lifelong enjoyment of movement.

Table 13.1. Implementing the Exploration Before Explanation Approach: Three Real-World Applications

Program	Structure	Key Elements
Before-School Health and Fitness Club (Grades 2–3)	6-week program 3 sessions/week, 45 minutes each First 2 weeks focus on exploration; 4 rotating activity stations: 1. Small-sided modified basketball or soccer 2. Strength exercises (burpees, push-ups, sit-ups) 3. Jump rope 4. Running/interval training or yoga	Students rotate through stations each session. Focus on experiencing different forms of physical activity. Regular reflection through exit tickets or partner discussions. Driving questions to guide exploration: • What was most challenging? • How did your body feel? • Which activities resonated most with you?
During-School PE Lessons: Net/Racket Sports Unit	6-week unit First 2 weeks dedicated to exploration Multiple stations featuring different sports: • Badminton • Table Tennis • Tennis • Pickleball	• Modified equipment for accessibility • Differentiated challenges at each station • Focus on individual and partner activities • Regular reflection and feedback • Emphasis on finding appropriate challenge levels
After-School Sports Clubs	• Sport-specific exploration stations • Modified equipment for different skill levels • Focus on discovery rather than drill-and-skill	• Multiple entry points for diverse abilities • Emphasis on personal challenge and growth

The Foundation: Making Learning Visible

As Hattie (2012) emphasizes,

> Good learning intentions are those that make clear to the student the type of level of performance that they need to attain, so that they understand where and when to invest energies, strategies, and thinking, and where they are positioned along the trajectory towards successful learning. (p. 52)

The very best educators and coaches excel at helping students understand not just expectations and routines, but what success truly looks like. They make this process student-driven, placing learners at the heart of their own journey and consistently empowering them by activating their voice throughout the process. You will see how the following strategies actively assist learners through exploration and self-reflection, allowing the learning (and hopefully success) to become visible.

Exit and Entrance Ticket Strategies. During the exploration phase of any movement or physically active lesson, we guide students through well-designed stations while asking key reflection questions:

- What was most challenging for you?
- What skills are necessary for you to be successful?
- What were you able to do well?
- What were these experiences like for you?

These questions can be implemented through several effective strategies that place students at the center of their own learning. This gives them ownership of their journeys and gets them more invested in developing important success criteria in the units being explored.

- ***Walk and Talk (2 minutes):*** Students pair up and walk around the gym or outdoor space, sharing their thoughts on the guiding questions. Upon return, they write answers on sticky notes and place them on a central board or poster. This strategy works both as an exit ticket and as an entrance ticket for the next session.
- ***Elbow Buddy Strategy:*** Like a walk and talk, but students remain seated and discuss with a partner nearby. They then document their reflections on sticky notes for the communal board of learning. Making this learning visible provides important anchors for both students and teachers.
- ***End-of-Session Line-Up:*** As students prepare to leave, they share one key insight with the teacher, who documents patterns in a journal. This efficient approach helps identify common themes quickly.

Seeking Patterns in Student Responses

Teachers analyze student responses during weeks 3–4 of a unit or club to identify common themes. For example, it could look like this:

Before-School Health and Fitness Club
- Early fatigue during exercise
- Limited endurance in skipping
- Challenges with body weight exercises
- Sprint endurance concerns

Net/Racket Sports Unit
- Challenges with forehand and backhand shots
- Difficulty controlling the ball/shuttlecock
- Struggles maintaining extended rallies
- Serving consistency issues

After-School Sports Clubs
- Stamina limitations
- Ball control challenges
- Passing accuracy
- Shooting precision

This pattern recognition helps teachers plan targeted activities for weeks 3–4 that address specific student challenges while maintaining appropriate differentiation that again emphasizes and supports a student-centered approach.

The Challenge Scale: A Powerful Self-Assessment Tool

One of the most effective strategies I've used as a teacher and shared through workshops is the Challenge Scale. This visual tool allows students to reflect on task difficulty using one of two options.

Option 1: Numbered Scale (1–10)
- Green: 1–3 (Easy)
- Yellow: 4–7 (Challenging but doable)
- Red: 8–10 (Too difficult)

Option 2: Color System
Three stations (paper or cones) spread out:

- Green: Comfortable/Easy
- Yellow: Challenging but achievable
- Red: Too difficult/Nearly impossible

Implementation. Implementation of this approach requires posting the scale so that it is visible on the gym wall or the learning space that students are using. The scale needs to be spread out so that there is ample enough distance between the colors green, yellow, and red. At any point in the lesson or the session, the teacher can simply blow the whistle or tell the students to stop the activity. At that point, the teacher instructs students to go and stand someplace between the far-left green and the far-right red to indicate, through self-assessment, how challenging whatever they were working on is for them.

The key is to look for students who are in the optimal zone, which is yellow. This is where the greatest learning occurs, as it is not too easy or too difficult for them. Chances are if they are in yellow, they will be experiencing some type of flow in their learning.

Sticky Dot Self-Assessments

An alternative approach using colored dots:

- Green: Mastering the skill
- Yellow: Making progress but challenged
- Red: Struggling significantly

The same idea applies during any lesson or session with the student. At any time during the lesson, teachers can have students write their names on dots and place them on a poster next to specific skills they are working on. One example is from a cycling unit I taught a few years ago. The focus was that students were working on finding "just right" challenges while working on very specific cycling options. It was great to see how they were self-assessing, and it always allowed me to step in when necessary to encourage students to keep them on track or to get them to either level up or level down their challenges.

BUILDING A CULTURE OF CONTINUOUS LEARNING

The key to success with the strategies previously described is consistency and authenticity. When implemented regularly, these constant formative assessment strategies empower students to own their learning and provides them with the autonomy needed to make it personally relevant to them. In addition, it creates natural opportunities for timely feedback and helps the teachers to adjust instruction based on learner needs. It also aligns well with Carol Dweck's work on growth mindset (Dweck, 2006), *Mindset: The New Psychology of Success*, as it helps students to build more resilience that uses possible failure and mistakes as steppingstones to real growth and progress.

Natalie's Story

There is no better example of a student making amazing progress using this style of assessment than Natalie. Natalie was a student of mine many years back while I was teaching in Saudi Arabia. At the beginning of the cycling unit, Natalie struggled with the basic skills needed to cycle with competence and confidence. As I had provided the conditions necessary for genuine exploration before explanation, Natalie had a chance, at her own pace, to tackle differentiated challenges that built her level of confidence on the bike.

After several weeks, Natalie found different challenges to take on and ended up building up the courage to try riding down small slopes. After taking on her first challenge of a small slope, the joy on her face was a perfect example of being in a flow state of learning.

After that lesson, Natalie told me that the bike she was using was old and in bad shape, and that she was enjoying the unit so much, she wanted a new bike. Natalie prompted me to ask her dad to buy her a new bike, and I did just that. The next week, her dad bought her a new bike and helmet. Natalie could not have been prouder. For the rest of the unit, she wanted to focus on off-road riding, setting one challenge for herself after another. Her growth was extraordinary, as was her level of confidence. This would not have been possible had I not set up learning that focused on differentiation and challenge. By placing the students at the center of their own learning, I put them in a position to safely pursue learning that was relevant to them. This was a win-win situation for me as their teacher and for my students.

TEACHER'S ROLE IN SUPPORTING SELF-ASSESSMENT

When students underestimate their abilities, the teacher must step in and redirect—which is why visible assessments play such a critical role in children exploring—and then the teacher explains. The teacher should always observe carefully to identify discrepancies between how the students are self-assessing and how the teacher feels they are doing. It is a perfect chance to conduct short mini-conferences aimed at providing timely, relevant feedback to correct the student course as needed. This process helps students to understand the value of honest self-assessments as it guides them toward finding their own appropriate challenge levels.

This approach creates a learning environment where mistakes are viewed as learning opportunities and students feel psychologically safe to challenge themselves accordingly. Progress is always celebrated as individual growth paths are respected and thoughtfully supported.

The goal is to build a culture where continuous learning and reflection become natural parts of every physical education experience, empowering students to take ownership of their development while maintaining high engagement levels (Clarke et al., 2003).

Helping to Develop Self-Assessment Capabilities With Our Young Learners

I often get asked about how we can best promote self-assessment in our younger learners. I think that this can be done in a variety of ways, but it really involves placing these younger students at the center of their own learning. Whether it be through storytelling or helping to guide them toward understanding important concepts, the driving questions we use must be pitched at their level.

Rather than the students doing actual exit tickets, we can get them to share their responses with the teacher, who can record their answers in a journal, on a whiteboard, or even on sticky notes. When we look at their responses, we can find patterns in their thinking and create visuals that highlight the success criteria that they have come up with. Getting young learners tuned into the success criteria can not only help to expand their vocabulary, but also provide them with opportunities to connect with important conceptual understanding in ways that are relevant to them. The visuals created were as friendly as possible.

At one point I had students working on further developing their fundamental movement skills. Through storytelling, we had the students imagine they were superheroes and had to find a skill that would be their defining strength. They set goals to improve this area and used the posters/visuals to self-assess their level of improvement.

Another example from my teaching is when I had students focus on demonstrating that they were a caring classmate. We used a story they had read in their kindergarten classroom as a provocation to unpack the different ways that they could demonstrate being a caring classmate. The students came up with five different ways they could show they were caring. The five areas of emphasis noted on the poster were (written on pictures from the stories):

1. I can keep my hands to myself.
2. I can work together with my friends and help them.
3. I can be caring and kind to others.
4. I can listen well! I can communicate nicely!
5. I can share with my friends and take turns.

At the end of the PE lessons/after-school clubs, the students let the teacher know what color they were regarding the chosen area of focus. During this lesson, students were focused on "keeping their hands to themselves."

Next, colored markers were used to help students identify where they self-assessed regarding "keeping their hands to themselves." The students who chose green believed they had done a good job, whereas the students in orange knew they needed to do better. The teacher signed their name on the poster by the "keeping hands to yourself criteria" in the color that the student had chosen as a self-assessment of how well they had kept their hands to themselves. It is possible to develop a younger learner's ability to self-assess themselves, but it must be done through intentional practice by teachers and coaches.

APPROACHING THE END OF UNITS OR CLUBS

This is a perfect time to focus on what the students most want to center their learning around. Through continued goal-setting, the students narrow their focus even further. A perfect example I can provide is a Net Games Unit that I taught in my last year as a physical educator.

After taking the students through the exploration before explanation phase, the middle part of the unit was focused on identifying challenges and goal setting. The students voted on which two net games they wanted to focus on in the last few weeks of learning. As my students had explored pickleball, tennis, badminton, and volleyball, they voted on pickleball and badminton to be the choices to end the unit.

At that point I had the students then vote on the one sport they individually wanted to play for the rest of the unit. Added to this, I had them choose if they wanted to play a tournament (proper rules and scoring) or if they wanted to play "just for fun," meaning recreationally. The last part of the unit was then set up accordingly. This is when I switched the focus from skill development to more of a social and emotional approach. I had set up tournaments for those who wanted to play in more of a tournament-style competition. For the students who only wanted to play recreationally, I set up an area of the gym for them to take part in this choice.

What I was most concerned about was the extent to which they were enjoying the choice they made. At the end of each class toward the end of the unit, the students self-assessed their level of enjoyment in relation to the choice they made. I looked at their self-assessments as important data that would provide me with relevant information to act on.

Colored stickers were used to determine the student's level of enjoyment. Criteria were listed on chart paper (1. Tournament, 2. Just for fun). In this case, green meant they were fully engaged and really enjoying it. Yellow meant they were enjoying it but not fully, and red meant they were not enjoying it at all. As an additional requirement, I had the students who had self-assessed as either red or yellow write on a sticky note (a third column on the chart paper) what they needed more of or less of to turn their red into a yellow or yellow into a green next lesson.

At this point, I had to look at their feedback and identify patterns. There were six main reasons why some students had self-assessed themselves as being either yellow or red. In concept map format, the criteria were spread around a poster. They were as follows:

- Some teams were breaking the rules.
- Sitting out and waiting for their turn to play was boring.
- They didn't like who their partner was.
- The teams were unfair.
- The games were not challenging enough.
- Their partner kept entering their space to hit their shot.

This was an excellent student feedback self-assessment, as it allowed me to design a learning strategy that I applied to the next lesson: to have the students come up with solutions to these issues, which they were able to do.

Some of the solutions were as follows:

- Some teams were breaking the rules. Have the teacher explain all rules more clearly so everyone understands.
- Sitting out and waiting for their turn to play was boring. Instead of just sitting out and watching, move to an area where partners could practice while waiting their turn to play.
- They didn't like who their partner was. Be flexible. You must play with whoever your partner is, so try your best no matter what.
- The teams were unfair. Try your best to compete against other teams. It is not about winning but working together well with your partner and communicating.
- The games were not challenging enough. Create new rules against other teams that makes it even more challenging, but all teams must agree on these new rules.
- Their partner kept entering their space to hit a shot. Create a dividing line between your partner's space and your space. Make sure that neither of you crosses that line so that you allow your partner to hit the shot in their own space whenever possible, unless they are out of position and cannot reach it in time.

After implementing these solutions, students continued to self-assess their level of engagement and enjoyment. In most cases, the data showed that students enjoyed it more, which means their co-constructed solutions had an immediate impact on their level of enjoyment.

ENGAGEMENT, MOTIVATION, AND AUTONOMY

My hope is that this chapter highlights the transformative power of movement, both as a personal joy and purpose, and as a tool for growth. As physical educators we all can create deep significance when it comes to providing meaning, connection, and purpose to our students, especially for the ones who need extra encouragement, love, and care.

The process that I have shared with you in this chapter reveals how physical activity, rooted in exploration and discovery, can cultivate essential life skills like self-confidence, resilience, and critical thinking. Through pedagogical approaches that place students at the center of their own learning, educators can foster an environment where movement is not just about fitness but about discovering personal meaning and lifelong engagement.

Ultimately, my main aim is that this chapter emphasizes the profound impact of student-driven exploration and self-assessment, creating pathways for all students to learn at their own pace, set meaningful challenges, and develop the autonomy needed to shape their own physical literacy journeys. Our before- and after-school activities and sports are a perfect avenue to apply these strategies as well, not just in our PE lessons and units. Any time we find ourselves responsible for guiding students toward a deeper understanding of the impact of physical activity, we must involve them more deeply in their own process of learning.

I have seen the pedagogical strategies shared here lead to lasting impact on student learning firsthand. In my consulting and coaching work, I have introduced these strategies face-to-face and virtually in over 50 countries around the world. The feedback I have had also told me that these strategies work. It is my hope that you try these approaches out in your own work. Tweak them in any way that you see fit, but most important, if you take anything away from this chapter, I hope that you continue to always place your students at the center of their own learning.

CONCLUSION

In closing, I want to share one last quote that inspires me, credited to the brilliant best-selling author Dr. Jim Loehr, who is a world-renowned performance psychologist:

> The power broker in your life is the voice that no one hears. How well we listen to the tone and content of our private voice is what determines the quality of our life. It is the master storyteller and the stories we tell ourselves, creates our reality.

As you reflect on this quote, what comes to mind? As an educator, how can you continue to create the conditions necessary for young people to thrive when it comes to physical activity, sports, and movement? How can you help learners to create more empowering personal narratives that help to give them the confidence needed to know they can learn anything and to develop the skills necessary to fully participate in and enjoy all forms of physical activity, sports, and movement under their own terms and conditions?

Best of success in your teaching journeys.

The QR code below will bring you to a printable version of all activities for Chapter 13. This material may also be accessed under the "Downloads" tab at https://www.tcpress.com/move-more-learn-more-9780807784051.

REFERENCES

Clarke, S., Timperley, H., & Hattie, J. (2003). *Unlocking formative assessment: Practical strategies for enhancing students' learning in the primary and intermediate classroom.* Hodder Moa Beckett.

Dweck, C. (2006). *Mindset: The new psychology of success.* Ballantine Books.

Greenberg, J., van der Mars, H., McKenzie, T., Battista, R., Chriqui, J., Cornett, K., Graber, K., Kern, B., Russell, J., Ward, D., & Wilson, W. (2024). The role of physical education within the national physical activity plan. *Journal of Physical Education, Recreation and Dance, 95*(2), 7–16.

Hattie, J. (2012). *Visible learning for teachers: Maximizing impact on learning.* Routledge.

Llewellyn, M., Cousins, A. L., & Tyson, P. J. (2022). "When you have the adrenalin pumping, it kind of flushes out any negative emotions": A qualitative exploration of the benefits of playing football for people with mental health difficulties. *Journal of Mental Health (Abingdon, England), 31*(2), 172–179.

Tomlinson, C. (2014). *The differentiated classroom: Responding to the needs of all learners.* ASCD.

CONCLUSION

Putting It All Together So Kids Will *Move More to Learn More*

Mike Kuczala, United States

Now it comes down to boots on the ground. If we want a better life for all our children, it must begin with you and me. Be an advocate for the physical life. Hopefully *Move More, Learn More* has given you a good starting point to understand how the brain and body connect with each other, a process that begins long before birth. The following is a reminder from Ali Golding's Chapter 11: The common misconception is that movement resides in and for the body when in fact it is really about the brain. If this sounds like a contentious idea, it is worth considering why we have brains at all. Our brains evolved to move.

You cannot separate the brain and body in any part of life, especially learning. The learning that occurs naturally in day-to-day life is both cognitive *and* physical. A home environment, day care, or classroom should look or feel no different. As a educator, parent, or caregiver, you might ask yourself each day, "How can I make my child's, or these children's, experience more physical?" You will then be creating learning experiences that more closely align with how the brain prefers to learn, through more implicit physical and emotional channels. There is no shortage of ideas about how to do this in the previous chapters.

It is also important to advocate for these experiences for children. Facilitating learning through movement does not come naturally to everyone, in part, because it is not how they were taught or trained. We have talked to tens of thousands of teachers, administrators, parents, and caregivers over the past several decades. Many have told us how students in general simply don't move enough during learning experiences or within a typical school day. As teacher training changes and improves based on cognitive science, more and more educators and administrators will come to understand how critical movement is to learning experiences. In the meantime, you can advocate to other parents, teachers, administrators, and school board members. Another point of advocacy should be centered around professional development. Movement activities that exist in the flow of a day or learning sequence need to be understood and well planned. This takes professional development. Movement activities can sometimes be perceived as "fluff," but that could not be further from the truth. It is critical that teachers and caregivers understand the science behind movement and how to implement these important activities. Using movement in a learning capacity needs to be carefully crafted and organized in order to keep a seamless flow in the learning experience. The way these activities are introduced, facilitated, and ended is all the "art" of education, which requires diligence and professional development to utilize successfully.

There has been an immense amount of science presented in *Move More, Learn More*. We thought it would be helpful to provide a big picture as we move on from learning to implementing. To capture its essence here, we elucidate the core messages of each chapter.

- **Chapter 1:** Physical activity profoundly influences brain development through multiple mechanisms. Neuroscientific research has established that movement experiences trigger neurochemical cascades that support neuroplasticity—the brain's ability to form new neural connections and modify existing ones. The science is clear: There is no time to wait—children need to move to learn.
- **Chapter 2:** Children's brains possess remarkable neuroplasticity, the ability to reorganize and form new neural pathways in response to experiences. This makes the early years a core period when movement and sensory experiences literally shape brain architecture. In this chapter, neuro-interventionist Ty Melillo builds upon the work of research scientists Robert Melillo and Gerry Leisman to clarify the developmental underpinnings of learning and cognition.
- **Chapter 3:** For over 30 years, occupational therapists Joann McFee and Kelly Barnhart have honed their multidisciplinary interventions to improve sensory-motor skills in children with neurodevelopmental differences. In this chapter, they provide the scientific rationale for strengthening sensory-motor skills with a sampling of activities that can be used daily in classrooms, clinics, and homes to enhance the motor foundations of learning.
- **Chapter 4:** Research has consistently shown that rhythm, timing, and tempo fundamentally influence neural processing, creating what is described as a "temporal scaffold" by Thaut et al. (2014), upon which cognitive functions are built. In this chapter, musical maestro, composer, and professor Angelo Molino provides educators and clinicians with evidence to bring music to all learning environments.
- **Chapter 5:** Advancements in psychophysiology, cognitive science, and kinesiology research have strengthened the neuroscience rationale for the beneficial effect of movement, music, and exercise on brain development and executive functioning in children and

adolescents. Introducing the dances, songs, and movement activities she uses in clinical practice, Dr. Lynne Kenney brings the field of motor cognition into the classroom and clinic.

- **Chapter 6:** Not only does incorporating music and movement into language therapy make it much more engaging and enjoyable, but it also activates multiple areas of the brain simultaneously, creating and strengthening connections that support language acquisition and literacy skills. Introducing the reader to the Alexander Integrated Method (AIM), dyslexia expert and speech pathologist Stacy Fretheim brings phonological instruction to life with motor activity.
- **Chapter 7:** Children with dysgraphia, dyspraxia, dyslexia, and other learning differences often have difficulties with fine and gross motor skills that can impact their classroom competence. Dyslexia expert Mary Mountstephen provides detailed activities to strengthen handwriting through whole-body work.
- **Chapter 8:** For over 30 years, Piero Crispiani and Eleonora Palmieri have refined the cognitive-motor techniques they use to promote neuroplasticity in children. Their intensive motor movement activities serve as a pathway to enhance functionality by quickly activating the brain and body.
- **Chapter 9:** As Mike Kuczala has taught for over 20 years, the research is clear: Young children need to move to learn. By utilizing the evidence-supported activities in this chapter, classrooms, clinics, and homes can transform into learning spaces that integrate cognitive movement and physical activity. Physical coordination and strength enhance cognition and learning; it's past time to allow children to move to learn.
- **Chapter 10:** Addressing the brain architecture underlying self-regulation development for all young children and supporting positive social skills requires activities explicitly targeting brain processes, with rhythmic movement being an ideal medium. With the evidence-based RAMSR approach, Dr. Kate Williams shows we can move all children toward academic, motor, and social achievement, beginning in the early years.
- **Chapter 11:** The peer-reviewed research shows that cognitive and motor development are more intertwined than previously thought, with both domains showing connected developmental trajectories. This is supported by imaging studies, observations in developmental diversity, and studies of typically developing children. Dance scientist Ali Golding shows us that dance in early childhood teaches executive function skills alongside motor competency, supporting academic and social achievement, specifically in autism.

- **Chapter 12:** Positive social interactions in early childhood foster emotional well-being and lay the foundation for essential life skills like cooperation, empathy, and effective communication. As an award-winning physical educator at New Trier High School, Andy Milne shows us how he employs physical education opportunities in a variety of settings so that children can develop cognitive, motor, and social skills.
- **Chapter 13:** International educator Andy Vasily demonstrates that physical education classes and sports provide optimal settings for teaching social collaboration, self-reflection, and confidence. Through group activities, children can develop self-awareness and interactive skills that will translate to their future relationships, sports, and academic environments. Providing genuine opportunities for exploration in a supportive setting is essential.

IN CLOSING

There has never been a better time to advocate for student-centered and whole-child education, leveraging the brain-body connection. Things have changed so rapidly in the last 2 decades that we risk forgetting or overlooking what initially drove the advances: an emphasis on whole-child and brain-friendly learning through numerous experiences away from screens. These experiences include exploration, physical activity, play, music, and the arts. Recognizing the critical importance of how the brain and body develop, and how to leverage that for our children's benefit in learning experiences, will provide future generations of children with a shift in trajectory toward greater life satisfaction, academic achievement, meaningful relationships, and overall success.

REFERENCE

Thaut, M. H., McIntosh, G. C., & Hoemberg, V. (2014). Neurologic music therapy: From social science to neuroscience. In M. H. Thaut & V. Hoemberg (Eds.), *Handbook of neurologic music therapy* (pp. 1–6). Oxford University Press.

Afterword
The Pediatric Perspective of the Family Experience and Why Returning to Our Roots in Pediatrics Matters for Children

As a pediatrician, I frequently treated children with developmental differences, which encompassed learning disabilities, speech and language disorders, feeding disorders, and neurodivergent conditions such as autism spectrum disorder (ASD), attention deficit disorder, anxiety, and Tourette's syndrome.

The incidence (frequency) of these conditions has been rising in recent decades, with approximately 10% of children diagnosed with ADHD and/or a learning disability and about 3% with ASD. Improved screening and diagnostic tools have been developed with increased awareness, permitting early diagnosis and treatment. Whether there is a real increase in the frequency of these conditions or whether the rise results from increased awareness and the broadening of diagnostic criteria, or epigenetics, remains under study.

Evidence has been accumulating that early intervention is effective at ameliorating the course of these conditions. Such intervention is provided by therapists (speech/language, physical, occupational, and behavioral therapy) and by preschool, public school, and private school programs with services directed to support the specific areas of developmental growth. In many programs, integration with typical peers provides role modeling that improves social acceptance of those with differences. Increasing accounts by adults diagnosed with these conditions who have achieved high levels of attainment has created a much more favorable prognosis.

When a child is diagnosed with autism, early recognition of developmental delays and differences leads to providing high-quality interventions to ameliorate their effects; the goal is to maximize adaptation as the child grows, and to make learning fun. The long-term goal is to help the child take their place in a world accepting of those with differences. With greater understanding by society, children with all disabilities fare better. Parents initially may grieve for the "normal" child they hoped for, then learn to appreciate the one they have, often marveling at their unique attributes and skills, and feeling proud of their child's accomplishments.

For decades, physical movement has been considered an essential component of early intervention programs, especially for children with motor skill, balance, and attention issues. Physical activity has long been associated with improved health parameters, well-being, and prevention of conditions exacerbated by inactivity. Physical education has also been a regular part of conventional educational programs. With an increased focus on top-down academic content delivery, we have lost opportunities in music, art, movement, and play, all central to the developing child. We can turn this around; we have the science. We can raise awareness to improve the lifelong outcomes of our children.

The authors offer various approaches to developmental activities, including movement, rhythm, music, and dance, for all children, especially those with a range of developmental issues. *Move More, Learn More* also documents the science behind these activities. The authors provide examples from an international array of experts on using movement at home, at school, and in clinical practice.

I have worked with Dr. Kenney for over 30 years. I have referred many patients to her for guidance and have appreciated her translational approach. As she points out, there is an urgent need to bring back "old-fashioned" physical activity, music, song, and play as part of education and provide opportunities for today's professional students to learn about the importance of movement in children's learning, something they may not have learned in graduate school.

You will find it easy to skip around chapters. Feel free to take in what is relevant to you, your students, your children, and your patients. Try a few of the activities, and watch your children flourish.

—Ronald S. Fischler, MD, FAAP
Pediatrician and Developmental Pediatrician
Former Medical Director at North Scottsdale Pediatrics
Musician, Husband, and Grandfather

Index

Academic integration, 73
Academic readiness and achievement, 11–12
Academic skills, 42
Activities. *See* Rhythmic movement activities
Activity Gym
   activities, 127–138
   Physio Praxis Vectors, 127–129
   practical elements of, 129
   results, functional, 138–139
ADHD (attention-deficit hyperactivity disorder), 11, 157, 215
   executive function, 68
   and rhythm perception, 53
Adjaye-Gbewonyo, D., 190
Adlof, S., 95, 96
Agrawal, K., 34
"Alert state of calm," 77
Alesi, M., 81
Alexander, Ann, 8, 97, 104
Alexander Integrated Method (AIM), 104–106
Algorithmic thinking, 76
Allen, Sheila, 8
Alotiby, A., 23
Alsaedi, R., 33
Amonkar, N., 171
Anvari, S., 100
Arrowsmith-Young, B., 170
Atypical Rhythm Risk Hypothesis (ARRH), 12
Auditory system, 35
   audio-motor coupling, 52
   auditory discrimination, 69
Autism Movement Therapy® (AMT), 170, 171–172, 177–180
   activities, 180–182
Autism spectrum disorder (ASD), 28–29
   and brain mapping, 169–170
   early intervention for, 215–216
   executive function, 68
   incidence of, 215
   music intervention, 53

Automaticity of learning, 69–70
Autonomic nervous system, 22–24
   autonomic nuclei, 21
   autonomic regulation, 26
Autonomy, 208–209
Ayres, A. Jean, 12, 37

Babbling, 93–94
Back to Sleep campaign, 36
Balance, 38, 42
   Dynamic Balance activity, 85
Bao, R., 68–69
Barbero-Alcocer, I., 10
Barnett, L., 13
Barnhart, Kelly, 212
Beat synchronization, 156–158
Becker, D., 10
Bell, M., 71
Belly crawling, 44–45
Bentley, L., 161
Berchtold, N., 10
Bernard, R., 167
Berthelsen, D., 70, 161
Best, J., 11
Bharathi, G., 75
Bhat, A., 53, 168
Bigelow, A., 34
Bipedalism and brain development, 24
Bloom, P., 94
Blundon, E., 154
Blythe, S., 22
Bonacina, S., 74
Bonding and interpersonal synchrony, 159–161
Bottom-up brain development, 21–22, 27
Bouwer, Fleur, 8
Brage, S., 143
brain-body connection, 73
Brain-derived neurotrophic factor (BDNF), 10

Brain development, 10
    asymmetric, 25–26
    bottom-up development, 21–22, 27
    Broca's area, 181
    "first 1,000 days," 33–34
    functional disconnection of networks, 27
    lateralization, 27–28
    left hemisphere, 28–29
    processing systems, 169–172
    vertical integration, 27
Brain Gym (Dennison), 141
Brain mapping, 169–170
Brain regions, 71
Brainstem maturation, 22
Braun Janzen, T., 59
Breathing ball, 182
Brian, A., 80, 87, 167
Briones, E., 190
Broca's area, 181
Brown, R., 96
Bruchhage, M., 71
Bryck, R., 169

Calmness. "alert state of calm," 77
Cannon, J., 156
Capio, C., 13
Carson, V., 12
Castelli, Darla, 8
"Caudal to rostral" development, 21–22
Centers for Disease Control and Prevention (CDC), 37, 143, 194
Cephalocaudal pattern, 36
Chaddock, L., 10
Challenge Scale, 203–204
Cheung, W. C., 113
Chinello, A., 25
Christmas, J., 116
Chung, P. J., 111
Cirelli, L. K., 52, 160
Clarke, S., 205
Clayton, Guy, 200
Clemente-Suárez, V. J., 114
Clevenger, K., 195
Clough, S., 171
CogniSuite Collection, 74–76
Cognitive development
    cognitive-motor movement, physiology of, 67–70
    cognitive sequencing, 75–76
    musical play, 55–56
Cognitive Motor Training (CMT), 127

Cognitive skill coaching, 73
Comizio, R., 10, 11, 42, 75
Comprehension in language development, 76, 98, 106
Contextual understanding, 76
Continuous learning, 204–205
    self-assessment for students, 205–207
    units and clubs, phasing out of, 207–208
Cooing, 93–94
Coordination, 38
Core strength, 38
Corriveau, K. H., 69
Cotman, C., 10
Crawling, 37
Crispiani, Piero, 81, 126, 127, 138, 139, 213
Crispiani Method, 126
    and neuroactivation, 126–127
    Physio Praxis Vectors, 127–129
    See also Activity Gym
Cross-body activities
    Activity Gym, 127–138
    cross hemispheric clapping, 181
    crossing midline, 117–119
    and neuroactivation, 126–127
    results, functional, 138–139
    See also Rhythmic movement activities
Cross patterns, 128
    cross-modal learning, 73
    cross-model integration, 74–75
Cundari, M., 9

Dadkhah, M., 10
Dancing, 75, 164–165
    dance classes, 71
Dapp, L., 13
Davis, E., 168
Deci, E., 14
Degé, F., 53
De Greeff, J. W., 82
Dennison, Gail, 141
Dennison, Paul, 141
De Rooij, S., 33
Desbernats, A., 155
Developmental coordination disorder (DCD), 110–111
    executive function, 68
Developmental Dance Movement® (DDM), 170, 171–172
    foundations of and typical sessions, 172–174
Developmental disabilities
    and autonomic nervous system, 22–24

developmental speech-language disorders (DSLDs), 12
   functional disconnection syndrome, 28–30
Developmental growth, 8–9, 215
Diamond, A., 10, 11
Dickinson, D., 95
The Differentiated Classroom (Tomlinson), 199
Doman, Alex, 8
Dondena, C., 53
Donnelly, J., 70, 82, 143
Dove, G. O., 12
Droit-Volet, S., 155
Duff, M., 171
Dweck, Carol, 204
Dyscalculia, 110
Dysgraphia, 110
Dyslexia, 53–54, 110, 111
   executive function, 68
Dyspraxia, 110

Early childhood development
   "first 1,000 days," 33–34
   sensory and motor skill integration, 38–43
   See also Infant development
Early Movements, Young Minds™ activities, 122–124
Ecological-Dynamic practices, 139–140
Eddy, L., 168
Education Endowment Foundation, 167
Ellefson, M., 70
Emotional co-regulation, 56–58
Engagement
   engaging children in activity, 80
   family and community, 60–61
   as tool for growth, 208–209
Engel, A., 170
Entrainment theory, 158–159, 171
Epigenetic factors, 26
Erwin, H., 143
Eunice Kennedy Shriver National Institute of Child Health and Human Development, 96
Evolutionary role of neonatal reflexes, 25
Executive function skills, 10–11, 67–87
   and musical play, 55
Exploration
   exploration before explanation, 200–201
   foundations of, 201–204

Face-to-face interactions, 95–96
Fain, E., 42

Family and community engagement, 60–61
Feng, X., 82
Fernandes, V. R., 82
Fight or flight mode, 22–23, 24
Fine motor (FM) skills, 38, 39, 42, 59, 75. *See also* Handwriting skills
Fiorentino, M., 36
Fischer, B., 9
Fisher, P., 169
Fiveash, Anna, 7, 8, 75, 157
Fluidity, 128, 139
Form recognition, 34
Foster Vander Elst, O., 71
Fretheim, Stacy, 213
Frischen, U., 51, 53, 74, 75
Frostig, Marianne, 114–115
Funato, K., 25
Functional disconnection syndrome, 28–30

Garcia-Hermoso, A., 70
Garcia-Madruga, J. A., 70
Generation A: Portraits of Autism in the Arts (documentary film), 170, 180
Gertrude Orff/Orff-Schulwer/Multi-Model (G.O./O.S./M.M.), 54–55
Getchell, N., 116
Goffman, L., 69
Golding, Ali, 169, 170, 171, 172, 183, 213
Goldstein, A., 178
González-Del-Castillo, J., 10
Gordon, Reyna, 8, 69, 104
Goswami, Usha, 8, 69
Goudas, M., 70, 80
Grandin, Temple, 170, 171
Gratz College, 142
Greenberg, J., 200
Greenfader, C., 10
Griffin, K., 118
Grip strength, 42
Gromko, J., 98, 100
Gross motor skills, 38, 59, 75
Group activities and social connections, 186–196
Guda, C., 26
Guo, Z. V., 135

Habibi, Assal, 8
Hall, J., 35
Hamilton, L., 171

Handwriting skills
    and crossing midline, 117–119
    and grip strength, 42
    observations of children, 116–117
    research concerning, 119
    sample activities, 119–122
    Specific Learning Differences (SpLDs), 110–111
    See also Fine motor (FM) skills
Hannaford, Carla, 141
Hansen-Tift, A., 95
Hardy, L. L., 80
Hardy, M., 53, 168
Hart, B., 92
Hattie, J., 201
Haywood, K., 116
Heavy work, benefits of, 79–81
Hebb, D., 96
Helen Arkell Dyslexia Charity, 110
Hillman, Charles, 8
Hobbs, A., 167
Hoberman sphere, 182
Hoemberg, V., 53
Hogan, Tiffany, 8, 95, 96
Horizontal plane, 81
Hosokawa, R., 186
Hu, C., 119
Human Kinetics, 8
Hutton, E., 111

Identity formation, 14
Immune function, 23
Improvisation, musical, 56–57
Incipit Praxis Vector, 128
Inclusivity, 80
Individual Habilitation Treatment Program (TAI), 127
Infant development, 20–21
    asymmetric hemispheric development, 25–26
    autonomic nervous system, 22–24
    head control, 36
    immune system, 26–27
    neonatal reflexes, 21–22, 25
    neurological foundations, 27–28
    See also Early childhood development
Inflammation, 23
International Classification of Function (ICF), 183
Iverson, J., 94

Jarraya, S., 70
Jaschke, A. C., 51
Jensen, Eric, 141
Jing, J., 71
Judson, G., 191
Jusczyk, P., 94
Jylänki, P., 9

Kasuya-Ueba, Y., 54
Kenney, Lynne, 10, 11, 42, 75, 213, 216
Ketcheson, L., 171
Khan, I., 20
The Kinesthetic Classroom (Lengel & Kuczala), 142–143
Kinesthetic classrooms
    applications, 146–149
    frameworks for, 143–146
    research concerning, 142–143
Kirk, M., 170
Kisilevsky, S., 154
Klotzbier, T., 115, 117
Koelsch, S., 51
Kohli, A., 119
Kolovelonis, A., 70, 80
Kong, J., 70
Koolwijk, P., 32
Kraus, Nina, 8, 51, 52
Kuczala, Mike, 11, 142–143, 145, 213
Kuhl, P. K., 9, 95, 96

Ladányi, E., 7, 12, 157
LaGasse, A., 53, 168
LaGasse, B., 54
Lambourne, K., 70, 143
Lane, S., 40
Language development, 12
    and Alexander Integrated Method (AIM), 104–106
    early development, 92–95
    and face-to-face interactions, 95–96
    and musical intervention, 58–59, 98–99
    oral language and transition to literacy, 96–98
    phonological skills, 98–103
    rhythm and language acquisition, 52
    vocabulary and syntax, 103–104
Lara, Joanne, 170, 171, 174, 177–180
Latino, F., 10, 67
Leaky gut, 26–27
Learning with the Body in Mind (Jensen), 141

Lebert, A., 12
Lee, C. C., 94
Lee, R., 194
Leisman, Gerry, 12, 111, 169, 212
Leman, M., 54
Lengel, Traci, 141–143, 145
Lense, M., 53, 69
Leon, M., 171
Leong, A., 11
Leventhal, B., 20
Levine, Y., 30
Lewkowicz, D., 95
Li, D., 11
Lind, R. R., 10
Lindner, N., 42
Ling, D. S., 11
Llewellyn, M., 198
Llinas, R., 169
Loehr, Jim, 209
Lubans, D. R., 14
Ludwig, K., 10
Lundetrae, K., 75
Luo, X., 67
Lyon, G. Reid, 8

Macdonald, K., 7
Mader, J., 194
Maes, P. J., 54
Makaton, 173
Malik, F., 187
Mao, F., 11
Martens, Marilyn, 8
Martens, Rainer, 8
Martial arts training, 11, 71
Martín-Rodríguez, A., 11, 196
Marz, A., 81
Mastrangelo, S., 9
math skills, 12, 76
Matthew Effect, 93
Mavilidi, M., 12
McClelland, M., 9
McCluskey, C., 12
McFee, Joann, 212
McGowan, A. L., 10, 11
Meeusen, R., 115
Melillo, Robert, 26, 212
Melillo, Ty, 212
Meltzoff, A., 160
Memory
  auditory, 69
  early formation of, 25
  and musical play, 51, 55, 104
  and rhythmic movement, 71, 72
Merlo, C., 68
Midline, crossing, 117–119. *See also* Cross-body activities
Miendlarzewska, E. A., 51, 74
Milne, Andy, 214
Mindset (Dweck), 204
Mitteroecker, P., 9
Moats, Louisa, 8
Moize, Jean, 8, 141
Molino, Angelo, 54, 55, 212
Monier, F., 155
Montroy, J. J., 10
Motivation, 208–209
Motor skill activities. *See* Rhythmic movement activities
Motor skill development, 12–13, 36
  fine motor development, 38
  gross motor development, 38
  and musical intervention, 59
  and sensory integration, 38–43
  sequential development, 9
Motor system
  functions of, 35–37
  and sensory system, in unison, 34–35
Mountstephen, Mary, 9, 213
Movement, advocacy for, 188
Movement, research concerning
  academic readiness and achievement, 11–12
  executive function, 10–11
  history of, 7–9
  motor skill development, 12–13
  neuroplasticity and brain development, 10
  sensory-motor integration and perceptual development, 12
  social and emotional development, 13–14
Movement detection, 34
Movement Education (Frostig), 114–115
MovementWorks®, 170, 171–172
  brain, information processing, 169–172
  foundations of, 168–169
Musgrave, J., 113, 119
Music
  and language development, 98
  musical play, 55–56
  musical thinking, 72–73
  and phonological skills, 99–103
  vocabulary and syntax, 103–104

Music interventions
    assessment of progress, 60
    cognition and learning, 54–56
    and cognitive-motor exercise, 71
    emotional co-regulation, 56–58
    improvisation, 56–57
    integration with family and community, 60–61
    language development, 58–59
    motor skills, 59
    synergy with movement, 51–54
Myowa, M., 155

National Reading Panel, 96, 97
Negi, S., 26
Neonatal reflexes, 21–22, 25
    integration of, 29
Neural activation, 71, 126–127
Neurodivergent learners, 167–168, 215
    music and movement, 53–54
    See also MovementWorks
Neurological development, 75
Neuroplasticity, 10, 38, 71
"Neurostorm," 127
Norris, E., 168
Numeracy, 76

Obsessive-compulsive disorder (OCD), 28
Ocklenburg, S., 135
Ohara, R., 168
Oller, D., 93
Overy, K., 54, 69

Palmer, K., 14
Palmieri, Eleonora, 81, 126, 127, 138, 213
Pangrazzi, Robert, 8
Paquette, K., 104
Parachute play, 192–193
Paschen, L., 80
Passarello, N., 37
Patel, Aniruddh, 8, 52, 99, 156
Pattern recognition
    and musical play, 55–56
    and network activation, 72
    pattern processing, 34
Perceptual development, 12
    perceptual narrowing, 93
    perceptual-motor training programs, 13
Pesce, C., 122
Phillips, D. A., 37

Phonemic awareness, 97–98
    activities that build, 100–103
    and music, 99–103
    phoneme blending, 102–103
    phoneme segmentation, 101–102
Phonetic discrimination, 93
Phonics, 76
Physical education, 115
Physio Praxis Vectors, 127–129
Pickup, I., 115
Planes of motion, 81
Pontifex, M., 10
Portwood, M., 111
Powell, L., 167
Praxis-Motor Theory (PMT), 126
Price, L., 115
Problem-solving, 76
Proprioceptive system, 35, 40
    proprioceptive-auditory relationship, 41
    proprioceptive sense, 77
Proximodistal pattern, 36
Pujari, V., 11

Rabinowitch, T., 160
Ramos-Campo, D. J., 114
Ratey, John, 8
Rauch, W. A., 10
Reading, 75
    oral language and transition to literacy, 96–98
    phonological skills, 98–103
    vocabulary and syntax, 103–104
Ready, Set, Go! The Kinesthetic Classroom 2.0 (Lengel & Kuczala), 143, 145
Recess, 193–195
Relay games, 191–192
Resaland, G. K., 12
Rest and digest mode, 23
Reverse patterns, 128
Rhodes, R., 170
Rhythm
    and cognition, 71
    and cognitive skills, 74–75
    and infant babbling, 93–94
    perception of, 53
    rhythm-based activities, 59
    rhythmic-coordinative training, 73
    value of, 154
Rhythm and Movement for Self-Regulation (RAMSR) program, 153, 161–165

Rhythmic movement activities
  Activity Gym activities, 129–138
  amoeba tag, 190
  animal walks, 45–46
  Autism Movement Therapy® (AMT), 180–182
  back-to-back ball passing, 43–44
  basic sports actions, 85–86
  beat matching, 158
  belly crawling, 44–45
  Big Ball Bounce, 83
  body writing, 146
  breathing ball—Hoberman sphere, 182
  Cardio Review, 147–148
  Comparison Review, 148
  Copy Me, 162–163
  Cross Patterns, 133–135
  dancing, 164–165
  Duck and Point, 147
  Dynamic Balance, 85
  Early Movements, Young Minds™, 122–124
  Editing on the Move, 148
  entrainment, 159
  Even/Odd Hop, 148
  Heads, Shoulders, Knees, Toes, 162
  hula hoop tower relay, 192
  I Clap, You Move Your Feet, 132–133
  Knee Up Down, 84
  Little Jane Fonda, 82–83
  Log Rolling Diagonal, 47–48
  lovely/unlovely walk, 190–191
  for motor skills and handwriting, 119–122
  Mouse, 180
  Move Freely, 129–130
  movements with sounds, 181
  moving in time with others, 160
  Name Pass, 147
  1-2 Cha, Cha, Cha, 83–84
  parachute igloo activity, 193
  parachute play, 192–193
  partner clapping, 181
  Rapid Responding, 131–132
  relay games, 191–192
  Reverse Patterns, 137–138
  rocking eggs, 46–47
  rolling on diagonals, 47–48
  Rotator Patterns, 135–137
  Show Your Size, 146
  tag games, 189–190
  Think-Ups, 77–79
  This Is the Way We . . . , 163–164
  tips for teachers, 86
  walking activities, 190–191
  whole-body group activities, 174–177
  See also Cross-body activities; Motor skill activities
Rieg, S., 104
Rintala, P., 171
Risley, T., 92
Rocha, S., 155, 157
Rodriguez-Gomez, D. A., 52
Role modeling, 80
Rosengard, Paul, 8
Rotator patterns, 128
Rough-and-tumble play, 14
Ryan, R., 14

Sagan, Carl, 200
Savanta, 167, 171
Schach, S., 33
Schaefer, R. S., 69
Schön, D., 98, 100
School readiness
  for children with learning differences, 111–114
  five domains of, 113
Schott, N., 115, 117
Self-assessment for students, 205–207
Self-concept, 14
Self-regulation development, 56–57, 153–165
  beat synchronization, 156–158
  bonding and interpersonal synchrony, 159–161
  entrainment, 158–159
  rhythm, value of, 154
  rhythm and movement for self-regulation (RAMSR) program, 161–165
  self-regulation skills, 10–11
  spontaneous motor tempo (SMT), 155–156, 157
Sensorimotor integration and synchronization, 12, 35, 156–158
Sensory processing, 37–38, 53
  musical intervention, 57–58
  sensory and motor systems, in unison, 34–35
Sequencing, cognitive, 75–76
Sequential processing, 73
  and musical play, 55
70 Play Activities for Better Thinking, Self-Regulation, Learning, and Behavior, 70

SHAPE America, 194
Sheffield University, 167
Shi, P., 82
Shils, B., 170, 171, 180
Shonkoff, J. P., 33, 37
Shore, Stephen, 180
Slater, J., 157
Slinger-Constant, A., 97
Smith, P., 14
Snow, C., 95, 97
Soan, S., 111
Soccer skills, 85–86
Social and emotional development, 13–14, 73
   group activities, 186–196
   musical experiences, shared, 52
   social interaction, 80
   social skill development, 14
Sowder, Nicolette, 1
Spatial awareness, 34
Special Educational Needs and Disabilities
   (SEND) curricula, 54–55
Specific Learning Differences (SpLDs)
   early years and primary practice, 114–116
   and school readiness, 111–114
Spiegel, J. A., 11
Spontaneous motor tempo (SMT), 155–156, 157
Sports
   basic sports actions, 85–86
   sport-inspired activities, 195–196
Spring, K., 13
Srinivasan, S., 53
Staiano, A., 13
Stamou, A., 171
Stanovich, K., 93
St. George, J., 14
Storytelling skills, 76
Students as teachers, 80
Su, W., 171
Sudden infant death syndrome (SIDS), 36
Sutapa, P., 13
Symanski, C., 71
Syntax skills, 103–104
   94–95

Tactile system, 35, 40
Tafuri, F., 10, 67
Tag games, 189–190
Tai chi, 71
Talero-Gutiérrez, C., 52
Tao, Y., 9, 68

Tate, M., 157
Taylor, R., 167
Team-based activities, 195–196
TEDXTalks, 170
Tees, R., 94
Thaut, Michael, 8, 51, 53, 158, 171, 212
Think-Ups, 77–79
   rhythmic supermans, 78–79
   rhythmic wall-sit, 77
   stand-squat-hold, 79
Thompson, R., 186
Thomson, J. M., 75
Tierney, Adam, 8, 51, 52
Timing and coordination, 52
Tomasello, M., 94
Tomlinson, C., 199
Tomporowski, Phillip, 8, 11, 67, 70, 115
Torjinski, M., 68
Tourette's syndrome, 215
Treffert, D., 28
Trost, W. J., 51, 74
Tummy time, 36
Tversky, B., 169

University of Leeds, 167
University of Stirling, 167

Van de Weyer, R., 116
Vasilopoulos, F., 70
Vasily, Andy, 214
Vertical plane, 81
Vestibular system, 34, 40
   vestibular-auditory integration, 41
   vestibular nuclei, 21
   vestibular-proprioceptive-visual systems, 40–41
   vestibular sense, 77
Vilarroya, Ó., 12
Visual system, 34
   visual acuity, 34
   visual-motor integration, 39
   visual-proprioception-tactile integration, 41
   visual-spatial skills, 39
Vocabulary development, 94, 103–104
Voight, R., 21

Walking activities, 190–191
A Walking Curriculum (Judson), 191
Wang, S., 70
Watson, A., 70, 143
Wellington-Alexander Center (WAC), 68, 104

Werker, J., 94
Wick, K., 82
Wiener-Vacher, S., 12, 40, 42
Williams, Kate, 70, 160, 161, 213
Willoughby, M., 7
Wolpert, Daniel, 168
Woo, C., 171
Wozniak, R., 94
Wright, K., 169

Yoshida, S., 25
Young, L., 119
Yu, L., 155

Zaatar, M., 53
Zelaznik, H. N., 69
Zelazo, P., 7, 11
Zeng, N., 110
Zhao, K., 11

About the Editors and Contributors

Mike Kuczala has delivered keynotes, given presentations, facilitated professional development, and taught graduate courses on four continents. His presentations, courses, books, and videos have reached more than 200,000 teachers, trainers, corporate executives, and parents. Kuczala is also the co-author of the Association of Educational Publishers' Distinguished Achievement Award–nominated, *The Kinesthetic Classroom: Teaching and Learning Through Movement*, a book and philosophy that has changed the view of teaching and learning around the world. Mike's other books include *Training in Motion: How to Use Movement to Create an Engaging and Effective Learning Environment, Ready, Set, Go! The Kinesthetic Classroom 2.0* (Corwin), and *The Peak Performing Teacher: 5 Habits for Success* (Corwin).

President of Kuczala Consulting and Chief Executive Officer at the Regional Training Center, Mike's presentations have been experienced in such diverse settings as the Educational Collaborative for International Schools, the East Asia Regional Council of Schools, the Francis Marion University Center of Excellence to Prepare Teachers of Children of Poverty Summer Institute, the American Society for Training and Development, the Forum for Innovative Leadership, the Association for Supervision and Curriculum Development, and the Society for Health and Physical Educators.

In his role with Regional Training Center, Mike leads a cadre of more than 70 graduate instructors who regularly provide graduate coursework to tens of thousands of teachers across Pennsylvania, Maryland, New Jersey, and beyond, in partnership with The College of New Jersey and La Salle University. During his tenure, he has overseen the development of RTC's online and virtual course offerings as well as the design and implementation of new coursework, certificate programs, and master's degree concentration options. Mike also manages college and university partnerships.

An expert in training, training design, and effective presentation, Mike has designed, or co-designed, four of the most successful graduate courses in the history of Regional Training Center. *Motivation: The Art and Science of Inspiring Classroom Success, Creating Health and Balance in Today's Classroom, The Kinesthetic Classroom: Teaching and Learning Through Movement*, and *The Kinesthetic Classroom II: Moving Across the Standards* are facilitated by a cadre of graduate instructors who have taught thousands of teachers the key principles of instructional movement, motivation, and wellness.

Mike is also a former American Fitness Professionals and Associates Certified Nutrition and Wellness Consultant and former competitive bodybuilder, and he's trained in the art of Effortless Meditation. He proudly and humbly comes from a family of educators, including his wife, sister, both parents, and three grandparents. He earned his Bachelor of Arts in Music from Kutztown University and Master of Music Education from the University of Northern Colorado. Mike enjoyed a 10-year band and choral directing career in both Colorado and Pennsylvania. "I am the product of three generations of teachers. Education is what I love and do. It is always an honor and pleasure to work with both educators in helping them to become true instructional leaders, corporate executives, and trainers in providing presentation skill and effectiveness. My background in education gave rise to my love of teaching, public speaking, curriculum and training design, and helping people create goals and live their dreams."

Lynne Kenney is an international educator and the nation's leading pediatric psychologist in the development of classroom cognitive-physical activity programs for students in grades K–8. Dr. Kenney develops curriculum, programming, and activities to improve children's cognition through rhythmic cognitive-motor movement, executive function skill-building strategies, and social-relational learning. Dr. Kenney has trained professional and Olympic athletes in fitness and mental wellness and enjoys writing songs for children to improve metacognitive awareness.

"Dr. Lynne" is a pediatric psychologist on the Language & Cognition Team at Wellington-Alexander Center for the Treatment of Dyslexia, Scottsdale, Arizona. She has advanced fellowship training in forensic psychology and developmental pediatric psychology from Massachusetts General Hospital/Harvard Medical School and Harbor-UCLA/UCLA Medical School. As an international educator, researcher, and author, Dr. Kenney is dedicated to improving the trajectory of children's learning, particularly in high-need, under-resourced communities.

In 2024, Fit and Fun Playscapes launched Cognitivities™, an original collection of portable mats that combine music, art, and movement for better self-regulation. This is the first Roll-Out Activities® mat of its kind, helping children practice cognitive skills, executive function, and self-regulation in a calming and engaging way. The lyrics, written by Dr. Kenney, incorporate the cognitive and social-relational lessons she brings to classrooms worldwide.

Dr. Kenney's books include *Brain Primers* (with Mike Kuczala); *70 Play Activities for Better Thinking, Self-Regulation, Learning and Behavior* (with Rebecca Comizio,); *Bloom Your Room™; Musical Thinking™*; and *Bloom: 50 Things to Say, Think and Do With Anxious, Angry and Over-the-Top-Kids* (with Wendy Young). Dr. Kenney is dedicated to shifting the trajectory of learning for neurodiverse children. She has spent 30 years bringing music, art, and movement to underserved communities to improve the course of children's lives.

Kelly Barnhart, OTR/L, CBIS, CSRS, is an occupational therapist based in Phoenix, Arizona, with over 20 years of pediatric experience. Her practice integrates neuroscience, sensory processing, motor skill development, and cognitive foundations to help children reach their full potential. A committed clinical educator and mentor, Kelly is known for her evidence-based approach, steadfast dedication to both clients and colleagues, and genuine delight in the children she serves. She is also deeply committed to continuing education, always seeking opportunities to expand her knowledge and refine her practice. Her contribution to this book reflects a firm belief that movement is not just physical but essential to how children grow, learn, and thrive.

Piero Crispiani is an Honorary Professor at the University of Macerata (Italy), Clinical Pedagogist and Scientific Director of the Dyslexia and Dyspraxia International Center, and President of the CO.MIS (Cognitive Motor International Society). Professor Crispiani is considered the premier motor-cognition expert in the treatment of dyspraxia and dyslexia in Italy. Professor Crispiani is a professor and researcher in special pedagogy, the science of movement, cognitive sience, and mental processes. He has also been a teacher and a didactic lead in education. Professor Crispiani is an Italian expert in dyslexia, dysgraphia, dyscalculia, dyspraxia, developmental disorders, executive function, and autism. He is the creator of a clinical and cognitive (CO.CLI.TE) system based on Praxic Motor Theory (PTM) and cognitive motor training. Publications include *The Crispiani Method* (2016, Champion Pressing), *Special Intensive Practices of Cognitive Motor Training* (2020), VTM 2016 (Video Motor Training), and *Dislessia come dispassia sequenziale* (2011).

Stacy Lawyer Fretheim, MS, CCC-SLP, is a licensed and certified speech-language pathologist with over 25 years of experience in the evaluation and treatment of language-based learning disabilities, particularly dyslexia. She is part of the founding team that established the Wellington-Alexander Center in 2003, and currently acts as its director. In this role, Stacy leads a multidisciplinary team providing comprehensive care for individuals with dyslexia, addressing language and linguistic skills, sensorimotor development, executive function skills, and social-relational growth. Stacy earned her Master of Science in Communication Disorders from The University of Texas, Dallas and has presented nationally on dyslexia, early intervention, and the science of reading. Stacy previously served for several years on the board of the Arizona Branch of the International Dyslexia Association. Beyond her professional life, Stacy is a proud wife and the mother of two amazing sons who inspire her daily to bring compassion, creativity, and excellence to everything she does.

Ali Golding, MSc, Post Grad Cert SEN, FRSA, is a dance scientist and specialist dance educator with a background as a professional choreographer. Ms.

Golding's research focus is on dance and cognition, with a particular interest in early years and special education. She is the founder and director of MovementWorks, a charitable organization dedicated to providing evidence-based applied research with an objective toward fostering interdisciplinary practice in education, health, and social sciences (www.movementworks.org). A published academic author, Ms. Golding has also contributed editorials for One Dance UK, Early Arts UK, The Royal Society of Arts, and Autism Eye. She's presented research at a wide range of conventions globally, including the British College of Occupational Therapists Conference, the Times Educational (TES) SEN Show, the National Autistic Society International Congress, and Movementis conferences at Harvard, Tel Aviv, and UCL. MovementWorks has been frequently featured at the National Autism Show and the National Autistic Society Professional Conference, with regular invitations to contribute internationally such as Adelphi University's Traditional Therapies and Expressive Modalities Course (Asia) and NYU's Nest program, NYC Public Schools' largest inclusion program for autistic students. Ms. Golding has delivered a TEDx talk you can find at movementworks.org.

Olivia Markan is a language technician on the multidisciplinary intervention team at Wellington-Alexander Center for the treatment of dyslexia in Scottsdale, Arizona. Olivia holds a BS in family and human development from Arizona State University (2021) and a master's degree in psychology from Pepperdine University (2023). Olivia is looking forward to beginning her doctoral program in psychology at Midwestern University in Fall 2025. Olivia is passionate about the intersection of language and cognition in children. She aims to become a neuropsychologist specializing in developmental and learning differences.

Joann McFee, MS, OTR/L, is an experienced occupational therapist with over 25 years in pediatric practice, specializing in learning disabilities and sensorimotor challenges. After recognizing a need for more targeted support for children who often went underreferred in traditional settings, she founded Pediatric Therapy Solutions in 2007. Through her clinic and collaborations with private schools, Joann provides both direct and consultative services, integrating the medical model of OT into educational environments. Her work emphasizes early identification, functional outcomes, and building strong partnerships with families and educators to support each child's unique development.

Ty Melillo, DC, is a lead clinician at the Melillo Method Centers working directly under Dr. Robert Melillo. Ty earned a BS in psychology with an autism study minor from Saint Joseph's University and a Doctorate of Chiropractic from Northeast College of the Health Sciences, Seneca Falls, New York. Ty has a certification in neurodevelopmental childhood disorders, and is a practitioner of advanced functional neuroscience and neuroimmunology. As a researcher, Ty co-authored several papers, including "Taking Sides: Asymmetries in the Evolution of Human Development in Better Understanding Autism Spectrum Disorder" and "Cognitive Effects of Retained Primitive Reflexes in Autism Spectrum Disorder." As a researcher, Ty is interested in the study of applied neuroscience in complex diagnoses. As a clinician, Ty appreciates neurodiversity and the contributions neurodivergent children and adults make to society.

Andy Milne's 29-year career in education has taken him to four continents as an international presenter and keynote speaker. He hosts the global slow-chathealth.com blog site, created the #sendateacher fundraising initiative, appeared on the TEDx stage with his popular "This Is Not Your Parents' Health Class," and was SHAPE America's National Health Teacher of the Year in 2017. Andy currently serves on the SHAPE America board of directors and teaches health and kinetic wellness (physical education) at New Trier High School in Winnetka, Illinois.

Angelo Molino has expertise in leading mental health initiatives to advance public policy change, including mental health access and parity, school-based behavioral health programs, and early intervention/prevention. Professor Molino is a devoted advocate for mental health and behavioral health globally. He has collaborated with and leveraged external partnerships, managing coalitions with the business community, educational institutions, and foundations internationally to achieve the goal of mental health awareness. Professor Molino has over 20 years of expertise in mental wellness, early childhood education, and special education. He has lectured in Europe, Asia, and the U.S. about music wellness for mental well-being.

Mary Mountstephen, MA (SEN), MA (RES), is a highly experienced specialist teacher who holds a master's degree in special educational needs and a second master's degree in research in education. She has studied at the doctoral level at the University of Reading and has published extensively. She is recognized internationally as an expert in the field of specific learning difficulties, with postgraduate qualifications in dyslexia, sensory processing, developmental delays, and associated assessment and intervention programs.

Mary has long-established academic and professional links with academics and practitioners in Europe (Cyprus, Italy, Latvia, Poland, Hungary, and Switzerland), in Asia (Singapore, Malaysia, Hong Kong), and in Australia and has collaborated on a number of projects and publications. She presents regularly at conferences; provides online training for schools, clinics, and families; and advises international organizations on innovative resources and the development of effective partnerships.

Current projects involve serving as advisory interim head for a new special school startup that aims to integrate various aspects of best practices for young children whose needs are not adequately met in either mainstream or specialist settings. She has published books and numerous articles and has served as the editor of the leading national publication for special educational needs in the United Kingdom. She continues as the reviews and products editor to maintain her connections with current innovations and leading experts in their fields.

Mary has worked with neurologically complex children for over 30 years, and she understands how movement can play a fundamental role in supporting children, teachers, other professionals, and parents in maximizing motor, emotional, and cognitive maturation.

Eleonora Palmieri is the director of the Psychological and Pedagogical Victor Center, Macerata (Italy), and director of Fidi Academy Support for Parental Education in the Crispiani Method, Macerata (Italy). As an Italian psychologist, she is an expert in dyslexia, dyspraxia, and autism, teaching and implementing the Crispiani Method practices internationally. Dottorressa Palmieri is a researcher in special pedagogy, disability, and neurocognitive activation training. She has been involved in international projects as a trainer, and she often attends as an expert speaker at international conferences. She has developed and coordinated partnerships with many experts in different countries, including universities (Poland, England, Spain, Hong Kong, Singapore, and the United States), to improve practice in training organizations, research centers, and guidelines for teachers and parents. Dottorressa Palmieri is the author of *Special Intensive Practices of Cognitive Motor Training* (2020), VTM (Video Motor Training, 2014), and articles, including "Improving the Fluidity of Whole Reading With Dynamic Coordinated Movement Approach" (2015), "Dyslexia and Champion L.I.R.M. Outcomes of a Research Study-Based Treatment of Cross Patterns" (2017), and "Early Markers of Executive Functions and Their Relation to Dyslexia: Cross Patterns and the Level of Initial Activation" (2019).

Kate Williams holds a PhD in developmental psychology, research masters in education, bachelor of music, and postgraduate qualifications in music therapy. An accomplished developmental scientist and registered music therapist, Dr. Williams is internationally recognized for her expertise in social-emotional and cognitive development, parent-child interventions, and the role of rhythmic movement in learning and wellbeing. Dr. Williams has authored over 70 research papers and secured over $3 million in research funding, often working in collaboration with international scholars. Dr. Williams is one of the founding researchers of the Australian Sing & Grow program, and she led the development of the internationally disseminated Rhythm and Movement for Self-Regulation (RAMSR) program. Dr. Williams's program of research ultimately aims to address inequities in health and education outcomes that often stem from early childhood adversity. She holds positions as professor of education and associate dean of research at the University of the Sunshine Coast and Adjunct at the Queensland University of Technology, and is Chair of Play Matters Australia.

Andy Vasily is a certified trust at work leadership/performance coach, pedagogical leader, educational consultant, and podcaster based in Antwerp, Belgium. He is currently the PYP Coordinator at the Antwerp International School. He has taught at fully authorized International Baccalaureate schools in 6 different countries over the past 20 years. His Run Your Life podcast has been downloaded more than 800,000 times in over 85 countries. He is passionate about working with all stakeholders in organizations to help bring out their best in regard to well-being, productivity, and motivation in the workplace. Andy has committed himself to better understanding the conditions needed for people to thrive both personally and professionally to best serve the people he coaches. He has presented his work virtually and in person in more than 40 countries around the world. Much of his work with international schools is focused on differentiation, assessment design, and how to deepen social and emotional learning to best meet the diverse needs of all students. Also, he works closely as an executive coach with many school leaders in Europe, Asia-Pacific, the Middle East, and North America.